10 April 2008

Dear Michael,

In admiration for your important policy thinking and trailblazing.

THE

PRICE WE PAY

Hank

Henry M. Levin

THE PRICE WE PAY

Economic and Social Consequences of Inadequate Education

CLIVE R. BELFIELD
HENRY M. LEVIN
editors

BROOKINGS INSTITUTION PRESS
Washington, D.C.

ABOUT BROOKINGS

The Brookings Institution is a private nonprofit organization devoted to research, education, and publication on important issues of domestic and foreign policy. Its principal purpose is to bring the highest quality independent research and analysis to bear on current and emerging policy problems. Interpretations or conclusions in Brookings publications should be understood to be solely those of the authors.

1775 Massachusetts Avenue, N.W., Washington, D.C. 20036
www.brookings.edu

Library of Congress Cataloging-in-Publication data

The price we pay : economic and social consequences of inadequate education / Clive R. Belfield and Henry M. Levin, editors.
p. cm.
Summary: "Highlights costs of inadequate education, attaching hard numbers to the relationship between educational attainment and critical indicators as income, health, crime, dependence on public assistance, and political participation. Explores policy interventions to boost the education system's performance and explains why demographic trends are so challenging to educating the nation's youth"—Provided by publisher.
Includes bibliographical references and index.
ISBN-13: 978-0-8157-0864-3 (cloth : alk. paper)
ISBN-10: 0-8157-0864-5 (cloth : alk. paper)
ISBN-13: 978-0-8157-0863-6 (pbk. : alk. paper)
ISBN-10: 0-8157-0863-7 (pbk. : alk. paper)
1. Education—Economic aspects—United States. 2. Education—Social aspects—United States. 3. Education—Costs—United States. 4. Educational equalization—United States. I. Belfield, C. R. II. Levin, Henry M. III. Title.
LC66.P735 2007
338.4'737—dc22 2007034882

9 8 7 6 5 4 3 2 1

The paper used in this publication meets minimum requirements of the American National Standard for Information Sciences—Permanence of Paper for Printed Library Materials: ANSI Z39.48-1992.

Typeset in Adobe Garamond

Composition by R. Lynn Rivenbark
Macon, Georgia

Printed by R. R. Donnelley
Harrisonburg, Virginia

Contents

PART TWO
Quantifying the Costs of Inadequate Education

PART THREE
Directions for Reform

Acknowledgments

THE OVERALL THEME of this book and much of its contents were developed for the First Annual Teachers College Symposium on Educational Equity, held by the Campaign for Educational Equity of Teachers College, Columbia University, on October 24–26, 2005. The symposium was dedicated to "The Social Costs of Inadequate Education," with empirical papers that attempted to identify the consequences for society of having a substantial portion of the population receive an education that is inadequate to the social, political, economic, and personal demands of adult life. We thank the authors of the symposium papers and the chapters in this volume, who are national experts on the topics that were covered.

A second and related source of input was the project titled "The Costs and Benefits of an Excellent Education for All of America's Children." This research project was devoted to documenting and comparing the costs to the public of increasing high school graduation with the public benefits that would accrue to that investment in the form of higher tax revenues and lower costs for crime, public assistance, and health care.

We thank the Laurie M. Tisch Foundation and the Campaign for Educational Equity for sponsoring the symposium and the Gerard and Lilo Leeds Foundation for funding the project on the costs and benefits of an excellent education. In addition, we thank Arthur Levine, Michael Rebell, and the Trustees of Teachers College for their roles in establishing the symposium and

Susan Fuhrman for her continuing support of the Teachers College focus on improving educational equity. The following people deserve our gratitude for making the symposium a success: Joe Brosnan, Laurie Dorf, Inez Gonzales, Joe Levine, Mark Noizumi, Judy Pryor, Karen Schnur, and Elisabeth Thurston. We are also grateful to Gerard and Lilo Leeds, Gerry House, Greg Jobin-Leeds, Dan Leeds, Rosa Smith, Bob Wise, and Doug Wood for reviewing the cost-benefit study and offering suggestions for improvement and to Jens Ludwig and Russ Rumberger for providing a valuable technical assessment of that study. We express our appreciation to Gwyneth Connell, Heather Schwartz, and Molly Sherlock for assistance in editing the manuscript and to Mary Kwak of the Brookings Institution Press for managing the logistics of publication. Finally, we acknowledge the important contributions of our research collaborators, Peter Muennig, of the Mailman School of Public Health at Columbia University, and Cecilia Rouse, of the Woodrow Wilson School at Princeton University.

THE
PRICE WE PAY

1 CLIVE R. BELFIELD HENRY M. LEVIN

The Education Attainment Gap: Who's Affected, How Much, and Why It Matters

Is excellent education for all America's children a good investment? We know that education is expensive, but poor and inadequate education for substantial numbers of our young may have public and social consequences that are even costlier. The contributors to *The Price We Pay* examine the costs of investing in services to provide excellent education and—equally important—the costs of not doing so.

A person's educational attainment is one of the most important determinants of his or her life chances in terms of employment, income, health status, housing, and many other amenities. Unlike other attributes, such as family background and personal characteristics, educational attainment can be chosen by the individual and influenced by public policy. In the United States we share a common expectation that all citizens will have access to high quality education that will reduce considerably the likelihood of later lifetime inequalities. Yet large differences in educational quality and attainment persist across income, race, and region. Even with similar schooling resources, educational inequalities endure because children from educationally and economically disadvantaged populations are less prepared to start school. They are unlikely to catch up without major educational interventions on their behalf.

In the United States we typically view educational inequality as a challenging public policy issue because of its implications for social justice. If life chances depend so heavily on education, then it is important that educational inequalities be redressed in order to equalize opportunities in a democratic society. But beyond the broader issue of fairness, such inequalities may create costly consequences for the larger society, in excess of what it would take to alleviate the inequalities. An excellent education for all of America's children has benefits not only for the children themselves but also for the taxpayer and society. A copious body of research literature has established that poor education leads to large public and social costs in the form of lower income and economic growth, reduced tax revenues, and higher costs of public services such as health care, criminal justice, and public assistance. Therefore we can view efforts to improve educational outcomes for at-risk populations as public investments that may yield benefits considerably in excess of investment costs.

In this volume we and our colleagues address these issues directly. To set the stage for the discussion, in this chapter we first review previous efforts to measure the costs of inadequate education. We then report on the current educational attainment and achievement of the U.S. population, adopting high school graduation as a minimum standard of education. We also suggest a feasible, if ambitious, goal for increasing high school graduation rates and estimate the further educational gains that would result. Finally, we provide an overview of the book as a whole.

Previous Studies of the Costs of Inadequate Education

Attempts to determine the social consequences of poor education and the returns on investments that might be gained by improving the situation have a modest history. In 1970 the U.S. Senate formed the Select Senate Committee on Equal Educational Opportunity to explore ways in which the federal government could build on the recent racial integration of U.S. public schools. Although the Supreme Court had decided in 1954, in *Brown* v. *Board of Education in Topeka*, to end the dual school system, the actual shift toward desegregating schools had not begun to gain traction until about 1968. The new Senate committee, under Senator Walter Mondale, held hearings on desegregation with the dual goal of supporting movement in that direction and identifying new ways to improve the education of minority and economically disadvantaged students.

Mondale's concern was that although many experts who testified before his committee argued that education would result in higher incomes and tax revenues and lower public costs of crime, public assistance, and health, no one was able to attach numbers to these claims. So the committee decided to commission a study that might provide at least an estimate of the benefits to the taxpayer of reducing the magnitude of inadequate education. What investment would it take, and what would be the return on such an investment? The results were reported in a study titled "The Costs to the Nation of Inadequate Education."[1]

The researchers who conducted the study attempted to estimate the effects of failure to attain a minimum of high school completion among males 25–34 years old in 1970. Using lifetime income patterns by race and education level, and adjusting for the presumed lower "ability" of high school dropouts, simulations were made to estimate the additional earnings associated with an increase in the number of high school completers (including the small number of additional graduates who might then undertake some postsecondary education). On the basis of this analysis it was estimated that $237 billion in lifetime income in 1970 dollars (about $1.2 trillion in 2004 dollars) was lost by failing to ensure that all persons attained a minimum of high school completion, including about $71 billion ($350 billion in 2004 dollars) in government revenues. The effects of inadequate education on public assistance and crime and their costs were also reviewed, as well as evidence on the effects of poor education on reduced political participation and intergenerational mobility and higher health costs. Because of data shortcomings, however, these estimates were highly speculative.

The study assumed that educational investments in compensatory resources would have to increase by 50 percent for every year of schooling, elementary through high school, in order to provide the resources that would lead to graduation. The overall cost of providing these additional resources for the dropout cohort that was analyzed was estimated at about $40 billion in 1970 dollars (about $200 billion in 2004 dollars). When this figure was compared with just the benefits of higher tax revenues from increased high school completion, the benefits were almost twice the costs. Under a substantial range of assumptions it appeared that investing in reducing the number of poorly educated people in the population would have public benefits well in excess of the costs.

Ramirez and del Refugio Robledo replicated this type of analysis for the cohort of Texas ninth graders in 1982–83 who were projected to drop out before their anticipated graduation in 1986.[2] They estimated the benefits of a dropout prevention program as those attributable to savings in public assistance, training and adult education, crime and incarceration, and unemployment insurance and placement and to higher earnings associated with the additional high school graduates. Such benefits were calculated at $17.5 billion, and the costs of eliminating dropouts in this cohort were estimated at slightly less than $2 billion, for a benefit to cost ratio of nine to one. Although

1. Levin (1972).

2. Ramirez and del Refugio Robledo (1987).

the specifics of this investment were unclear, estimates of additional tax revenues were 2.5 times greater than the costs to taxpayers.

James Catterall undertook a similar analysis of children who dropped out of high schools in Los Angeles for all students in the class of 1985.[3] He concluded that because of the dropouts, the Los Angeles class of 1985 was likely to generate more than $3 billion less in lifetime economic activity than it would have if all its members had graduated. Catterall suggested that the cost of investing successfully in dropout reduction would be a mere fraction of this amount. Furthermore, he found that Los Angeles was addressing the dropout problem with programs that were spending the equivalent of only about $50 per dropout, or less than one-half of 1 percent of school spending, even though 40 percent of its students were not graduating.

Although the authors of each of these studies made serious attempts to identify the benefits to society or to the taxpayer of improving the education of those with the most serious educational inadequacies, each study has serious shortcomings because of the early vintage of the research. Only recently have detailed data that enable the linking of educational levels to participation in crime, health, public assistance, and tax revenues become available. This is also true of research studies that have provided insights into ways to separate out non-educational influences on income and behaviors that increase the cost of public services. Moreover, in recent decades the benefits of education have grown, leaving high school dropouts farther behind. The contributors to this book capitalize on both the rich data resources and the research on these topics that have emerged in recent years.

Inadequate Education Today

What do these data say about the current state of education in the United States? In attempting to answer this question in this chapter, we focus on the flow of new entrants into the labor market (approximately 4 million persons in 2005) rather than the stock of the total workforce (approximately 150 million persons). Specifically, we describe the educational attainment levels of the cohort of persons aged 20 in 2005. We then consider potential improvements in education levels that might be feasible and realistic. Such improvements can be used to calculate the economic consequences of ensuring an adequate education.

Consistent with previous analyses, we adopt high school graduation as a minimally adequate educational standard. We recognize that precisely what consti-

3. Catterall (1986).

tutes an adequate education differs among observers. Some argue for high student performance on standardized achievement tests. Others say that all students should meet meaningful levels of proficiency in key subjects. Still others emphasize the ability to solve problems and analyze complex situations. We focus on high school graduation because it is viewed as a minimum requirement for developing both the cognitive and noncognitive attributes that are important for success in adulthood. It is usually a minimum requirement for engaging in further training and higher education, and it opens up a range of future possibilities that would otherwise be closed. Most important, we focus on high school graduation because for the population as a whole the United States is far from fulfilling even this educational goal. International comparisons show that the United States lags behind other industrialized countries in rates of high school graduation.[4]

High School Graduation Rates

There is no consensus on definitions of high school graduation, completion, and dropout status.[5] Some students may complete high school but not graduate—that is, complete school with a level of knowledge and skills deemed appropriate by age 18. Some may take an examination such as the General Educational Development (GED) exam in lieu of completing secondary school, but this may not fully capture what is learned by attending school.[6] Some may drop out and then return to school later. Further, states vary in the exit standards they impose on graduates. Increasingly, states are requiring students to pass an exit examination in addition to completing a specified set of courses.

Research studies typically use a uniform method for estimating graduation rates: the number of completers divided by the student population for a given age or grade cohort. However, some studies use contemporaneous figures (for example, diplomas awarded relative to the age cohort size in a given year), and others compare the number of twelfth grade graduates with the size of the ninth grade cohort three years earlier. Also, studies vary in the way they account for private school enrollments, special education students, and migration.

Two population-level data sets—the Current Population Survey (CPS) of the U.S. Bureau of the Census and the Common Core of Data (CCD) of the U.S. Department of Education—are typically used. Both have shortcomings

4. Organization for Economic Cooperation and Development (2006).

5. See Barton (2005); Educational Testing Service (2004); Greene (2002); Haney and others (2004); Holzman (2005); Kaufman (2004); Mishel and Roy (2006); National Center for Education Statistics (2003); Orfield and others (2004); Swanson (2004); Warren (2005).

6. On the lack of equivalence between graduation and the GED, see Cameron and Heckman (1993).

Table 1-1. *National Graduation Rates*
Percent

Measure	*Graduation rate*
High school completion rate[a]	67
Graduates/population rate[b]	68
Cumulative proportion index[c]	68
Basic completion ratio[c]	68
Diploma/population rate[c]	69
Diploma/population rate[d]	70
Department of Education CCD enrollment rate[e]	70
National Center for Education Statistics rate[c]	80
Inverse dropout promotion rate[c]	82

a. From Warren (2005).
b. From Haney and others (2004).
c. From Swanson (2004).
d. From Barton (2005).
e. From Greene and Forster (2003, app. table 1).

for calculating graduation rates. Neither is longitudinal or based on actual student transcripts, as recommended by Mishel and Roy.[7] The CPS has poor population coverage (especially for black males), counts only the civilian noninstitutionalized population (but includes immigrants), and classifies GED holders as high school graduates. In contrast, the CCD relies on public school administrative data, estimates "event status dropout" in terms of whether a student graduated on time or not, and classifies GED holders as dropouts. In addition, both self-reported and administrative data are likely to have significant measurement biases (misreporting and overstatement), particularly for persons with low education levels.

Notwithstanding these methodological issues, there is reasonable agreement across data sets on the high school graduation rate for public school students. Table 1-1 summarizes nine separate measures. Seven of them report rates of 67 to 70 percent, and two report rates of 80 to 82 percent, but these last have lower coverage rates of districts and schools and so may be overstated.[8] Separately, the authors of a recent federal study comprehensively documented ways of measuring the high school graduation rate.[9] Identifying eleven measures from the literature, they found strong correlations across the estimates (with

7. Mishel and Roy (2006).
8. Swanson and Chaplin (2003).
9. Seastrom and others (2007).

Table 1-2. *Public School Graduation Rates and High School Dropout Rates*[a]
Percent

Subgroup	*On-time graduation rate*	*High school dropout rate*
Male		
White	71	8
Black	42	13
Hispanic	48	32
Female		
White	77	7
Black	56	9
Hispanic	59	22

Sources: Column 1 from Swanson (2004, table 5) for 2001 school year. Column 2 from Greene and Forster (2003, app. table 1) for ages 16–24.

a. Recipients of GED credentials are counted as high school completers. Data are based on sample surveys of the civilian non-institutionalized population.

the weakest correlations at 0.5 and most at 0.8). Thus, rather than focus on the precision of the estimates of the dropout rate, we emphasize the overall consensus. Specifically, we can conclude with reasonable confidence that roughly three of every ten students in the United States are not graduating from high school on time.

There are significant differences in dropout rates by race and by gender.[10] Table 1-2 reports the figures for two studies that tabulate on-time graduation rates and dropout rates by race and gender. Graduation is measured at one point in an individual's life, whereas being a dropout is a state that a person can move out of at any time by passing a high school equivalency exam. Table 1-2 shows that educational attainment, whether measured as an event or as a status, is very low, especially for minority groups. The black male public high school graduation rate is 42 percent, in comparison with 48 percent for Hispanic males and 71 percent for white males. The disparities are smaller for females, but they follow the same pattern: black females graduate at a rate of 56 percent, Hispanic females at 59 percent, and white females at 77 percent.

Attainment for New Cohorts Entering the Labor Market

To model the economic consequences of high school graduation, we focus on a single age cohort. Specifically, we use the Current Population Survey (CPS)

10. Kao and Thompson (2003).

Table 1-3. *Educational Attainment of the Population Aged 20 in 2005*[a]
Thousands except as indicated

Subgroup	*< 9th grade*	*9th–11th grade (GED)*	*High school*	*College level*	*Total*	*Dropouts (percent)*
Male	63	450	638	1,101	2,252	23
White	18	194	402	749	1,362	16
Black	6	69	99	127	301	25
Hispanic	38	168	104	48	358	58
Other	1	19	33	177	230	9
Female	33	259	508	1,183	1,983	15
White	6	100	297	822	1,225	9
Black	0	71	96	129	296	24
Hispanic	25	63	81	114	283	31
Other	2	26	33	118	179	16

Source: Current Population Survey, March 2005.

a. The category 9th–11th grade includes persons with GEDs. College level includes persons with some college and those with at least a B.A. Dropout percentages include all persons with less than high school education. Race-specific adjustments for rates of institutionalization are from Raphael (2004): the average rate for blacks and other [whites] is 9 percent [2 percent]; for those with less than high school education it is 23 percent [4 percent]. Race-specific adjustments for GED receipt are from Rumberger's (2004) analysis of the National Educational Longitudinal Survey (2000). Of all graduates, 15 percent of blacks and other races and 8 percent of whites are GED holders.

for educational attainment levels for the cohort of young adults who were 20 in 2005. We choose age 20 to allow for those who did not graduate on time.

The distribution of attainment is given in table 1-3. We adjust the raw figures to account for two ways in which the CPS is less than ideal (see table note). First, we adjust for persons who are incarcerated and so are not counted in the CPS; we use data on incarceration rates by education level from Stephen Raphael.[11] Second, we adjust for those who have earned a GED, because this is not equivalent to a regular high school diploma; here we use data from the National Educational Longitudinal Survey (NELS) derived by Russell Rumberger.[12] We separate persons by gender and by race or ethnicity—white, black, Hispanic, and other.

As shown in table 1-3, a large number of males aged 20 are not high school graduates. Of the 2.3 million males, 0.5 million are dropouts, with 0.6 million having completed high school and another 1.1 million attending or having

11. Raphael (2004).
12. Rumberger (2004).

completed college. The overall male dropout rate is 23 percent. After accounting for those who graduate late from high school, this rate corresponds to the national estimates reported in table 1-1. The dropout rate is much higher for black and Hispanic males than for white males.

A similar pattern can be seen for females. There are 0.3 million dropouts, which is 15 percent of the age cohort. For white females, fewer than one in ten is a dropout. For black females, one in four is a dropout; for Hispanic females the ratio is almost one in three.

Overall, table 1-3 shows that a significant number of persons entering the labor market lack an adequate education. Although there are about 800,000 noncompleters, we assume that the 709,000 who have succeeded in reaching at least tenth grade might be considered prospects for high school graduation. (If we do not adjust for incarceration and the GED, there are approximately 600,000 dropouts). This subgroup of persons might become graduates if effective educational interventions were implemented.

Increasing Educational Attainment after High School

Increasing the numbers of people graduating from high school will also enable and motivate more of them to attend college. These may be the same new graduates or they may be people who would have graduated in the absence of new interventions but were motivated by the programs to attend college and to raise their employment prospects. Regardless, failing to ensure that a person graduates from high school, and so foreclosing the opportunities of college, should be counted as one of the costs of inadequate education. Raising educational standards in high school would mean more college education, resulting in additional economic benefits. To capture these effects we can conceive of an "expected high school graduate," a person who is a new high school graduate and in addition now has some probability of progressing to college and completing a degree.

Progression to college—conditional on high school graduation—can be divided into attendance and completion, both of which may vary across race, gender, and many other variables (for example, occupational choice, region, parental education). Table 1-4 shows rates of college attendance and completion by sex and race or ethnicity. We calculated attendance rates directly from NELS-1988, a longitudinal survey that followed students who were in eighth grade in 1988. For attendance rates we looked only at those who were in the lowest quartile for reading. For completion rates we used tabulated results from the Beginning Postsecondary Students Longitudinal Study, which followed persons through five academic years from college entry in

Table 1-4. *College Attendance and Completion Rates by Age 20*[a]
Percent

	Attendance rates for lowest quartile in reading		*Completion rates for lowest third of socioeconomic status*	
	Two-year college	*Four-year college*	*Two-year college*	*Four-year college*
Male				
White	18	12	64	56
Black	17	16	48	49
Hispanic/other	18	9	55	53
Female				
White	24	6	58	65
Black	21	10	47	54
Hispanic/other	21	6	48	57

Sources: For attendance, 1988 National Educational Longitudinal Survey; for completion rates, 1996–2001 Beginning Postsecondary Students Longitudinal Study (National Center for Education Statistics 2002, table 311).

a. College attendance rates are as of 1994 for those aged 20 who were in the lowest quartile for reading. College completion rates are within five years of first enrollment.

1995. We restricted the analysis to those in the lowest third of socioeconomic status.

Using these progression rates we construct an "expected high school graduate" by sex and race. The probabilities that a person in each category will graduate from high school, attend some college, and obtain a B.A. or more advanced degree are reported in table 1-5. Based on data for persons from the most disadvantaged backgrounds, these are very conservative progression rates. They reflect the fact that only education levels are being changed, not ability or family resources. Approximately 80 out of 100 new high school graduates are expected to terminate their education after high school, and of the remainder, three-quarters are likely to attend but not complete college. Nevertheless, for all groups it is likely that inducing expected dropouts to graduate will yield a further upgrading of education into college. This upgrading effect must also be counted in examining the cost to the nation of inadequate education.

Aggregate Effects of Raising the Number of High School Graduates

Aspirationally, we wish to find ways for all students to graduate from high school and to receive an excellent education. The literature on the causes of dropping out, however, suggests that this will not be accomplished by even the

Table 1-5. *Expected High School Graduate Progression Rates*[a]
Probability

	Highest level of attainment conditional on high school graduation		
	High school	*Some college*	*B.A. or above*
Male			
White	0.80	0.12	0.07
Black	0.75	0.17	0.08
Hispanic/other	0.77	0.18	0.05
Female			
White	0.81	0.14	0.05
Black	0.83	0.11	0.06
Hispanic/other	0.85	0.11	0.04

a. Probabilities are derived from table 1-4. Those who failed to complete four-year college are classified as "some college." These rates are for new graduates who were on the margin of completing high school. Rates do not sum to 1 because of rounding.

most promising educational interventions. Both statistical studies and surveys of dropouts suggest that the quality or type of education received is not a sole factor.[13] Family problems, frequent residential moves and school mobility, limited cognitive or physical abilities, psychological problems, pregnancies, and financial constraints all exert pressure on students to drop out. Experts agree that a more complete response will require changes not only in schools but also in the combined support and additional resources of families and communities. In addition, some of the dropouts are immigrants, many of whom did not attend U.S. schools throughout childhood. Their educational deficiencies cannot be fully addressed by educational reforms within the United States. On the basis of our reading of the literature and on expert opinions, we believe that perhaps half the school dropout rate can be influenced by school interventions that have been proven to be effective.

Realistically, we might expect a reduction of the dropout rate by up to 50 percent for persons who currently have a ninth to eleventh grade education—that is, those on the margin of graduation. As shown later in this volume, each effective intervention typically raises the number of on-time high school graduates by 10 out of 100 students, and school officials are not restricted to applying only one intervention per student. Moreover, we believe

13. Rumberger (2004).

Table 1-6. *Increase in Educational Attainment for Persons Age 20 in 2005*[a]
Projected numbers of persons

	Increase in educational attainment if 50 percent of those with 9th–11th grade education became high school graduates		
	High school	*Some college*	*B.A. or above*
Male	175,470	34,335	14,225
White	77,600	11,640	6,790
Black	25,875	5,865	2,760
Hispanic	64,680	15,120	4,200
Other	7,315	1,710	475
Female	107,790	15,800	6,410
White	40,500	7,000	2,500
Black	29,465	3,905	2,130
Hispanic	26,775	3,465	1,260
Other	11,050	1,430	520

a. Cohort numbers from table 1-3. College progression derived from table 1-5.

other strategies can further reduce dropout rates, although they will draw more heavily upon policies for providing support and resources to families and communities in conjunction with schools.[14] These are discussed later in the book.

In absolute terms, even half of those who reach ninth grade but drop out is still a large number. The age cohort in our analysis includes 450,000 males and 259,000 females who are dropouts. The projected effect on educational attainment of reducing the dropout rate by 50 percent is shown in table 1-6. Such a reduction would mean 354,030 new high school graduates. Most of them would terminate their education after high school, but 50,000 would progress to some college education, and 20,000 would obtain a four-year college degree. Ensuring an adequate education for this number of persons would yield a significant economic gain for taxpayers and society.

About This Book

The remaining chapters in this volume are divided into three parts. The contributors to part 1 examine the broader context of efforts to improve education in the United States. Part 2 is focused on calculating the economic gains pro-

14. Levin and Belfield (2002); Rothstein (2004); Rumberger (2004).

duced by improved education in the form of higher graduation rates. The contributors to part 3 examine specific policy interventions and their potential to achieve the desired gains.

Richard Rothstein and Tamara Wilder lead off part 1 by highlighting the complexity of any effort to reduce inequality, whether in educational attainment or economic outcome. Focusing on differences between blacks and whites, they catalog the many interrelated inequalities associated with low education, from birth through adulthood. Their discussion makes it clear that inadequate education is often a joint product of social disadvantage both outside and inside school. Moreover, even if educational inequality is eliminated, significant disparities in outcomes across the population will remain.

In chapter 3 Marta Tienda and Sigal Alon analyze the demographic trends that make the problem of improving education, particularly for the disadvantaged, so urgent today. As they argue, the United States is experiencing a school-age population bulge, largely as a result of high immigrant fertility. These future workers have parents with relatively little education and lower incomes, making them both a potential asset and a potential liability. If we make major educational investments on their behalf, they can play a crucial role in helping the United States cope with the consequences of an aging population. If we do not rise to the occasion, we will see a decline in both the education and the productivity of the future labor force. This conflux—large numbers of poorly educated people set against an aging population—has been dubbed the "perfect storm."[15]

In chapter 4 Thomas Bailey also focuses on labor force productivity, but he expands the boundaries of the discussion by analyzing the importance of higher education in an increasingly competitive global economy. Bailey agrees with Tienda and Alon that without a major push for educational improvement among the children of immigrants, minorities, and low-income families, the future labor force will be less skilled than the present one. In addition, Bailey asserts that increasing high school graduation is a necessary but insufficient solution. Vast increases in postsecondary participation will also be necessary, requiring public policies that overcome both academic and financial obstacles to higher educational progress.

Beyond the need to invest now to markedly improve the educational attainments of the future labor force, we need to ask what kinds of returns the taxpayer will obtain on such an educational investment. Or, to turn the question around, what does it cost taxpayers not to make that investment? The chapters in part 2 offer some answers by addressing the way inadequate education

15. Kirsch and others (2007).

reduces potential tax revenues and raises public expenditures on crime, health, and public assistance.

In chapter 5 Cecilia Rouse provides estimates of the incomes associated with different levels of education. She converts the additional income from greater educational attainment into the additional tax revenues the U.S. government would receive. The additional tax payments received from high school graduates as opposed to high school dropouts are substantial, and they are even greater for people who undertake some postsecondary education as a consequence of high school graduation. Even the completion of one more year of schooling by age 20 yields to the government the present-value equivalent of $50,000.

In addition to paying less in taxes, high school dropouts are costlier to society because of their dependence on publicly subsidized health care. With lower incomes and poorer health than their more educated counterparts, they draw heavily on public programs such as Medicaid and Medicare in the event of disabilities. In chapter 6 Peter Muennig estimates the effects of poor education on public health care costs using recently available data sets that provide great detail on public health expenditures. He finds that each additional high school graduate would save the government the present-value equivalent of $39,000 over his or her lifetime from age 20.

In chapter 7 Enrico Moretti documents the strong association between education and crime. Dropouts are incarcerated at rates twice those of high school graduates, leading to much greater public spending on policing, the court system, and the prison system. Moretti uses statistical modeling to estimate the likely effects of increased schooling on engagement in criminal activity. He finds that a one-year increase in average schooling reduces murder and assault by almost 30 percent, motor vehicle theft by 20 percent, arson by 13 percent, and burglary and larceny by about 6 percent. Increasing the high school completion rate by just 1 percent for all men ages 20–60 could save the United States more than $1 billion a year in the costs of criminal justice.

Jane Waldfogel, Irwin Garfinkel, and Brendan Kelly show in chapter 8 how poor education raises the probability that a person is on welfare, directly increasing the costs of providing public assistance. The obvious link is that high school dropouts face economic circumstances so poor that they often require financial and other assistance just to meet basic needs. With more education, their economic prospects rise, reducing their dependence on such public assistance. For example, single-mother high school graduates are from 24 to 55 percent less likely to be dependent on assistance from the Temporary Assistance for Needy Families program than are high school dropouts. This chapter highlights the relationship between low levels of educational attainment and the cost of public assistance and the way in which improved education would reduce the taxpayer's burden.

In part 3 the two of us, in chapter 9, begin to join these separate analyses by looking at interventions that might improve the educational situation of people who would normally be recipients of inadequate education. In our view, the best solution would be to invest in educational interventions that ensure that as many students as possible graduate from high school, with an increasing portion of these proceeding to postsecondary education. We identify five interventions that have proved effective in increasing graduation rates, and we estimate the costs for each intervention. We also aggregate the public benefits of additional high school graduates in terms of increased tax revenues and reduced public costs for crime, health care, and public assistance. We then compare the intervention costs with the public benefits. Our analysis clearly shows that the public benefits are substantial and considerably greater than the costs of effective education programs.

Given the scale of inadequate education across the United States, we and our colleagues pay particular attention to policy solutions that might yield significant improvements in the rate of high school graduation. In chapter 10 Clive Belfield focuses on preschool programs. On the basis of a large and rigorous body of evidence, preschool programs are often heralded as a major part of the solution to inadequate education. Belfield reviews this evidence and offers a critical view of whether an expansion of preschool really can deliver what is needed. It is noteworthy that two of the interventions discussed in chapter 9 that have shown strong evidence of increasing high school graduation are preschool programs.

In chapter 11 Ronald Ferguson considers a farther-reaching solution, one in which communities collectively address the problem of inadequate education through social empowerment. Ferguson supports high quality preschools as part of the solution, but he also calls for more skillful parenting along with "transformative school reform." He focuses on both more resources and better programs for children from impoverished and minority backgrounds.

Finally, in chapter 12 Michael Rebell returns the discussion to the issue of fairness and equity. Many high school dropouts come from disadvantaged families in impoverished communities. Rebell reinforces our initial contention that, coupled with strong economic arguments in favor of increased educational investments, U.S. society has an important moral imperative to ensure that all children have the opportunity to secure their own economic well-being.

Conclusion

By focusing resources on students who are receiving inadequate education, it is possible to obtain benefits far in excess of the costs of those investments. Increases in tax revenues and reductions in taxes paid into public health, criminal justice, and public assistance would amount to many billions of dollars a year in excess of the costs of educational programs that could achieve these results. Even these benefits of more and better education as a good investment do not include the gains in political participation or civic engagement that are also causally influenced by education. Effective investments to ensure high school graduation therefore produce high yields from the taxpayer's perspective.

According to the National Opinion Research Center's General Social Survey (2006), three-quarters of respondents thought the government was spending too little on education.[16] This proportion was greater than the proportions of respondents who thought all other government spending items, including health care, welfare assistance, and the environment, were too low. Political support for public investment in education is strong and justified by the economic returns. But it is important to note that this is due to more than just good public investment policy with monetary returns. A society that provides fairer access to opportunities, is more productive, and has higher employment, better health, and less crime is a better society in itself. It is simply an added incentive that the attainment of such a society is profoundly good economics.

References

Barton, Paul. E. 2005. *Unfinished Business: More Measured Approaches in Standards-Based Reform.* ETS Policy Information Report. Princeton, N.J.: Educational Testing Service.

Cameron, Steven V., and James J. Heckman. 1993. "The Nonequivalence of High School Equivalents." *Journal of Labor Economics* 111, no. 1: 1–47.

Catterall, James. 1986. "On the Social Costs of Dropping Out of School." Report SEPI-86-3. Stanford, Calif.: Stanford Educational Policy Institute.

Educational Testing Service. 2004. *One-Third of a Nation.* ETS Policy Information Report. Princeton, N.J.

Greene, Jay. P. 2002. *High School Graduation Rates in the United States.* New York: Manhattan Institute for Policy Research.

Greene, Jay P., and Greg Forster. 2003. "Public High School Graduation and College Readiness Rates in the United States." Working paper. New York: Manhattan Institute for Policy Research.

16. National Opinion Research Center (2006).

Haney, William, and others. 2004. *The Education Pipeline in the United States, 1970–2000.* National Board on Educational Testing and Public Policy, Boston College.

Holzman, Mark. 2005. "Public Education and Black Male Students: A State Report Card." Policy paper. Boston, Mass.: Schott Foundation for Public Education.

Kao, Grace, and Jennifer Thompson. 2003. "Racial and Ethnic Stratification in Educational Achievement and Attainment." *Annual Review of Sociology* 29, no. 2: 417–42.

Kaufman, Phillip. 2004. "The National Dropout Data Collection System: History and the Search for Consistency." In *Dropouts in America,* edited by Gary Orfield, pp. 107–30. Cambridge, Mass.: Harvard Education Press.

Kirsch, I., and others. 2007. *America's Perfect Storm: Three Forces Facing Our Nation's Future.* ETS Policy Brief. Princeton, N.J.: Educational Testing Service.

Levin, Henry M. 1972. *The Cost to the Nation of Inadequate Education.* Select Senate Committee on Equal Educational Opportunity, 92nd Congress. Government Printing Office.

Levin, Henry M., and Clive R. Belfield. 2002. "Families as Contractual Partners in Education." *UCLA Law Review* 49, no. 6: 1799–1824.

Mishel, Lawrence, and Joydeep Roy. 2006. *Rethinking High School Graduation Rates and Trends.* Washington, D.C.: Economic Policy Institute.

National Center for Education Statistics. 2002. *Short-term Enrollment in Postsecondary Education: Student Background and Institutional Differences in Reasons for Early Departure, 1996–98.* NCES 2003-153. Department of Education.

———. 2003. *Public High School Dropouts and Completers from the Common Core of Data: School Year 2000–01.* NCES 2004-310. Department of Education.

National Opinion Research Center. 2006. "Trends in National Spending Priorities." Chicago.

Orfield, Gary, and others. 2004. *Losing Our Future: How Minority Youth Are Being Left Behind by the Graduation Rate Crisis.* Civil Rights Project, Harvard University.

Organization for Economic Cooperation and Development. 2006. *Education at a Glance.* Paris (www.oecd.org/document/7).

Ramirez, David, and Maria del Refugio Robledo. 1987. "The Economic Impact of the Dropout Problem." *IDRA Newsletter* (April). San Antonio: Intercultural Development Research Association.

Raphael, Stephen. 2004. "The Socioeconomic Status of Black Males: The Increasing Importance of Incarceration." Working paper. University of California, Berkeley.

Rothstein, Richard. 2004. *Class and Schools: Using Social, Economic, and Educational Reform to Close the Black-White Achievement Gap.* Washington, D.C.: Teachers College Press and Economic Policy Institute.

Rumberger, Russell. 2004. "Why Students Drop Out of School." In *Dropouts in America,* edited by Gary Orfield, pp. 243–54. Cambridge, Mass.: Harvard Education Press.

Seastrom, Marilyn, and others. 2006. *User's Guide to Computing High School Graduation Rates,* vol. 2: *Technical Evaluation of Proxy Graduation Indicators.* NCES 2006-605. National Center for Education Statistics, Department of Education.

Swanson, Chris. B. 2004. "Who Graduates? Who Doesn't? A Statistical Portrait of Public High School Graduation, Class of 2001." Working paper. Washington, D.C.: Urban Institute.

Swanson, Chris B., and D. Chaplin. 2003. "Counting High School Graduates When Graduates Count: Measuring Graduation Rates under the High Stakes of NCLB." Working paper. Washington, D.C.: Urban Institute.

Warren, John. 2005. "State-Level High School Completion Rate: Concepts, Measures, and Trends." *Education Policy Analysis Archives* 13: 51.

PART I

Assessing the Scope of the Challenge

these domains run in multiple directions, and because, in the absence of controlled experimentation, it would be impossible to establish the extent to which inequality in any domain causes inequalities in others, we think it useful to make this presentation of consistent inequalities across all domains without attempting to draw conclusions about their relative importance.

Many indicators of inequality are not truly comparable. For a rough comparison, we estimate each indicator as black and white percentile rankings in a national distribution. In other words, we describe the experience of a typical (the mean or, where more appropriate—as in the case of family income—the median) African American as being at a certain percentile rank in a national distribution, in comparison with the typical white experience, which is at a different (and almost always higher) percentile rank in that national distribution. In each case, the national distribution includes data for the most recent year available, between 1998 and 2005, on the experiences of all individuals, not only non-Hispanic blacks and whites.

Our effort to transform each indicator of inequality into percentile rankings requires an assumption that the national experience in each of the domains we measure is normally distributed, an assumption that may not be as faithful to reality as we would like. In other words, our method forces us to assume that if we were to plot all experiences in any domain, a bell-shaped curve for that domain would result. In such a distribution, the mean rank in the population is the 50th percentile. When, as is almost always the case, the distribution of white outcomes is shifted to the right of that of black outcomes, the white mean percentile is above 50 and the black mean below 50. In the most commonly reported academic subject areas, for example, we describe average white student outcomes as being generally close to, and sometimes even slightly above, the 60th percentile. Those of black students are at about the 30th percentile, reflecting roughly a 30 percentile gap in academic achievement.[2]

In other cases the data themselves cannot be distributed normally because they are dichotomous. What we assume in such cases is that there is an underlying, normally distributed risk of experiencing an indicator. For example, we consider teen pregnancy and report that 9 percent of black teenagers and 2 percent of white teenagers become pregnant or get someone pregnant.

2. This assumption of a normal distribution is more valid for some indicators than for others. Norm-referenced academic achievement tests, such as the National Assessment of Educational Progress (NAEP), produce a close-to-normal distribution of results, but even there the matter is not straightforward. Testing experts vigorously dispute whether academic achievement truly is normally distributed or whether tests such as the NAEP assume, without evidence, that ability is unidimensional, whether those tests are constructed to include only questions that confirm this assumption, and whether their distributions of responses conform to a preconceived normal distribution.

Applying our assumption that these outcomes reflect underlying normal distributions of "risk of pregnancy"—in this case, one might think of the risk as the degree of "risky behavior"—we infer that the average black teenager is at the 35th percentile in the national distribution of avoiding teen pregnancy, whereas the average white teenager is at the 61st percentile. We are aware that a teenager cannot be only a little bit pregnant. But this need not mean that all teens who become pregnant face identical probabilities of becoming so, on the basis of their sexual practices, nor that those who do not become pregnant have not risked becoming so. This way of thinking about teen pregnancy, not as a dichotomous outcome (being pregnant or not) but as the culmination, on average, of a set of risks of pregnancy, has the advantage of enabling us to compare the percentile rankings of blacks and whites for teen pregnancy with their rankings for test scores, wealth, illness, and other measures.

When we summarize indicators in each of the ten broad domains, we arbitrarily weight each indicator equally. Reasonable arguments can be made that some indicators should have more weight than others—for example, eighth grade test scores incorporate not only eighth grade learning but also fourth grade learning, because eighth grade scores are affected by how well prepared eighth graders were by their fourth grade teachers. Thus it might be reasonable to weight eighth grade test scores more heavily than fourth grade test scores in an academic achievement summary. For another example, it might seem that in assessing differences in civic participation, whether a young adult votes should be weighted more heavily than whether he or she engages in volunteer activity. Yet because at this point we have no basis for a consistently appropriate weighting scheme, we utilize an equal-weight-within-domain approach, which we acknowledge is arbitrary. Because inequalities are so consistent within domains, however, this arbitrariness makes less difference than it might at first appear.

Academic Achievement

We begin with conventional measures of academic achievement, with data from the National Assessment of Educational Progress, or NAEP, produced by the National Center for Education Statistics of the U.S. Department of Education. Although we discuss these and subsequent data in the present tense, it should be remembered that they were collected between 1998 and 2005.

For fourth grade reading, average black student scores are at the 30th percentile in a distribution of all students. White fourth graders, on average, are at the 62nd percentile. In the eighth grade the reading gap is roughly the same, with black students at the 31st percentile and whites at the 60th. In writing, black fourth graders perform at the 35th percentile, and eighth graders seem to have fallen to the 32nd percentile. Whites are at the 57th percentile in both grades. In mathematics, black fourth graders are, on average, at the 26th percentile, in comparison with whites at the 63rd percentile. At eighth grade, black students are at the 25th percentile, in comparison with whites at the 62nd percentile.[3]

Turning to the gap in social studies, in American history, black students perform at the 29th percentile in the fourth grade and at the 28th in the eighth grade. In knowledge of civics and government, black students perform at the 31st percentile in both the fourth and eighth grades. And in geography, black fourth graders perform at the 24th percentile and eighth graders at the 21st percentile. In each of these subject areas and grades, whites are at, just below, or just above the 60th percentile.

In the arts, the NAEP has tested only eighth graders, and only once, in 1997. On a test in which students listened to music and then demonstrated their skill in identifying, analyzing, and describing important aspects of the work, black students performed on average at about the 28th percentile, and whites at the 59th percentile. On a similar test of the visual arts in which students were asked to identify, analyze, and describe works of art, black students performed at about the 23rd percentile, and whites at the 60th.[4]

Is it possible to render a judgment about the overall gap in academic achievement between black and white students? To do so, we would need data on other subject areas and grade levels. We would also require a theory about the relative importance of these different measures. Notwithstanding the danger of misleading from a failure to evaluate relative importance, we summarize the academic achievement gap simply by averaging the various indicators of academic achievement just described, finding that black students are at about the 27th percentile of achievement using such an unweighted average of indicators and that white students are at the 61st percentile.

Pregnancy, Childbirth, Neonatality, and Infancy

We now turn to the wider set of inequalities, beginning with those that affect a child even before birth. We have collected a number of indicators of inequality from pregnancy through infancy. Space permits us to describe only a few of them here.

3. National Center for Education Statistics (2005a). Except where otherwise indicated, this publication is the source for each indicator in this section of the chapter.

4. Persky, Sandene, and Askew (1998).

Inequality begins shortly after conception. One indicator of a child's healthy birth, making other lifetime outcomes more likely to be successful, is that the mother receives early medical attention during pregnancy. Twenty-five percent of black mothers receive no prenatal care during the first trimester, whereas 11 percent of white mothers receive none. Six percent of black mothers receive no prenatal care at all (or get it only during the last trimester, when it is almost too late), but only 2 percent of white mothers, one-third the number of blacks, receive no care or too-late care.[5]

These data, describing only care during pregnancies that end with live births, probably understate the disparity. We have no good data on unsuccessful pregnancies, but it is probable that black women also miscarry more frequently than whites. Data on neonatal deaths strengthen this conclusion. For black newborns, there are 9 deaths within the first month for every 1,000 live births. For whites, there are only 4 such deaths. Considering infant mortality during the first year of life, there are 14 deaths for blacks and 6 for whites per 1,000 live births.[6] Adequate prenatal care perhaps could have prevented some of these deaths.

These differences in pregnancy and childbirth are reflections of racial inequality itself and are not eliminated by controlling for maternal education. For black mothers who are high school dropouts, 15 of every 1,000 newborns die within the first year; for white dropouts, 9 do so. For mothers who graduate from high school but receive no further education, infant deaths are 13 for blacks and 6 for whites. And for mothers with at least one year of college, infant deaths are 12 for blacks and 4 for whites.[7]

Racial differences in pregnancies and live births are paralleled by differences in birth weight. Low birth weight predicts special education placement, lower academic achievement, emotional maladjustment, and likelihood of criminal behavior. For blacks, 3 percent of newborns have very low birth weights, less than 1,500 grams, the condition most likely to lead to adverse educational and lifetime outcomes. For whites, the rate is only one-third as great. For low birth weight (less than 2,500 grams), a condition still putting children at risk, 13 percent of black babies qualify, versus 7 percent of whites.[8] Again, these disparities narrow only slightly after controlling for education.[9]

Black mothers are less likely than whites to follow practices recommended for the best infant outcomes. One of the few measures for which we have data

5. National Center for Health Statistics (2004, table 6).
6. National Center for Health Statistics (2004, table 19).
7. National Center for Health Statistics (2004, table 20).
8. National Center for Health Statistics (2004, table 12).
9. National Center for Health Statistics (2004, table 13).

is breast-feeding. Fifty-four percent of black mothers breast-feed their infants in the early postpartum period, in comparison with 73 percent of white mothers. When infants are 6 months of age, the disparity is even greater, with 19 percent of black mothers and 36 percent of white mothers breast-feeding. For mothers of infants 1 year of age, the rates are 12 percent and 21 percent, respectively.[10]

As with academic achievement, some of these indicators of racial gaps in pregnancy, childbirth, neonatality, and infancy are more important than others. For example, if one closed the gap in prenatal care, then the low and very low birth weight gaps might, at least partly, resolve themselves. Nonetheless, with all the cautions we mentioned earlier, we can summarize the overall black-white gap by weighting each indicator equally, concluding that the average black experience with healthy and successful pregnancy, childbirth, neonatality, and infancy is at the 37th percentile of the experience of all U.S. mothers and babies, whereas the average white experience is at the 54th percentile.

Access to Health Care

Inequalities in the probability of lifetime success attributable to characteristics of pregnancy, childbirth, neonatality, and infancy stem partly from inequalities in health insurance coverage. For children under 18, 14 percent of blacks lack health insurance, including Medicaid and CHIP (federally subsidized children's insurance), versus 7 percent of whites.[11]

The shortage of health insurance for black families is compounded by the inaccessibility of primary care physicians, even when families have insurance. In many low-income minority communities, insurance cards practically confer only the right to wait in line at clinics or emergency rooms, because few obstetricians, pediatricians, and other primary care physicians practice in these communities. We have no national data on this, but a California analysis found that urban neighborhoods with high poverty and large concentrations of black and Hispanic residents had one primary care physician for every 4,000 residents. Neighborhoods that were neither high poverty nor high minority had one per 1,200.[12]

Black children are thus less likely to get primary and preventive medical care than are white children. Although 87 percent of black children and 90 percent

10. Centers for Disease Control and Prevention (2005b, Focus Area 16-19).

11. U.S. Bureau of the Census, Current Population Survey, July supplement, 2005 (table H101).

12. Komaromy and others (1996).

of white children (under 18) have seen a doctor in the previous year,[13] this relatively small disparity does not reflect much larger disparities in the average number of doctor visits and type of medical facility visited. This inequality has both a racial and a socioeconomic aspect. Relatively more poor black children lack medical care than do poor whites, and relatively more non-poor black children lack medical care than do non-poor whites.

Inequality in access to medical care influences the treatments children receive. By the age of 35 months, 25 percent of black children have not received standard vaccinations for diphtheria, tetanus, pertussis, polio, measles, and influenza. For whites, the unvaccinated share is 16 percent.[14]

These inequalities in access to health care compound the inequalities of birth outcomes in contributing to differences in health between black and white children. Differences in health in turn contribute to differences in educational and lifelong outcomes.

Again, assuming that each of these indicators of health care access (as well as other indicators not explicitly described here) reflects normally distributed characteristics and that each has equal weight, black children, on average, are at the 43rd percentile in the distribution of children's access to good health care. White children, on average, are at the 56th percentile.

Health of Young Children

Black children get less adequate nutrition, lacking not calories but some essential nutrients. For example, iron deficiency anemia, which adversely affects cognitive ability and predicts special education placement and school failure, is more prevalent among black children than among whites. Iron deficiency anemia also predisposes a child to lead absorption, which further depresses cognitive ability. In federal programs for low-income children, 19 percent of blacks under the age of 5 are anemic, versus 10 percent of whites.[15]

Disparate rates of lead poisoning also exacerbate the academic achievement gap. Children who live in older buildings have more lead dust exposure, which harms cognitive functioning and behavior. High lead levels also contribute to hearing loss.[16]

13. National Center for Health Statistics (2004, table 74).

14. National Center for Health Statistics (2004, table 72).

15. Centers for Disease Control and Prevention (2005c, table 8).

16. Rothstein (2004, p. 158 n. 83, 84). Three percent of black children but only 1 percent of whites, ages 1–5, have blood lead levels that are dangerously high (Centers for Disease Control and Prevention 2005a, p. 515).

Educational inadequacy also results from disparities in vision—not only in near- or farsightedness but also in poor eye-muscle development, which leads to less facility in skills needed for reading, such as tracking print, converging, and focusing. Optometrists who have tested children in low-income black communities report that as many as 50 percent of children may come to elementary school with vision difficulties that impair reading ability, in comparison with 25 percent of children in non-poor communities.[17] These difficulties do not always require correction with eyeglasses; vision exercise therapy may suffice.

At this early age, racial differences in oral health are relatively small. Twenty-five percent of black children between the ages of 2 and 5 have untreated dental cavities; for whites, the figure is 23 percent. As we show later, however, these small disparities grow large as children mature.[18]

Again, assuming that each of these (and other) indicators of young children's health reflects normally distributed characteristics and that each indicator has equal weight, we conclude that young black children, on average, are at the 41st percentile for good health characteristics, whereas young white children, on average, are at the 52nd percentile.

Early Childhood Preparation and School Readiness

Disadvantaged black children are more likely to have vision difficulties that impede reading than are middle-class white children. One reason for this inequality is that disadvantaged children are less likely to engage, as infants and toddlers, in the kind of supervised play that develops hand-eye coordination. Instead, disadvantaged children are more likely to watch television. We have data for fourth graders, among whom 42 percent of black children watch six hours or more of television a day, in comparison with 13 percent of white children.[19] We include these data here because, with actual data on television watching by preschool children unavailable, we assume that the disparities are similar for preschool children.

Young children who watch a lot of television are less likely to be read to by parents or other family members. Young children who are read to not only become familiar with books and words but also learn about the broader experiences described in books, to which they can later relate their instruction in school. In the preschool years, 87 percent of black children ages 3–5 are read

17. Rothstein (2004, p. 157 n. 70, 73).

18. National Center for Health Statistics (2004, table 80).

19. National Center for Education Statistics (2005b, table 143).

to regularly by a family member, less than the 96 percent of white children who are read to regularly. In other words, 13 percent of black children come to school without having benefited from being read to by a family member at least once a week.[20] When they get to kindergarten, only 35 percent of black children benefit from *daily* reading by a parent or other family member; 49 percent of white children do so.[21]

Newly analyzed data from the federal government's Early Childhood Longitudinal Study (ECLS) show that the most powerful predictor of elementary school reading and math skills is not whether children enter school knowing the alphabet, how to sound out words, or how to count. Rather, it is their level of fine motor skills.[22] Fine motor skills are developed not by watching television, no matter how educational, but by playing games of imagination with toy cars, blocks, dolls, and other manipulable objects. In the distribution of all children who are 5 years of age, fine motor skill development for black children is, on average, at the 35th percentile; for white children, it is at the 53rd percentile.[23]

Behavioral characteristics of kindergartners also predict their reading and mathematics success in school.[24] These characteristics include measures of attention span, curiosity, self-control, interpersonal skills, and problem behaviors. These data also confirm what kindergarten teachers contend: the abilities to sit still, pay attention, and take turns are more important indicators of school readiness than early academic skills.[25] Black kindergartners are at the 37th percentile on a composite of these behavioral characteristics; whites are at the 53rd percentile.[26]

20. U.S. Bureau of the Census, "Survey of Income and Program Participation, 1996 Panel, Wave 12, P70-89"; "A Child's Day: 2000 (Selected Indicators of Child Well-Being)" (table D7); "Reading to Children by Any Family Member: Characteristics of Children and Parents: 2000" (www.census.gov/population/socdemo/well-being/p70-89/00tabD07.xls [August 2005]).

21. Denton and Germino-Hauskens (2000, table 20). These apparent racial differences may result partly from the fact that black parents are likely to have less education themselves than white parents. This means not only that they are less comfortable with leisure reading but also that their similarly educated peers are less likely to model such behavior by reading to their own children. Yet a racial difference remains even after controlling for these gross measures of parental education. Where mothers have at least a high school education, 35 percent of black kindergartners benefit from daily reading by a family member, in comparison with 50 percent of white kindergartners. Where mothers have less than a high school education, 32 percent of black kindergartners benefit from daily reading by a family member, in comparison with 43 percent of white kindergartners.

22. Grissmer (2005). These ECLS predictive data only confirm what kindergarten teachers themselves contend. The ECLS survey of kindergarten teachers finds that they are more likely to consider the ability to use pencils and paint brushes to be an important indicator of school readiness than the ability to count or know alphabet letters (see National Center for Education Statistics 2005b, table 50).

23. Grissmer (2005).

24. Grissmer (2005).

25. National Center for Education Statistics (2005b, table 50).

26. Grissmer (2005).

The development of these behavioral characteristics, as well as of fine motor skills, reflects, among other environmental characteristics, the quality of child care experienced by preschool children while their parents are at work. Inadequate data exist on the quality of child care received by preschool children, but the National Institute of Child Health and Human Development has conducted a survey in which researchers characterized the quality of nonmaternal child care settings by measures such as adult-to-child ratios, group sizes, caregiver education levels, and physical space per child, all factors shown to contribute to improved child development.[27] Although the sample sizes are too small for comfort, the direction of the findings is worth noting. About 35 percent of black children from 6 months to 4.5 years of age were in high quality child care settings, in comparison with 55 percent of white children.[28]

Partly these differences in quality of care reflect that, among children not cared for at home by their mothers, black preschoolers are more likely than whites to be cared for by relatives or in other homes and less likely to be in child care centers (38 percent of black children are in center care, versus 41 percent of whites). In addition, the child care centers in which black preschoolers are placed are of poorer quality than those which white preschoolers attend.[29]

More black than white children are enrolled in full-day kindergartens.[30] This is probably because public school districts are more likely to offer full day kindergartens in communities where the need is greatest. But it suggests that if affordable, quality preschool options were offered, black parents would likely take advantage of them.

We can summarize these indicators of early childhood preparation and school readiness, again assuming that each reflects normally distributed characteristics and has equal weight. Young black children, on average, are at the 40th percentile of early childhood preparation and school readiness, whereas young white children, on average, are at the 57th percentile.

Use of Non-classroom Hours in the School Years

During children's school years, inequality is further compounded by differences in out-of-school experiences that contribute to school success.

We earlier speculated that differences in the quality of child care might contribute to black preschool children's watching more hours of television than

27. National Institute of Child Health and Human Development (1999).
28. Bub and McCartney (2005).
29. Bub and McCartney (2005).
30. Walston and West (2004, chap. 4).

white preschool children, and this might interfere with the development of fine motor skills that predict later reading ability. This racial difference in television watching continues through adolescence, perhaps reflecting the relative accessibility of organized cultural, athletic, and academic programs in the after-school hours. On an average school day, 67 percent of black high school students watch three or more hours of television, whereas only 29 percent of white high school students watch this much television.[31]

Outside of school, 14 percent of black elementary and secondary students take music lessons, in comparison with 18 percent of white students. Twenty percent of black students take part in scouting programs, versus 27 percent of white students. Thirty percent of black students take part in organized sports such as soccer and Little League, relative to 48 percent of white students.[32] Considering combined participation on either in-school or out-of-school sports teams, 53 percent of black students participate, in comparison with 61 percent of white students.[33]

Such inequalities continue during the summer, when white children are more likely to gain additional organizational, athletic, and leadership experiences than are black children. Twenty-five percent of black schoolchildren participate in organized summer activities of all kinds, in comparison with 45 percent of white children. Eight percent of black teenagers either get unpaid internships or perform community service during their summer breaks from school, relative to 13 percent of white teenagers.[34]

Yet on a few measures of activities that parents conduct with their children, black parents raise their children in ways that are more conducive to success than the ways white parents raise their children. Black school-age children are more likely than white children, 22 percent to 19 percent, to be taken by their parents each month to visit an art gallery, museum, or historical site. They are more likely than white children to be taken monthly by their parents to visit a zoo or an aquarium, 15 percent to 9 percent. Black children are more likely than white children to be taken each month by their parents to a religious event, 62 percent to 54 percent, or to an event sponsored by a community or ethnic organization, 29 percent to 24 percent.[35]

Although white schoolchildren are more likely to be enrolled by their parents in after-school activities such as scouting, music lessons, and sports

31. Centers for Disease Control and Prevention (2004, table 56).
32. Vaden-Kiernan and McManus (2005, table 11).
33. Centers for Disease Control and Prevention (2004, table 56).
34. National Center for Education Statistics (1998, p. 42).
35. Vaden-Kiernan and McManus (2005, table 8).

leagues, black children are more likely to be enrolled in religious activities or educational programs, including college admission test preparatory classes.[36]

When school-age children see neighbors, parents of friends, or friends of parents who are well educated, have professional jobs, and are otherwise successful, they have models to which they can aspire. Thus, for disadvantaged students, living in communities with diverse populations can contribute to their success. For all the reasons that social and economic disadvantages contribute to children's failure, living amid concentrated social and economic disadvantage accelerates that contribution.[37] Black children are more likely than whites to live amid concentrated social and economic disadvantage, whether that disadvantage is caused by racial or economic segregation or both. Seventy-two percent of black children attend schools in which more than half their fellow students are members of minority groups, in comparison with 11 percent of white children. Fifty-one percent of black children attend schools in which more than three-fourths of their fellow students are members of minority groups, in comparison with 3 percent of white children.[38] Sixty-one percent of black children attend schools in which more than 50 percent of their classmates are from low-income families, eligible for subsidized lunches. Only 18 percent of white children live in such communities. Twelve percent of black children attend schools in which more than 90 percent of their classmates are from low-income families, in comparison with only 1 percent of white children.[39] In such extremely distressed neighborhoods, peer and community influences toward success are less available.

Although blacks make up only 15 percent of the juvenile population, they commit 55 percent of all known juvenile murder offenses.[40] Twenty-five of every 100,000 black 14- to 17-year-olds are known murder offenders. The corresponding rate for white juveniles is 4 per 100,000; the black juvenile murder offender rate is more than six times the white rate.[41]

Again we summarize these indicators of non-classroom hours, including those for which black experience is more positive and those for which it is

36. Vaden-Kiernan and McManus (2005, table 11).

37. Massey and Denton (1993); Wilson (1987).

38. National Center for Education Statistics (2005b, table 95).

39. Orfield and Lee (2005, tables 6 and 7).

40. U.S. Bureau of the Census, *DataFerrett* (dataferrett.census.gov [July 2005]); National Center for Juvenile Justice (2002). The census data were used to define the age-relevant population for purposes of calculating a population rate.

41. U.S. Bureau of the Census, *DataFerrett* (dataferrett.census.gov [July 2005]); National Center for Juvenile Justice (2002). The census data were used to define the age-relevant population for purposes of calculating a population rate.

more negative. Assuming once more that children's experiences are normally distributed and each of the indicators has equal weight, then black children, on average, are at the 46th percentile of all children on measures of positive out-of-classroom experiences, whereas white children, on average, are at the 54th percentile.

Health of School-Age Children

We described earlier the inequalities in the health of young children who enter school. As they move through school, inequalities persist but take somewhat different forms. We mentioned that black children enter school with a rate of vision difficulty that makes reading success less probable. For children under 18, the rates of the most severe cases of blindness and vision difficulty that cannot be corrected by eyeglasses are 2.6 percent for blacks and 2.3 percent for whites.[42]

Because the environments of neighborhoods where disadvantaged children reside contain more allergens, minority and low-income children are more likely to suffer from asthma. Seventeen percent of black children suffer from asthma, versus 11 percent of white children. (Because black children receive less adequate primary medical care and are less likely to be diagnosed, these numbers may understate the disparity.) Again, this is both a racial and a socioeconomic disparity; although poor children suffer from asthma more than non-poor children, the disparity for poverty (15 percent for poor children versus 12 percent for non-poor) is smaller than the racial disparity.[43]

Asthma is generally believed to be the single greatest cause of chronic school absenteeism.[44] It keeps children up at night, and if they do attend school the next day, they are more likely to be drowsy and less attentive. Middle-class asthma sufferers typically get treatment for its symptoms, whereas disadvantaged children get relief less often. As a result, low-income asthmatic children are about 80 percent more likely than middle-class asthmatic children to miss more than seven days of school a year from the disease.[45] Children with asthma refrain from exercise and so are less physically fit. Irritable from sleeplessness, they also have more behavioral problems that depress achievement.[46]

42. Centers for Disease Control and Prevention (2005b, Focus Area 28-04).

43. National Center for Health Statistics (2005, table 1).

44. Philip J. Hilts, "Study Finds Most States Lack System for Monitoring Asthma," *New York Times*, May 22, 2000, p. A-12.

45. Halfon and Newacheck (1993).

46. Forrest and others (1997).

Although lead poisoning has diminished in the United States, black preschoolers have three times the rate of whites. Disparities in blood lead levels continue during the school years. There is no clear cutoff between dangerous and safe blood lead levels. Many school-age children have less-than-"dangerous" levels that still have subtle depressing effects on cognitive ability. In particular, school-age children with levels even half as high as those considered dangerous have lower reading scores, lower math scores, lower nonverbal reasoning scores, and less short-term memory. For black and white children from the ages of 6 to 16, 22 percent of blacks have this half-dangerous level, more than three times the white rate of 6 percent.[47]

Perhaps from differences in diet, perhaps from differences in opportunities for sports and physical activity, black children are more likely to be overweight than whites. Excessive television watching is a significant predictor of obesity in children,[48] and we have already mentioned that black children, perhaps because of less adequate child care arrangements, watch more television than whites. In the elementary school years, 20 percent of black children are overweight, versus 14 percent of whites. Including those who are not overweight but are heavy enough to be seriously at risk of becoming so, the figures rise to 34 percent of black elementary school children and 29 percent of whites.[49] In high school, 16 percent of black students are overweight, in comparison with 10 percent of whites. And 34 percent of black high school students are either overweight or at risk of being overweight, in comparison with 24 percent of whites.[50]

Black students are more likely to engage in irresponsible sexual behaviors than are whites. Nine percent of black high school students have either been pregnant or gotten someone pregnant, in comparison with 2 percent of whites.[51] Engaging in unprotected sexual activity is an indicator of poor health, because of its potential to result not only in pregnancy but in AIDS and other sexually transmitted diseases. Black teenagers are diagnosed with new cases of AIDS at nearly 20 times the annual rate of whites—for every million black teenagers, there are 29 new cases; for every million whites, 1.5 new cases.[52]

In a few important respects, the health of black teenagers is superior to that of whites. For example, black high school students are less likely to engage in

47. Centers for Disease Control and Prevention (2000); Lanphear and others (2000).

48. Hancox and Poulton (2006).

49. Hedley and others (2004).

50. Centers for Disease Control and Prevention (2004, table 58).

51. Centers for Disease Control and Prevention (2004, tables 46).

52. Centers for Disease Control and Prevention (2005b); *DataFerrett* (dataferrett.census.gov [July 2005]).

substance abuse than whites. Only 9 percent of black twelfth graders regularly smoke cigarettes, in comparison with 28 percent of whites. Only 11 percent of black twelfth graders engage in binge drinking, versus 32 percent of whites. One percent of black twelfth graders use cocaine regularly, half the percentage of whites who do so.[53] These patterns, in which fewer blacks than whites engage in self-destructive behaviors, are established by the eighth grade. Although black and white eighth graders seem to experiment with marijuana to similar extents, as these students move through high school, use of marijuana by blacks accelerates much less than does that by whites.

Despite these few contrary indicators, the data together reflect an overall disadvantage in the health status of black schoolchildren. Assuming that children's experiences are normally distributed for each of the indicators of school-age children's physical and mental health, and weighting each indicator equally, we find that black school-age children, on average, are at the 48th percentile in a distribution of favorable health characteristics, whereas white children, on average, are at the 55th percentile.

Educational Attainment

A consequence of these accumulated inequalities is a gap in educational attainment. Absolute levels of attainment are reported in chapter 1 of this volume, so we focus on the disparities between blacks and whites. Our best estimates of the shares of black and white students who earn regular high school diplomas are 74 percent for blacks and 86 percent for whites.[54] Inequality also exists in the academic content of diplomas awarded to blacks and whites. Only 30 percent of black high school graduates take higher level mathematics courses such as precalculus, calculus, and trigonometry in high school, in comparison with 45 percent of white graduates.[55] Ten percent of black graduates take higher level chemistry, physics, or biology, versus 16 percent of white graduates.[56] Overall, blacks with high school diplomas have earned about 2 percent fewer academic course credits than have whites with high school diplomas.[57]

Some dropouts obtain high school equivalency certificates, or GEDs. Although they are commonly termed "equivalency" certificates, a GED is not truly equivalent to a high school diploma. GED holders have worse labor mar-

53. National Center for Health Statistics (2004, table 64).
54. Mishel and Roy (2006).
55. Hoffman and Llagas (2003, p. 57).
56. National Center for Education Statistics (2005b, table 139).
57. Wirt (2005).

ket outcomes, for example, than high school graduates, even when their cognitive skills, measured on a common test, are the same. Nonetheless, having a GED is better than remaining in dropout status, partly because a GED creates eligibility for postsecondary education. Fourteen percent of black youths get GEDS, as do 7 percent of whites. Yet even when GED holders are included, there remains an inequality in high school completion. Eighty-eight percent of blacks have completed high school, including those who dropped out but later acquired a GED, in comparison with 92 percent of whites.[58]

This difference in high school completion is compounded by differences in the college enrollment and completion rates of high school graduates. Forty percent of black high school graduates enroll in four-year colleges the following year, relative to 51 percent of white high school graduates. As a share of the entire college-age population, 24 percent of blacks enroll, and 36 percent of whites.[59] Enrollment in postsecondary education is valuable, but not nearly as much so if students do not complete it with an associate's or bachelor's degree. Of those who enroll in two-year colleges, 9 percent of black students have an associate's degree five years later, and another 3 percent go on to a four-year college to earn a bachelor's degree, for a total of 12 percent. For whites who enroll in a two-year college, 18 percent have an associate's degree and another 11 percent a bachelor's five years later, for a total of 30 percent. For students who enroll in a four-year college, 43 percent of blacks and 62 percent of whites have earned a bachelor's degree five years later. Of those who have not yet completed a degree, some are still enrolled and will get a degree later. Five years after starting college, 72 percent of blacks have either gotten a degree or are still enrolled, whereas 81 percent of whites have similarly persisted.[60] Another way to think of this statistic is that black college students drop out at a rate that is half again as great as the white college dropout rate.

One consequence of these inequalities in college completion is that blacks continue to be underrepresented in the nation's elementary and secondary teaching force. Only 8 percent of all public school teachers are black, whereas 15 percent of the school-age population is black.[61] Another serious consequence is lack of employability. In chapter 4 Thomas Bailey discusses the implications of inequalities in educational attainment for the future workforce.

Of course these inequalities are further compounded when we consider advanced degrees. Blacks make up 12 percent of 35-year-olds, but only 5 percent of all doctoral degrees (outside the field of education) are awarded to

58. Mishel and Roy (2006).

59. Knapp and others (2003); *DataFerrett* (dataferrett.census.gov [July 2005]).

60. Matriculation rates are from National Center for Education Statistics (2005b, table 313).

61. National Center for Education Statistics (2005b, tables 16 and 67).

blacks.[62] Only 7 percent of all M.D. degrees (not including those awarded to nonresident aliens) are awarded to blacks. Only 4 percent of all dentistry degrees are awarded to blacks, as are only 2 percent of all degrees in optometry.[63]

In education, however, blacks receive advanced degrees in numbers proportional to their representation in the population. Again, keeping in mind that blacks are 12 percent of the age-relevant adult population, they receive 13 percent of all doctoral degrees in education. Although blacks continue to be seriously underrepresented in the nation's teaching force, they are less so in school leadership: 11 percent of all public school principals are now black, partly because they are more likely than whites to possess advanced degrees in education.[64] This parity may make greater equality in other professional occupations more achievable by future generations.

Nonetheless, assuming that each of the indicators of educational attainment reflects a normal distribution, and weighting each of them equally, we find that black youths and young adults, on average, are at the 38th percentile in the distribution of educational attainment, whereas whites are at the 51st percentile.

Economic Security

Black and white adults lead unequal lives as well. As at previous stages of life, these inequalities partly continue the inequalities of earlier stages, and partly they are accelerated. About 11 percent of black workers are unemployed, in comparison with 5 percent of white workers.[65] In part this is because black labor force participants have less education than whites, and unemployment rises for workers with less education. But black workers suffer additional labor market disadvantages, even after their education is taken into account. Among 20- to 24-year-olds without high school diplomas, 65 percent of blacks are employed, in comparison with 84 percent of whites. Among 20- to 24-year-old workers with only high school educations, 80 percent of blacks are employed, in comparison with 91 percent of whites.[66] For inequalities after college, we can consider workers from the ages of 25 to 34. Among workers with some college education but who are not college graduates, 91 percent of

62. *DataFerrett* (dataferrett.census.gov [July 2005]); National Center for Education Statistics (2005b, table 298).

63. National Center for Education Statistics (2005b, table 274).

64. National Center for Education Statistics (2005b, tables 84 and 298).

65. Mishel, Bernstein, and Allegretto (2005, table 3.1).

66. National Center for Education Statistics (2006, table 370).

blacks are employed, and 95 percent of whites. Among workers with college degrees, 97 percent of blacks are employed, and 98 percent of whites.[67]

Some analysts suggest that this inequality is only apparent, not real, because the educations received by blacks are less adequate than those of whites with similar educational attainment. If this is the case, then unemployment rates for blacks and whites with comparable educational adequacy might not differ, even if it appears that blacks and whites with similar amounts of education are not equally successful in finding employment. But although this may be part of the explanation, it is not all of it. National data on this point are unavailable, but the continuing findings of audit studies, in which blacks and whites with identical educational backgrounds have differences in job-seeking success, show that labor market discrimination against black workers persists.[68]

The most serious form of unemployment is long-term unemployment, or joblessness that lasts more than six months, often with the loss of unemployment benefits. Here, too, we find inequality. Three percent of black workers are long-term unemployed, in comparison with 1 percent of white workers. Although 20 percent of all unemployed workers are black, 25 percent of the long-term unemployed are black.[69]

Some workers are not counted as unemployed because they are not actively seeking work. They may not want work or may be discouraged from looking for work because recent job searches have been fruitless. So another way to look at inequality in employment is to use the percentage of the total working-age labor force that is employed. Those not employed, the non-workers, include the unemployed as well as discouraged workers. Sixty-six percent of the black working-age population is employed, in comparison with 75 percent of the white working-age population.[70] The lower black employment rate is primarily attributable to the lower employment rate for black males, not females.

These data may misrepresent the inequalities, because they are calculated only for the civilian non-institutionalized population. Because black adults are more likely than white adults to be incarcerated, the employment of blacks as a share of all working-age adults (especially the younger ones) is relatively lower than we show here. But this would be offset, to some degree, by the greater likelihood of blacks being employed in the military.

Income inequalities among workers who are employed are well known. The average hourly wage for all employed black workers was $14.23 in 2003, in comparison with $18.35 for white workers. In other words, black workers' hourly

67. National Center for Education Statistics (2005c, table 17-1).

68. For example, Pager (2003).

69. Allegretto and Stettner (2004).

70. Mishel, Bernstein, and Allegretto (2005, table 3.9).

wages were 76 percent of white workers'.[71] Again the explanation is partly that black workers have less education than white workers. In chapter 5 Cecilia Rouse discusses the economic repercussions of low educational attainment.

But not all wage inequality is explained by differences in educational attainment. For black workers with less than high school educations, hourly wages are 90 percent of the wages of whites with comparable educations. Among people with only high school educations, black workers' hourly wages are 85 percent of whites'. For those with some college education, the ratio is 87 percent, for those with four-year college degrees, it is 83 percent, and for those with advanced degrees, it is 80 percent.[72] It is particularly noteworthy that the inequalities mostly increase as blacks and whites get more education. These data contradict the conventional view that inequalities diminish as educational levels increase. Some of these inequalities may be attributable to differences in the quality of education that blacks and whites receive, but direct evidence of discrimination suggests that educational quality is not the entire explanation.

Inequalities in compensation contribute to inequalities in household income. Median household income for blacks in 2004 was 62 percent of median household income for whites. The United States has made very slow progress in this regard. The ratio of black to white median family income in 2004 was only 3 points higher than the 59 percent rate in 1967.[73]

Even more unequal than earnings and incomes are family assets. Median black wealth, defined as net household worth, is only 10 percent of median white wealth. A higher proportion of the net worth of black than of white households is in home equity. Forty-eight percent of black families own their homes, compared to 72 percent of white families: black net worth in home equity is 67 percent of that of white households. If we look separately at financial wealth, racial inequalities are even more dramatic. Black households have median financial assets of $1,100, only 3 percent of median white household financial assets of $42,000.[74]

All these inequalities in income and wealth have direct effects on the likelihood of educational success for children. Families with less income have less money to devote to the welfare of children. Families with less financial wealth

71. Mishel, Bernstein, and Allegretto (2005, tables 2.6 and 2.17).

72. Mishel, Bernstein, and Allegretto (2005, table 3.9).

73. Mishel, Bernstein, and Allegretto (2005, table 3.9). The ratio of black to white household income was smaller than the ratio of black to white average wages that we described earlier. In part this may be due to there being more employed adults in white families than in black families, which itself is partly attributable to the greater share of black families headed by single mothers. And it may be in part that when black workers are employed, they have fewer hours of work than do white workers.

74. Mishel, Bernstein, and Allegretto (2005, tables 4.6 and 4.11).

are less able to save for college. Assuming that the indicators of employment, wages, and income we have collected each reflect a normal distribution, and weighting each indicator equally, black families, on average, are at the 41st percentile in measures of financial security, whereas white families are at the 54th percentile.[75]

Adult Non-Economic Characteristics

Inequalities in economic security, compounding educational and health inequalities, contribute to differences in the adult lives of blacks and whites in American society. Some of these inequalities would be redressed by raising black youths' educational attainment, but not all of them. Moreover, these inequalities in adult lives cycle back into differences in the ways black and white adults are able to support and nurture their children, perpetuating the inequalities for another generation. In the descriptions of adult life that follow, we focus mostly on activities of young adults, because their lives are presumably more reflective of contemporary educational, social, and economic institutions. Racial inequalities in the lives of older adults can more reasonably be attributed to schools and social conditions of the past.

Black young adults are less likely than whites to participate fully in civic life and democratic governance, perhaps because they are less prepared for it in their schools and communities and perhaps because they have fewer opportunities for involvement. In the 2004 presidential election, 45 percent of young black adults (ages 18–24) voted, in comparison with 49 percent of young white adults. Only 15 percent of young black adults (ages 20–24) engage in volunteer activities, versus 24 percent of whites.[76]

Health inequalities, for which foundations are laid in early childhood and the school years, continue and in some cases increase for young adults who are less able to care for their own children and pass good health habits on to the next generation. The poor health of parents is therefore another determinant of children's lower achievement. Among adults in prime childbearing years, ages 18–34, only 68 percent of blacks are covered by health insurance (including employer-provided, individually purchased, and government-provided insurance such as Medicaid), in comparison with 79 percent of whites.[77] Of

75. It is impossible to include the wealth measures just discussed in these percentile conversions, because the inequalities are expressed as differences in median wealth, not average wealth. If there were a meaningful way to include wealth in these estimates, then the differences in percentile rankings would be even greater.

76. *DataFerrett* (dataferrett.census.gov [July 2005]).

77. U.S. Bureau of the Census, Current Population Survey, July supplement, 2005.

every 100,000 young black adults (ages 20–24), 18 are newly diagnosed each year with AIDS. For whites of the same age group, there is only one diagnosis per 100,000.[78]

Unequal exercise habits also persist into adulthood. Fifty-one percent of black young adults (ages 18–24) engage in the minimal amount of physical activity recommended for good health (including recreational exercise or activity integrated into household work or employment). Among whites, 61 percent of young adults do so. Considering adults from 25 to 34 years old, 44 percent of blacks engage in the minimal amount of physical activity, in comparison with 54 percent of whites.[79] These data are consistent with differences in adults' overweight status. Sixty-three percent of black young adults (ages 20–39) are overweight, in comparison with 55 percent of whites. Considering only those who are obese, 36 percent of blacks and 24 percent of whites in this age group are in this category.[80]

Just as the foundations for physical health in adults are laid in childhood and adolescence, so, too, are patterns of culture and literacy. Thirty-seven percent of black adults have read a play, a poem, or a novel in the last year, relative to 51 percent of white adults.[81]

Black young adults commit more crimes than whites, a continuation of the pattern observed for juvenile offenders. For every 100,000 black young adults (ages 20–24), there are 56 murder offenders; for every 100,000 whites in this age group, there are 7.4.[82]

Among young adults between the ages of 20 and 24, 6 percent of blacks are in prison or jail, in comparison with 1 percent of whites. In this age group, black men are incarcerated at 18 times the rate of black women; for whites, the male-female ratio is half that. These incarceration rates and male-female ratios remain nearly the same for young adults from the ages of 25 to 29.[83]

Bringing together these differences in other adult life experiences, assuming that each of these indicators of adult health, civic participation, and crime reflects a normal distribution, and weighting each of them equally, black adults, on average, are at the 41st percentile in these measures of adult experience, whereas white families are at the 55th percentile.

78. *DataFerrett* (dataferrett.census.gov [July 2005]); Centers for Disease Control and Prevention (2005b).

79. Centers for Disease Control and Prevention (2005d).

80. Hedley and others (2004). For more on health inequalities and the individual health benefits of increasing one's educational attainment, see Muennig (this volume).

81. National Endowment for the Arts (2004, table 9).

82. *DataFerrett* (dataferrett.census.gov [July 2005]); Federal Bureau of Investigation (2003, table 2.5).

83. Harrison and Beck (2005, tables 13, 14).

Conclusion

In summarizing ten domains of black-white inequalities from before birth through adulthood, we have made no attempt to judge which are more important than others or which result from independent forces of inequality in American society as opposed to being simply direct consequences of the others. Certainly the prevailing opinion in the United States today is that of all the inequalities we have described, the gap in education is the most important, and that if this gap were addressed forthrightly, then other inequalities would, with the passage of a generation, take care of themselves. It is true that the black-white gap in academic achievement is greater than the gap in any other domain (table 2-1). This may be partly an artifact of our method, if it is the case that academic achievement is reported from data that are constructed to be more normally distributed than are outcomes in other domains. If this were the case, then our assumption of a normal distribution in other domains could understate the extent of black-white inequality in those domains.

Nonetheless, a plausible inference from the greater inequality in academic achievement might be that our schools themselves produce greater inequality than other social and economic institutions, and therefore schools should be our primary object of reform. We are cautious about drawing this inference, however, for it implicitly assumes that the causal relationships between domains are neither additive nor compounded.

In fact, the inequalities documented here are likely to compound one another.[84] And if risk of academic underachievement is additive (or even compounded), then we should not be surprised if gaps in academic performance turn out to be greater than any gap, considered separately, in the social, economic, or other family characteristics that contribute to academic success. Children whose health, on average, is 7 percentile points worse than that of other children, whose school readiness, on average, is 16 percentile points inferior to that of other children, and whose out-of-school experiences that contribute to

84. Consider this example: if black students' poorer health led them to be absent from school 10 percent more often than white students, it would not be reasonable to assume that these health differences explain only a 10 percent deficit in black students' achievement. Students who are absent from school may suffer not only from missing the learning that could have taken place if they had been present. Because knowledge is cumulative, they may also fall farther behind and be less able to benefit from teaching that takes place after they return to school. In this case, a 10 percent increase in health-related absenteeism is responsible for more than a 10 percent decrease in learning opportunities. So although it might initially seem plausible that the greater inequality in academic achievement (an estimated black-white gap of 34 percentile points) than in school-age health (an estimated black-white gap of 7 percentile points) suggests a greater failure of educational than of health institutions, no such suggestion can be confirmed by these data alone.

Table 2-1. *Rankings of Blacks and Whites in a National Distribution across Ten Domains of Life*
Percent

Indicator	*Blacks*	*Whites*	*Gap*[a]
Academic achievement	27	61	33
Well-being from pregnancy through infancy	37	54	17
Children's access to health care	43	56	14
Health of preschool children	41	52	11
School readiness	40	57	16
Purposive use of nonschool hours	46	54	8
Health of school-age children	48	55	7
Educational attainment	38	51	13
Economic security	41	54	13
Adult non-economic characteristics	41	55	14
Average gap	...	...	15
Average non-academic gap	...	...	13

a. The gap does not always appear to be identical to the difference because of rounding.

school success are, on average, 8 percentile points worse than those of other children could well have a cumulative deficit in academic achievement that exceeds the separate deficits in any of these contributing domains. The gap in academic achievement could be greater than the gap in any of the contributing institutional domains, even if disadvantaged children received academic educations equivalent to those received by middle-class children—and disadvantaged students seldom receive adequate educations or even educations equal in quality to those of middle-class students.

Inequality in other domains contributes to academic inequality in many ways. For example, to the extent that black children suffer more from asthma than white children, and to the extent that such suffering causes black children to be absent from and perform worse in school, health inequalities lead to inequalities in academic achievement. To the extent that black parents suffer greater economic stress—more frequent unemployment, lower incomes, more crowded housing, and so on—their children may exhibit behavioral problems that interfere with learning. It is also the case that if children had higher quality educations, they would be economically more secure as adults and better able to provide for their own children. If children had higher quality educations, they would also, as adults, be better able to keep their own children in good health—for example, by attempting to minimize exposure to allergens or by getting prompt treatment for symptoms of asthma.

It is also apparent that the relationships between other domains are nonlinear. For example, inequalities in economic security, health, and parents' educational backgrounds have a compound effect on children's early childhood experiences, which in turn affect academic achievement, educational attainment, and economic security in the next generation. Therefore we conclude that efforts to eliminate black-white inequality in American society should be mounted across all domains, including schools, but not in schools alone. No single policy focus is likely, by itself, to make the nation equitable.

The greatest importance of these inequalities may be that they are cumulative. When combined with many other inequalities, some small, some larger, the differences in, for example, the rate of vaccination and preschool reading contribute to and compound a system of pervasive inequality. For the present, all we can conclude from the data presented here is that the pattern of racial inequality in American society is consistent across domains. We can also say that some, perhaps most, of the racial inequality reflects racial differences in social and economic circumstances, but some racial inequality cannot be explained simply by social and economic disadvantages. To some extent this systematic pattern of inequality suggests a society organized along caste, not class, lines. Despite the systematic inequalities we have described, some progress has been made, and this leads to the hope that further progress is possible. Perhaps highlighting the extensive costs to society of permitting these inequalities to continue will help spur Americans to further action.

References

Allegretto, Sylvia, and Andy Stettner. 2004. "Educated, Experienced, and Out-of-Work: Long-Term Joblessness Continues to Plague the Unemployed." EPI Issue Brief 198. Washington, D.C.: Economic Policy Institute.

Bub, Kristin, and Kathleen McCartney. 2005. Unpublished analysis of the database of National Institute of Child Health and Human Development, Study of Early Child Care and Youth Development, provided to the authors.

Centers for Disease Control and Prevention. 2000. "Blood Lead Levels in Young Children: United States and Selected States, 1996–1999." *Morbidity and Mortality Weekly Report* 49, no. 50: 1133–37.

———. 2004. "Youth Risk Behavior Surveillance: United States, 2003." *Morbidity and Mortality Weekly Report* 53, no. SS-2.

———. 2005a. "Blood Lead Levels: United States and Selected States, 1999–2002." *Morbidity and Mortality Weekly Report* 54, no. 20: 513–16.

———. 2005b. *CDC Wonder: Data 2010. The Healthy People 2010 Database.* Department of Health and Human Services (wonder.cdc.gov/data2010/focus.htm [July 2005]).

———. 2005c. *Pediatric and Pregnancy Nutrition Surveillance System: Pediatric Data Tables.* Department of Health and Human Services (www.cdc.gov/pednss/pednss_tables/index.htm [July 2005]).

———. 2005d. *U.S. Physical Activity Statistics: 2003 State Demographic Data Comparison.* Department of Health and Human Services (apps.nccd.cdc.gov/PASurveillance/DemoComparev.asp [July 2005]).

Denton, Kristin, and Elvie Germino-Hausken. 2000. *America's Kindergartner's: Findings from the Early Childhood Longitudinal Study, Kindergarten Class of 1998–99, Fall 1998.* NCES 2000-070 (revised). Department of Education, Office of Educational Research and Improvement.

Federal Bureau of Investigation. 2003. *Crime in the United States, 2003: Uniform Crime Reports.* FBI 20402-9328. Department of Justice (www.fbi.gov/ucr/cius_03/pdf/toc03.pdf [August 2005]).

Forrest, Christopher B., Barbara Starfield, Anne W. Riley, and Myungsa Kang. 1997. "The Impact of Asthma on the Health Status of Adolescents." *Pediatrics* 99 (February): 2.

Grissmer, David. 2005. Unpublished analysis of data from the Early Childhood Longitudinal Survey–Kindergarten (ECLS–K), provided to the authors.

Halfon, Neal, and Paul W. Newacheck. 1993. "Childhood Asthma and Poverty: Differential Impacts and Utilization of Health Services." *Pediatrics* 91 (January): 56–61.

Hancox, R. J., and R. Poulton. 2005. "Watching Television Is Associated with Childhood Obesity: But Is It Clinically Important?" *International Journal of Obesity* 30 (January): 171–75.

Harrison, Paige M., and Allen J. Beck. 2005. *Prison and Jail Inmates at Midyear 2004.* NCJ 208801. Department of Justice, Bureau of Justice Statistics (www.ojp.usdoj.gov/bjs/pub/pdf/pjim04.pdf).

Hedley, Allison A., and others. 2004. "Prevalence of Overweight and Obesity among US Children, Adolescents, and Adults, 1999–2002." *Journal of the American Medical Association* 291, no. 23: 2847–50.

Hoffman, Kathryn, and Charmaine Llagas. 2003. *Status and Trends in the Education of Blacks.* NCES 2003-034. Department of Education, Institute of Education Sciences.

Knapp, Laura G., and others. 2003. *Enrollment in Postsecondary Institutions, Fall 2001, and Financial Statistics, Fiscal Year 2001.* NCES 2004–155. Department of Education, Institute of Education Sciences (nces.ed.gov/pubs2004/2004155.pdf).

Komaromy, Miriam, and others. 1996. "The Role of Black and Hispanic Physicians in Providing Health Care for Underserved Populations." *New England Journal of Medicine* 334, no. 20: 1305–10.

Lanphear, Bruce P., and others. 2000. "Cognitive Deficits Associated with Blood Lead Concentrations < 10 microg/dL in US Children and Adolescents." *Public Health Reports* 115, no. 6: 521–29.

Massey, Douglas S., and Nancy A. Denton. 1993. *American Apartheid: Segregation and the Making of the Underclass.* Harvard University Press.

Mishel, Lawrence, Jared Bernstein, and Sylvia Allegretto. 2005. *The State of Working America 2004/2005.* Washington, D.C.: Economic Policy Institute.

Mishel, Lawrence, and Joydeep Roy. 2006. *Rethinking High School Graduation Rates and Trends.* Washington, D.C.: Economic Policy Institute.

National Center for Education Statistics. 1998. *The Condition of Education 1998.* NCES 1998-013. Department of Education, Office of Educational Research and Improvement.

———. 2005a. "NAEP Data: The NAEP Data Tool" (nces.ed.gov/nationsreportcard/naep data).
———. 2005b. *Digest of Education Statistics 2003.* NCES 2005-025. Department of Education, Institute of Education Sciences.
———. 2005c. *The Condition of Education 2005.* NCES 2005-094. Department of Education, Institute of Education Sciences.
———. 2006. *Digest of Education Statistics 2005.* NCES 2006-030. Department of Education, Institute of Education Sciences.
National Center for Health Statistics. 2004. *Health, United States, 2004: With Chartbook on Trends in the Health of Americans.* DHHS 2004-1232. Department of Health and Human Services, Centers for Disease Control and Prevention (www.cdc.gov/nchs/data/hus/hus04 trend.pdf).
———. 2005. *Summary Health Statistics for U.S. Children: National Health Interview Survey (NHIS), 2003.* Series 10, no. 223. Department of Health and Human Services, Centers for Disease Control and Prevention (www.cdc.gov/nchs/data/series/sr_10/sr10_223.pdf).
National Center for Juvenile Justice. 2002. "Easy Access to the FBI's Supplementary Homicide Reports: 1980–2000." Department of Justice, Office of Juvenile Justice and Delinquency Prevention (ojjdp.ncjrs.org/ojstatbb/ezashr).
National Endowment for the Arts. 2004. *Survey of Public Participation in the Arts.* NEA 003027809 (www.nea.gov/pub/NEASurvey2004.pdf).
National Institute of Child Health and Human Development, Child Care Research Network. 1999. "Child Outcomes When Child Care Center Classes Meet Recommended Standards for Quality." *American Journal of Public Health* 89, no. 7: 1072–77.
Orfield, Gary, and Chungmei Lee. 2005. *Why Segregation Matters: Poverty and Education Inequality.* Civil Rights Project, Harvard University (www.civilrightsproject.harvard.edu/research/deseg/Why_Segreg_Matters.pdf).
Pager, Devah. 2003. "The Mark of a Criminal Record." *American Journal of Sociology* 108, no. 5: 937–75.
Persky, Hilary R., Brent A. Sandene, and Janice M. Askew. 1998. *The NAEP 1997 Arts Report Card: Eighth Grade Findings from the National Assessment of Educational Progress.* NCES 1999-486. Department of Education, Office of Educational Research and Improvement.
Rothstein, Richard. 2004. *Class and Schools: Using Social, Economic, and Educational Reform to Close the Black-White Achievement Gap.* Teachers College Press.
Vaden-Kiernan, N., and J. McManus. 2005. *Parent and Family Involvement in Education: 2002–03.* NCES 2005-043. Department of Education, Institute of Education Sciences.
Walston, Jill, and Jerry West. 2004. *Full-day and Half-day Kindergarten in the United States: Findings from the Early Childhood Longitudinal Study, Kindergarten Class of 1998–99.* NCES 2004-078. Department of Education, Office of Educational Research and Improvement.
Wilson, William Julius. 1987. *The Truly Disadvantaged: The Inner City, the Underclass, and Public Policy.* University of Chicago Press.
Wirt, John. 2005. Unpublished analysis of High School Transcript Study, provided to the authors.

3

MARTA TIENDA
SIGAL ALON

Diversity and the Demographic Dividend: Achieving Educational Equity in an Aging White Society

THE UNITED STATES IS facing a unique moment in its demographic history, for two reasons. First, as the third largest nation in the world, behind prosperous China and India, the United States has a vital resource that gives it a productive advantage over its industrialized peers—namely, people. In contrast with several western European nations that have been coping with the challenges of below-replacement fertility for several years, the United States sees its population continue to grow, albeit slowly, owing to high levels of both immigration and fertility.[1] Population growth replenishes the labor force with new workers, but in today's global economy, the quality of workers matters as much as the quantity.

Second, because of the increased salience of migration as a component of population growth, the U.S. population is among the most diverse in the world.[2] When its white non-Hispanic population fell below 50 percent, Texas became the fourth state to be declared a "majority minority" state, joining California, New Mexico, and Hawaii.[3] Population diversification will continue well into the future, even as immigration ebbs, because a larger share of new births will be to foreign-born women. Not only were immigration and births

1. The United Nations estimates the U.S. total fertility rate at 1.9, but the CDC's National Center for Health Statistics puts it at 2.1.

2. Prewitt (2001).

3. U.S. Bureau of the Census (2005). With a nonwhite population of 70 percent, the District of Columbia also qualifies as a "majority minority" political entity.

to immigrant women responsible for about 60 percent of demographic growth during the 1990s, but currently white women have below-replacement fertility, whereas the total fertility rate of Hispanic women is around 3.1.[4] Although immigration outpaced births as a component of Hispanic population growth during the 1980s and 1990s, during the first decade of the twenty-first century Hispanic births were projected to surpass net immigration from Latin America by approximately 1.6 million.[5]

The components of demographic growth have direct implications for changes in the sizes of the labor force and the school-age population and for old-age dependency burdens. In 2005, for example, the U.S. Bureau of the Census announced that school enrollment surpassed the previous all-time high of 48.7 million set in 1970 by the baby boom generation.[6] The recent school-age population bulge, produced largely by high immigrant fertility, represents a potential demographic dividend that can help assuage population aging, but that dividend can be realized only with appropriate educational investments. Viewed as returns on an investment portfolio, dividends reaped from population growth depend crucially on the caliber of investments made throughout the educational career, but especially during the early years.[7]

That the most ethnically diverse youth cohorts in U.S. history are coming of age with an aging white majority also poses formidable social and policy challenges because, on average, the fastest growing cohorts are more likely to have parents with little education and lower incomes than are the cohorts they are replacing.[8] Census 2000 revealed that the median age of the population reached a new high of 35.3 years, rising 2.5 years since 1990.[9] The challenges of population aging could become acute as the baby boom cohorts increase their dependency on the Social Security earnings of the young, especially if racial and ethnic educational gaps are not closed. At the same time, the costs of underinvesting in education pose a serious risk not only to youths themselves—because the returns on investments in schooling are higher now than in the past—but also to a nation facing greater international competition for goods, services, and highly qualified labor.[10]

We argue that the demographic dividend afforded by the modest but transitory minority age bulge will be lost if the nation's investment priorities are

4. Landale, Oropesa, and Bradatan (2006); Taylor and others (2002, fig. 2.2).
5. Tienda and Mitchell (2006, fig. 2-1).
6. Shin (2005).
7. Heckman (2006); Knudsen and others (2006).
8. McPherson and Shapiro (2004).
9. U.S. Bureau of the Census (2001).
10. Cox and Alm (2004).

diverted away from education. To make our case, we briefly describe the demography of diversification, emphasizing changes in the school-age population. Subsequently, we summarize recent trends and differentials in secondary and postsecondary educational attainment according to race and Hispanic origin, both to illustrate how diversity challenges equity as a social goal and to underscore the importance of prompt action, because the window of opportunity to harness the demographic dividend will soon close. Finally, we discuss the myopia of educational underinvestment by juxtaposing the social and political interests of dependency at young and old ages.

Demography of Diversification

Three overarching trends characterize the changing demography of the total and the school-age population in the United States over the past half century: racial and ethnic diversification, the growth of the foreign-born population, and the growing concentration of minority students in large central cities.[11] All three have profound implications for the future contours of educational inequality, and consequently for economic disparities. The relatively recent geographic dispersal of immigrants to new, Southern destinations adds yet another layer of complexity to the challenge of equalizing educational opportunity, both because of the intensity of the flows and because many school districts in the South are ill-equipped to handle students who speak limited English.[12]

Ethno-racial diversification is largely a post–World War II phenomenon that gained momentum after 1970. The composition of the U.S. population changed little during the first half of the twentieth century; whites made up about 88 percent of the total, and blacks were the dominant minority group during this period of relatively slow demographic growth.[13] Although population diversification began to unfold during the 1960s, as recently as 1970 whites composed nearly 84 percent of the national population (table 3-1). In that year Hispanics were estimated to make up fewer than 5 percent of the total population, with blacks accounting for roughly 11 percent. Triggered by changes in U.S. immigration laws, U.S. population diversification accelerated during the 1980s and 1990s.

Census 2000 recorded the largest "minority" population in U.S. history—28 percent of the total—with blacks and Hispanics each accounting for more

11. Fry (2005); Orfield and Lee (2004); Schneider, Martinez, and Owens (2006).

12. Fischer and Tienda (2006).

13. Hirschman (2006, table 1); U.S. Bureau of the Census (2001a, table 10).

Table 3-1. *Composition of Total and School-Age Populations, 1970, 1990, and 2005*
Percent

Group	Total population			School-age population
	1970	*1990*	*2005*[a]	*2005*[a]
White	83.6	75.7	66.9	60.7
Black	11.1	11.8	12.8	15.4
Hispanic	4.5	9.0	14.4	18.4
Asian	0.7	2.8	4.4	4.3
Other[b]	0.1	0.7	1.5	1.2

Sources: U.S. Census 1970 (www.census.gov/population/www/documentation/twps0029/tab08.html); U.S. Bureau of the Census (2007, tables 11, 15).

a. Based on intercensal estimates.

b. Includes Native Americans and "other race not allocated."

than 12 percent, Asians for around 4 percent, and other groups combined for the rest.[14] Although the Asian population share continued to rise over time, from around 1 percent in 1970 to more than 4 percent by 2005, the main story since 1970 has been the dramatic growth of the Hispanic population. In 2003 the Census Bureau announced that Hispanics had surpassed blacks as the largest minority group and projected their share to rise well into the current century. By 2030 some 40 percent of the U.S. population is projected to be black, Hispanic, or Asian.[15] Beyond its historical significance, this shift in the demographic makeup of the population has profound implications for future labor force productivity and global competitiveness, because Hispanics have, on average, lower levels of education than both African Americans and Asians.

The relative youthfulness of minority populations, especially Hispanics, means that they will drive future demographic growth. The school-age population already is more diverse than the total population, particularly in the major immigrant-receiving states. This is because larger shares of minority women are in their reproductive years than are non-Hispanic white women

14. Tienda (2002, table 1). Precise estimates of the ethnic groups differ, depending on the identifiers used to sort the population. Hirschman (2006, table 1) reported that nearly 13 percent of the population was African American in 2000, 11.5 percent was Hispanic, and nearly 5 percent was Asian. Enumeration methods also contributed to the growth of some groups, especially Native Americans and Hispanics, after 1980.

15. Passel (2004).

and because the fertility rate of white women is lower than that of minority, especially foreign-born, Hispanic women.[16]

Demographers project that population diversification will continue well into the current century as fertility overtakes immigration as the major component of demographic growth.[17] Notwithstanding uncertainty about the future course of undocumented immigration, legal immigration already has begun to fall and is expected to continue on a downward path as fertility decline proceeds apace in the major immigrant-sending countries. By 2030 the entire baby boom generation will be drawing Social Security checks, and the solvency of the system will depend on the productivity of youths currently in school.

The sea change in the ethno-racial composition of the school-age population acquires added significance because it coincides with equally profound shifts in the residential distribution of the population from rural to urban and suburban areas; an industrial transformation of employment away from unskilled, blue-collar jobs to service jobs requiring higher skill levels; and a bifurcated skill distribution among new immigrants. Immigration dropped precipitously after 1930, and by 1950 only 7 percent of the U.S. population was foreign-born; the percentage dropped further to 5 percent by 1970.[18] After the 1965 amendments to the Immigration and Nationality Act lifted quotas on previously barred countries, the volume of immigration began its steady ascent, and the regional origins of new arrivals changed from Europe to Asia and Latin America. The foreign-born share of the U.S. population climbed to 12 percent in 2003, double its 1980 share.[19] With legal and illegal immigrants topping 14 million, the 1990s registered the highest level of immigration in U.S. history, but continuing recent trends, the first decade of the twenty-first century is likely to reach a new zenith.[20]

Reflecting the change in the source countries of immigrants since 1960, the foreign-born share of Asian and Hispanic minorities rose faster than that of whites. As figure 3-1 shows, approximately 16 percent of all Hispanics were foreign-born in 1960, but this share had more than doubled by 1990 and increased to 40 percent over the next decade. The effect of recent immigration on the Asian population is even more striking. Before the recent surge in immigration, one in three Asians was foreign born; by 1990 this share had roughly doubled; and by 2000 it had risen to 70 percent. The foreign-born

16. Landale, Oropesa, and Bradatan (2006).

17. Passel (2004).

18. Gibson and Jung (2006).

19. Larsen (2004).

20. Meissner and others (2006).

Figure 3-1. *Foreign-Born Share of Major Population Groups, by Decade*

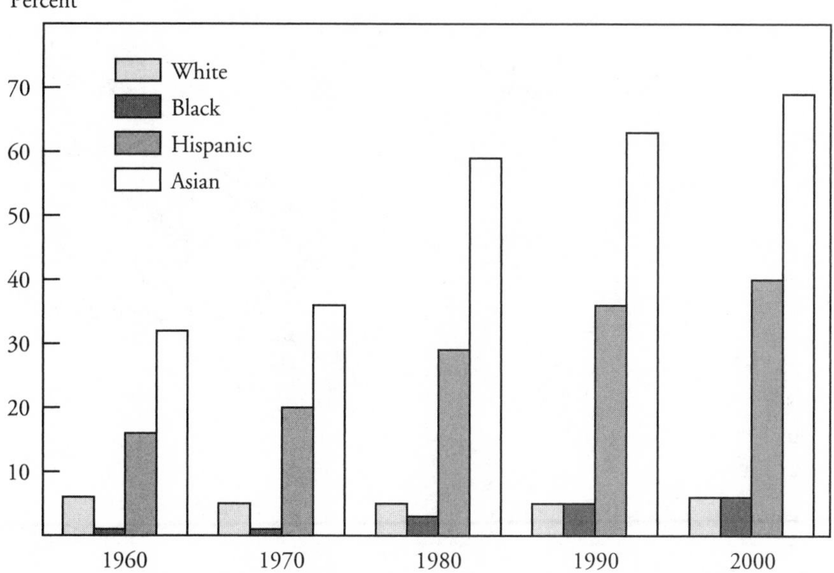

Source: Gibson and Jung (2006, tables 8, 10).

share of the non-Hispanic white population hovered around 5 to 6 percent throughout the period, but the black share rose gradually over the second half of the twentieth century, largely involving immigrants from the Caribbean.

International migration disproportionately involves persons of working age. The Migration Policy Institute reports that nearly half the growth in the U.S. labor force during the 1990s was due to new immigrants, and it projects that net growth in the domestic workforce over the next twenty years will primarily involve foreign-born workers.[21] Although only 7 percent of the foreign-born population is under 15 years of age, international migration contributes to the future labor force through the reproductive behavior of foreign-born women, which is manifested in the generational transition of ethno-racial groups. As figure 3-2 shows, however, substantial shares of the Asian and Hispanic school-age population are either immigrants or children of immigrants. In comparison with Hispanics, a larger share of the Asian school-age population is foreign born, but because the Asian population is appreciably smaller, there are more than three times as many foreign-born Hispanic as Asian

21. Migration Policy Institute (2007).

Figure 3-2. *Generational Composition of School-Age Population, 2006*[a]

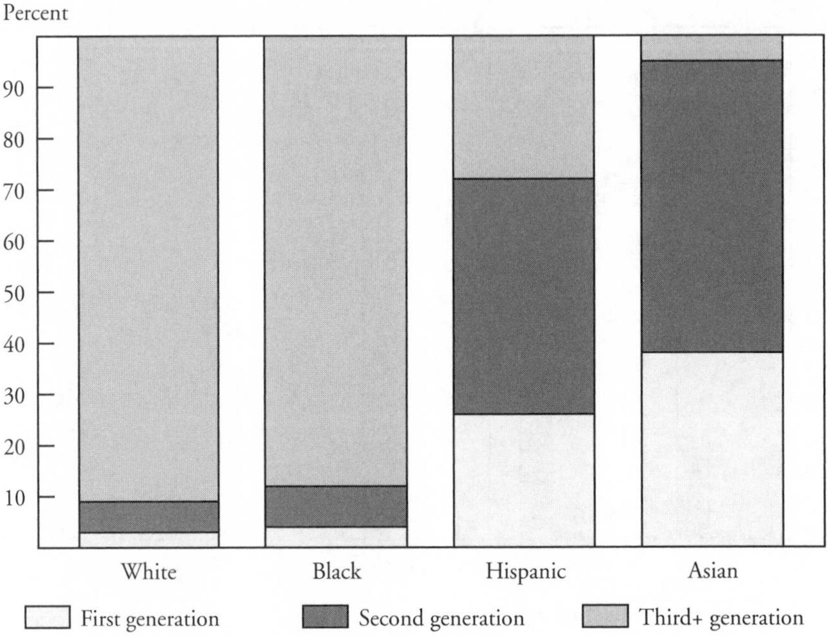

Percent

90
80
70
60
50
40
30
20
10

White Black Hispanic Asian

First generation Second generation Third+ generation

Source: Authors' tabulations from 2006 Current Population Survey.
a. Ages 5–24.

youths. Overall, the Hispanic school-age population is 4.6 times that of its Asian counterpart. Thus the importance of immigration for future labor force growth will increasingly depend on the children of immigrants, the fastest growing segment of the U.S. population.

These ethno-racial differences in the generational composition of the school-age population are important because they signal educational needs that depend partly on parents' educational status and English proficiency and partly on the unequal educational opportunities associated with settlement patterns. Rubén Rumbaut reports that 51 percent of non-Hispanic foreign-born persons age 5 and over who spoke a language other than English at home were proficient in English, in comparison with only 30 percent of Hispanics.[22] Disadvantages in English proficiency dissipated by the second generation, in which three in four persons who reported speaking a language other than English at home claimed proficiency in English. Whether and by how much these

22. Rumbaut (2006, table 2-9).

differences undermine educational achievement remains highly controversial, because English proficiency is often conflated with bilingualism, which in a global economy represents an asset to be cultivated rather than a liability to be diminished. Bilingualism becomes problematic only when proficiency is not achieved in either language. Moreover, group differences in English proficiency conceal considerable variation by length of U.S. residence, age at arrival, and parental educational attainment. Second-generation Asian youths have a marked advantage over their Hispanic counterparts because their parents, on average, possess higher levels of formal schooling and because they are less residentially segregated in large, urban schools.[23]

Historically, six states—California, Texas, Florida, New York, New Jersey, and Illinois—have served as hosts to the majority of the foreign-born population, although the first four receive the largest number of immigrants now, whereas the last two were dominant historically.[24] Given the salience of immigration in the diversification of the school-age population in these states, a few indicators help to denote the risks of educational underinvestment and opportunities to capitalize on the minority demographic dividend. For example, the four largest immigrant-receiving states rank in the lower half of all states on the basis of their overall and child poverty rates as well as their high school graduation rates. In 2003 California, Florida, and New York were tied for 34th place in their child poverty rates, and Texas ranked lower still—43rd out of 50 states.[25] Using a cohort-derived index to estimate high school graduation rates, Christopher Swanson ranked California 32nd, Texas 37th, New York 43rd, and Florida 50th.[26] These indicators do not bode well for the educational prospects of the swelling school-aged minority populations of these states, which will shoulder the burden of the aging baby boom generation.

Although per capita education spending does not guarantee quality instruction, in 2003 only New York ranked above the national average in expenditures per pupil in public elementary and secondary schools.[27] California, Texas, and Florida ranked 27th, 34th, and 43rd, respectively. Yet except for Florida, which according to estimates by the State Science and Technology Institute ranked 38th in gross state product per capita in 2003, three of these immigrant-receiving states hardly qualify as poor: New York ranked 5th, California 12th, and Texas 22nd.[28] Together these four states hold one-quarter of

23. Schneider, Martinez, and Owens (2006); Tienda and Mitchell (2006).

24. Tienda (2002).

25. Annie Casey Foundation (2005).

26. Swanson (2003).

27. National Center for Education Statistics (2006).

28. State Science and Technology Institute (2005). As the sum of all net industrial activity within a state, Gross State Product is a measure of the "value added" by a state's economy.

the seats in the U.S. Congress, which represents significant political power deriving from their population size.[29] Whether this political asset will be converted into an economic asset depends on educational investments in future generations.

Taken together, recent trends in the demography of the school-age population pose both opportunities and formidable challenges for the nation, not because diversity per se is problematical but because diversification coincides with rising economic inequality, and Hispanic and black youths are more likely to be poor and to have parents with low education levels. Linguistic diversity may temporarily stymie school systems unprepared to educate large numbers of foreign-born students, but it need not become a source of enduring inequality, particularly for students who enter the U.S. educational system at young ages.

Although bilingualism is often blamed for educational underachievement, our practical experiences indicate that this underachievement signals difficulties in the ability of parents to provide strong links between their children and the schools they attend, rather than the ability of youths to learn English, especially at the lower grades. Put differently, it is not that immigrant parents do not value education; rather, their limited communication skills significantly reduce their ability to engage with the school system and to provide help with homework and school activities.[30] More than length of U.S. residence or age at arrival, parental education is the single most powerful indicator of English mastery and scholastic success.[31]

If language diversity was the main reason for the academic underachievement of minority youths, then Asians, too, would score lower than whites on standardized tests, because, in comparison with Hispanics, a larger share is foreign born. In fact, white, black, Hispanic, and Asian youths enter the school system at very uneven starting lines. This is clearly evident in the large differences in math and reading scores of minority and nonminority children upon arrival at the schoolhouse. Even before entering first grade, Asians outperform whites and, especially, blacks and Hispanics.[32] Rather than linguistic diversity, these differences reflect large social and economic gaps that exclude significant numbers of minority students from the resources associated with high socioeconomic status.

Trends in the living arrangements of children further aggravate the achievement gap. The share of youths living with one parent more than doubled from

29. Tienda (2002).

30. Schneider, Martinez, and Owens (2006).

31. Rumbaut (2006).

32. Schneider, Martinez, and Owens (2006).

1970 to the present, and although the figure has leveled off in the past decade, 30 percent of all children did not live with two parents as of 2003.[33] Yet this overall change conceals large differences by race and Hispanic origin. In 1970 fewer than 10 percent of white children and just over one in four black children lived with a single mother. By 2003, 22 percent of white children, 34 percent of Hispanic children, and 62 percent of black children lived with a single parent. Parent absence places youths at high risk of educational failure and behavioral transgressions, largely because these children are more likely to be poor.[34] Youths reared in poverty are significantly more prone to scholastic underperformance and low educational attainment than those reared in affluent families.

Trends in poverty are both encouraging and troubling. Apparently the robust economy of the late 1990s did more to reduce poverty than a decade's worth of antipoverty programs; by 2000 child poverty rates had fallen to their lowest level since 1975.[35] Yet racial and ethnic differentials in child poverty rates have proved resistant to change. In the mid-1970s, a black child was four times as likely as a white child to be poor, and a Hispanic child, three times as likely. Although the racial and ethnic gaps in child poverty narrowed slightly during the 1980s, absolute rates rose, especially for Hispanic youths. The uptick in child poverty after 2001 reveals the vulnerability of youths to economic cycles and the weak safety net above which the near poor balance. It may also reflect the lower levels of education and income of recent influxes of Hispanic immigrants.

If all K–12 schools offered quality instruction, then urban and suburban residence would merely reflect lifestyle choices. Unfortunately, this is not the case, and several scholars have reported evidence of rising school segregation.[36] Indeed, the distribution of minority students among urban, suburban, and rural schools has become more unequal over time, such that black and Hispanic students are more likely not only to attend highly segregated schools but also to delay school entry and to withdraw prematurely.[37] Orfield and Lee reported that in 2000 most black and Hispanic students attended segregated schools in which two out of three students were poor or near poor; further, 88 percent of the students enrolled in hypersegregated minority schools (that is, with fewer than 10 percent white students) were poor, in comparison with only 15 percent of students attending equally segregated white schools.[38] Even

33. Annie Casey Foundation (2005).

34. McLanahan and Sandefur (1994); Stier and Tienda (2001).

35. Annie Casey Foundation (2005).

36. Fry (2005); Orfield and Lee (2004); Reardon and Yun (2001).

37. Schneider, Martinez, and Owens (2006).

38. Orfield and Lee (2004).

as minority youths become more suburbanized, their chances of enrolling in segregated schools are significantly higher than those of white youths. For example, Reardon and Yun showed that schools located in Southern metro counties were 40 percent less segregated than housing markets in 1990, but a decade later the schools were only 27 percent less segregated.[39]

The pernicious effects of school segregation stem from its divisive class underpinnings, namely, that schools in which minorities are disproportionately concentrated are poorer, on average, than predominantly white schools. Resource-poor schools have more unqualified teachers and offer more remedial courses and fewer advanced placement courses. Hence their students—disproportionately black and Hispanic—fare poorly on standardized achievement tests and are less likely to graduate.[40] According to Christopher Swanson, graduation rates for central city high schools averaged 58 percent in 2001, in comparison with 73 percent for suburban schools.[41]

The long-term social and economic significance of population diversification depends crucially on changes in the educational attainments of students currently enrolled and those completing their education before 2030, by which time the U.S. age structure will begin to stabilize. Because socioeconomic differences among families are the major sources of inequality in student performance, closing achievement gaps requires targeting economically disadvantaged students at very young ages.[42] Whether the growing number of school-age children will be prepared to sustain the rising service needs of baby boom retirees depends on the educational investments made over the next decade, and especially on progress in closing test score gaps in the early years. As we show in the following section, the news is both encouraging and disturbing.

Trends and Differentials in Educational Attainment

According to Cox and Alm, in 2000 the United States led the world in the average number of years of school completed per capita—12.3 years. Trends in both high school graduation and college completion contributed to the high average attainment level. Currently, 26 percent of persons ages 25 and over and 29 percent of this group—the 25- to 29-year-olds—are college graduates. At the turn of the twentieth century only about 2 percent of the adult population

39. Reardon and Yun (2003).

40. Schneider, Martinez, and Owens (2006); Swanson (2003).

41. Swanson (2003, table 7).

42. Heckman (2006); Knudsen and others (2006).

Figure 3-3. *Attainment of Postsecondary Education, by Country, 2002*

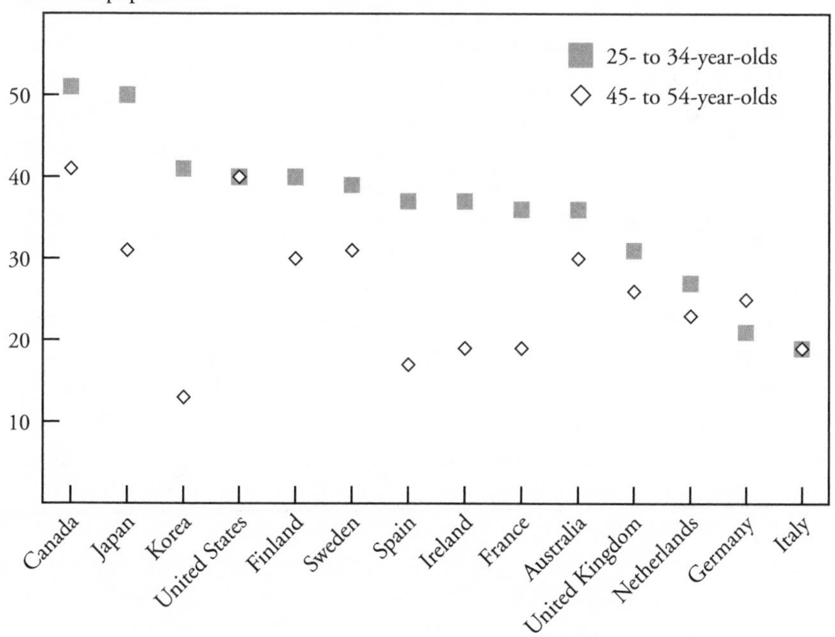

Source: Organization for Economic Cooperation and Development (2004, table A3.3).

consisted of college graduates, and as recently as 1950 a scant 6 percent achieved college degrees.[43]

Yet there are troubling signs that the United States is losing ground to its industrialized peers. Recent data from the Organization for Economic Cooperation and Development (OECD) reveal that thirteen countries had equaled or achieved the U.S. educational benchmark by 2004, and four nations surpassed it, whereas in 1991 only Canada and Finland registered larger shares of young people with college degrees. Among the thirty OECD countries, U.S. college participation rates currently rank in the bottom half. Figure 3-3 compares schooling for two cohorts in fourteen industrialized nations observed in 2002—one ages 25–34 and the other 45–54. All the nations compared except (reunified) Germany and the United States show signs of improvement in the share of adults with postsecondary degrees.[44] Given their smaller economies, it is noteworthy that both

43. Cox and Alm (2001).

44. Haveman and Smeeding (2006); Kelly (2005).

Canada and Japan surpassed the United States in their shares of college-educated young adults.

Moreover, the United States does not hold the top rank in quality of educational outputs or broadened access. Despite higher expenditures per student, the United States is losing ground to other industrialized nations in terms of students' performances in math and science. Haveman and Smeeding claim that if U.S. colleges and universities had increased their postsecondary graduation rate during the 1980s and 1990s, they would not only have served larger shares of low-income youths but also weakened the link between socioeconomic status and postsecondary education. Indeed, Peter Sacks has argued that the chance of a low-income child's obtaining a bachelor's degree has not changed in three decades; in both 1970 and 2002, only 6 percent of students from the lowest-income families earned college degrees.[45]

Aggregate trends in school attainment provide signs of hope, because educational levels have risen steadily for all demographic groups during the period of massive ethno-racial diversification. Recent trends, however, also highlight vexing problems that bear directly on the social costs of inadequate education, notably widening disparities between whites and Hispanics, blacks, and Native Americans.[46] In particular, rates of noncompletion of high school remain unacceptably high, particularly for Hispanic youths. Between 1972 and 2003 the high school status dropout rate for whites was cut from 14 to 8 percent, and that for blacks was nearly halved, from 28 to 15 percent.[47] Although the Hispanic status dropout rate also declined 14 percentage points over the period, from 44 to 31 percent, the 2003 rate for Hispanics was double that of blacks and nearly four times that of whites.[48] Status dropout measures have been criticized on the grounds that many foreign-born Hispanics who lack high school diplomas never attended U.S. schools.[49] But measures based on single-year periods for enrolled students also reveal that Hispanics and blacks are more likely than whites to discontinue their schooling before achieving a diploma.[50]

Given the changing demography of the school-age population and the influx of large numbers of unskilled immigrants since 1970, improvements in high

45. Haveman and Smeeding (2006); Sacks (2007).

46. Kelly (2005).

47. The status dropout rate measures the percentage of 18- through 24-year-olds who are not enrolled in high school and who do not hold a high school diploma or GED equivalent.

48. National Center for Education Statistics (2006, table 11).

49. Fry (2003).

50. Shin (2005, table D). These dropout rates are optimistic in comparison with Swanson's (2003, table 3) estimates based on the cumulative promotion index, which imply an average dropout rate of 32 percent. The range was from around 50 percent for blacks, Hispanics, and Native Americans to 25 percent for whites and Asians.

school and college graduation rates are heartening. Yet persisting differentials are worrisome, because they imply intergenerational reproduction of inequality over time. Using time as a metric, as of 2000 the Hispanic high school graduation rate was almost three decades behind that of whites (see figure 3-4). In that year, 57 percent of Hispanics ages 25 and over achieved high school diplomas, whereas 55 percent of whites did so in 1970. Although unskilled immigration may exacerbate Hispanics' educational attainment gap, it does not explain why African Americans with high school diplomas trailed whites by more than a decade through the beginning of the twenty-first century.

Similarly, in higher education there is much progress to celebrate. College-going rates are at an all-time high for every demographic group, and the number of postsecondary institutions available to promote this trend continues to grow. Yet despite steady gains, race and ethnic differentials in college graduation rates not only are larger than those for diploma holders but are widening over time. Only 11 percent of Hispanics ages 25 and over were college graduates in 2000, a rate comparable to whites thirty years before. Throughout the period Asians stand out as the most highly educated U.S. racial group, with 44 percent achieving baccalaureate degrees as of 2000. Partly this reflects the fact that the majority of immigrants from Asia enter under occupational preference visas, which are highly selected toward advanced degrees. Latin American immigrants, by contrast, gain admission under visas allotted for family reunification and tend to have low levels of education.[51] Thus Asian immigration adds to the college-trained population, but newcomers from Latin America mainly swell the ranks of persons lacking high school degrees.

Although the college-educated population also is now more diverse than ever before, today's college graduates look the way the U.S. population did in 1970, with whites making up 82 percent of degree recipients. The key difference is that Asians, who made up a tiny share of the 1970 population and roughly 4 percent of the 2000 population, represent 7 percent of degree holders today. African Americans represent only 6 percent of college graduates—less than half their population share—and Hispanics make up only 4 percent of the college educated, or about one-third their population share.[52] We are not suggesting that proportionality should be used as a measure of social justice, but rather that these disparities will likely widen as the minority share of young cohorts continues to rise.

Population comparisons understate Hispanics' educational progress because they include large numbers of immigrants who never studied in the United

51. Hirschman (2006); Tienda (2002).
52. Tienda (2006).

Figure 3-4. *High School and College Graduation Rates for Persons 25 and Older, by Decade*

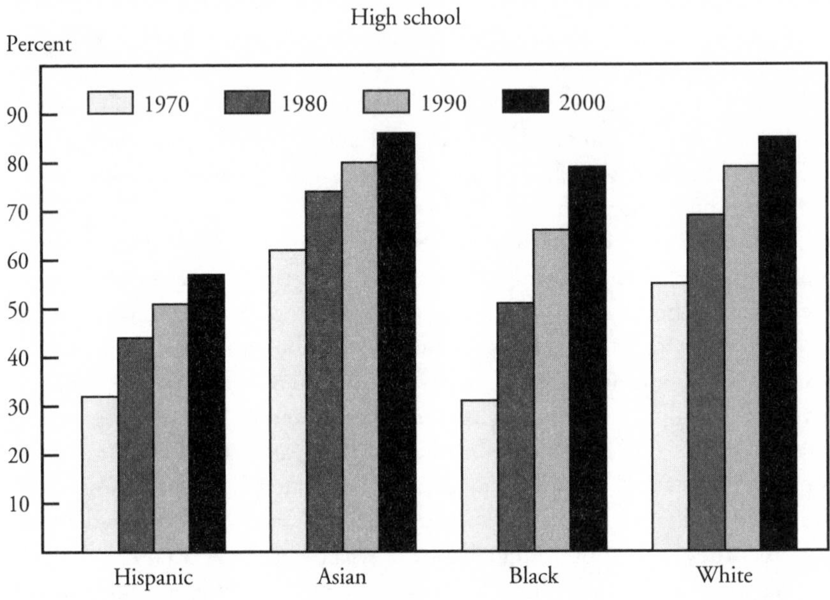

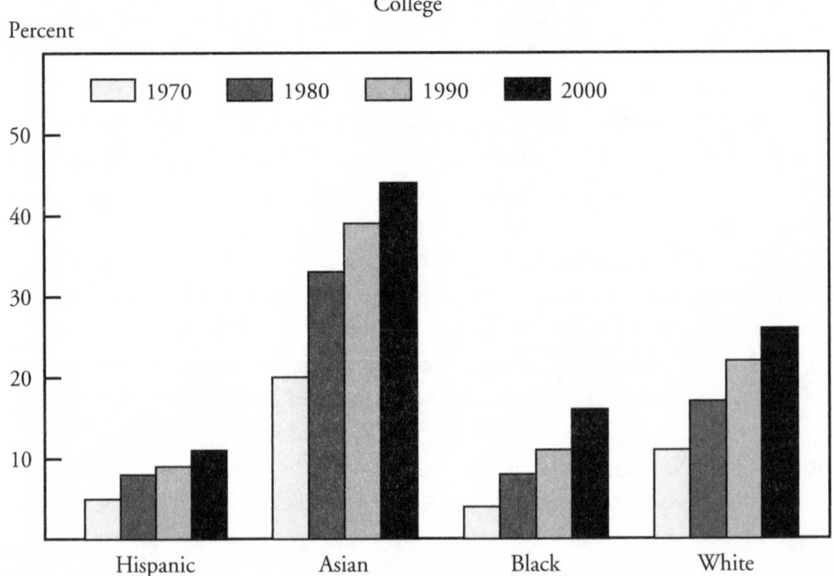

Source: U.S. Bureau of the Census, *Statistical Abstract of the United States* (2006, table 214).

Figure 3-5. *College Enrollment Rates by Immigrant Generations, 2000*

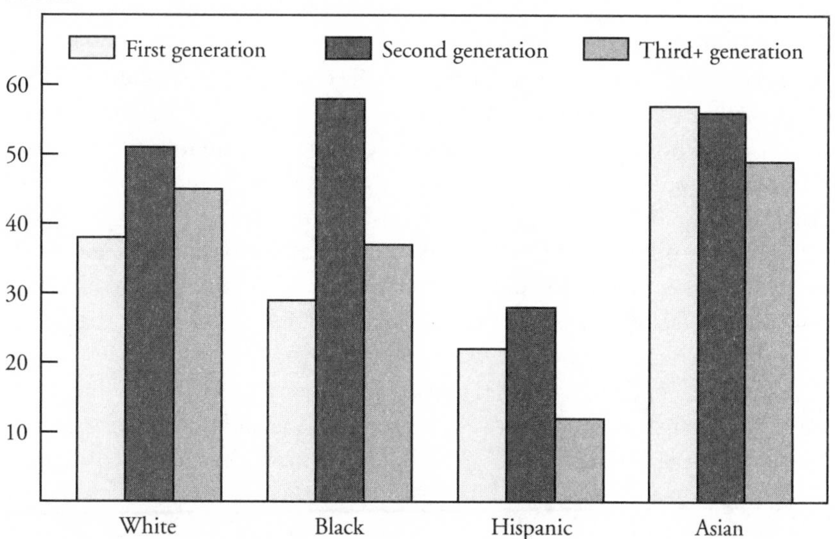

Source: Authors' tabulations from 2000 Current Population Survey.

States,[53] and they conflate the changing educational attainments of successive cohorts by averaging the lower attainments of older generations with the higher achievements of successive cohorts.[54] Comparisons in educational attainment across "generations" better portray educational progress. Census data provide an approximate measure of generational status, where the foreign-born represent the first generation, the native-born offspring of foreign-born parents represent the second generation, and the native-born offspring of native-born parents represent third and higher-order generations. This metric provides strong evidence of educational progress, as Hispanics more than doubled their college enrollment rates between the first and second generations (figure 3-5). Still, second-generation Hispanics were only half as likely as their Asian and black counterparts to enroll in college in 2000. This disparity could be magnified in the future because children of Hispanic immigrants are the fastest growing segment of the youth population and hail disproportionately from

53. Fry (2003).

54. Smith (2003). Still, the pattern of differentials is relatively similar if the focus is restricted to a young cohort, such as persons aged 25–34, or to a cohort of recent graduates. See Tienda (2006).

families with limited economic resources. Thus, despite clear evidence of educational progress among second-generation Hispanic youths, the continued educational advancement of Asian, white, and black students results in larger college enrollment gaps over time.[55]

Large differentials in college enrollment rates reflect socioeconomic differences—mainly disparities in parental education—but also values that do or do not make educational attainment a priority for both parents and their children. Even among families of low socioeconomic status, almost 80 percent of Asian youths enroll in college, in comparison with about 30 to 40 percent of others. At the other extreme of the socioeconomic distribution, college enrollment rates do not differentiate among whites, Hispanics, and Asians, although high-status blacks are significantly less likely to enroll in college than their high-status white, Hispanic, or Asian counterparts.

These differentials indicate that for Hispanics, ameliorative policy measures, such as use of race-sensitive admission criteria and policies that diminish the financial burden of college, will likely narrow the college enrollment and graduation gaps vis-à-vis whites.[56] Recent trends in financial aid, however, are not encouraging. Policy choices made in the late 1970s redirected financial aid away from the neediest students, toward those in middle income groups, and eventually toward upper income students. Enrollment disparities among the high-status groups suggest that a one-size-fits-all financial aid policy may not have uniform effects on blacks and Hispanics from disadvantaged backgrounds.

Parental education is essential to promoting educational success because it drives the expectations parents set for their children and the resources they invest to promote their offspring's achievements.[57] Yet parental education not only is less amenable to policy levers but also is inefficient as a policy instrument to achieve social equity.[58] Owing to the low average educational level of recent Hispanic immigrants, the burgeoning Hispanic school-age population is clearly the most disadvantaged in this regard: only 10 percent of Hispanic youths had college-educated fathers in 1999, a share barely changed since 1974. By contrast, one in three white youths had college-educated fathers in 1999, as did half as many school-age blacks.[59] Data for mothers tell the same story, except that the scenario is even bleaker, because fewer mothers than fathers attain college degrees.

55. Kelly (2005).

56. McPherson and Shapiro (2003).

57. Schneider, Martinez, and Owens (2006).

58. Heckman (2006); Knudsen and others (2006).

59. National Center for Education Statistics (2003).

The priority policy challenge, then, is to narrow achievement gaps for low-income youths at all stages of the educational pipeline, but particularly during early childhood, in order to weaken the link between social class and minority group status. To what extent low levels of parental education will slow intergenerational mobility in the future is unknown. George Borjas cautions that the rate of social mobility enjoyed by prior immigrants will not continue, because unlike the manufacturing jobs filled by the foreign born at the turn of the twentieth century, the economic sectors in which contemporary immigrants are employed do not provide avenues for economic betterment.[60]

Although it is common to blame slow improvement in Hispanics' high school and college graduation rates on the drag of low-skill immigration, doing so deflects attention from inadequate investments in educational institutions. Underinvestment in early childhood education is particularly important, because a growing body of neurobiological, economic, and behavioral evidence indicates that social equity can be achieved most efficiently by reducing achievement gaps during early childhood.[61] Knudsen and associates argue that the most cost-effective strategy for strengthening the American workforce is to strengthen the cognitive environments of the most economically disadvantaged, who have the most to gain because their social environments are least likely to provide the stimulation that is necessary to prepare the brain architecture for later learning.[62]

The large immigrant-receiving states have the most to gain in future labor force productivity. With immigrant fertility driving population growth in these states, their age structures are more bottom heavy, which implies an important opportunity to capitalize on the demographic dividend. A few illustrations dramatize these points while strengthening our case for the urgency of harnessing the demographic bonus via educational investment.

Reflecting the baby boom "echo," figure 3-6 shows that the number of high school graduates nationally increased 19 percent between 1994 and 2004, but this average conceals wide variation among states. Despite elevated high school dropout rates in Texas, California, and Florida, rapid growth of the school-age population, combined with improved graduation rates, resulted in larger cohorts of high school graduates—in Texas, double the national average. New York, on the other hand, lagged far behind.[63]

The sizable growth in the college-eligible population is projected to slow over the decade from 2005 to 2015 as the children of baby boomers move

60. Borjas (2006).

61. Heckman (2006).

62. Knudsen and others (2006).

63. Western Interstate Commission for Higher Education (2003).

Figure 3-6. Actual and Projected High School Graduates, 1994–2015

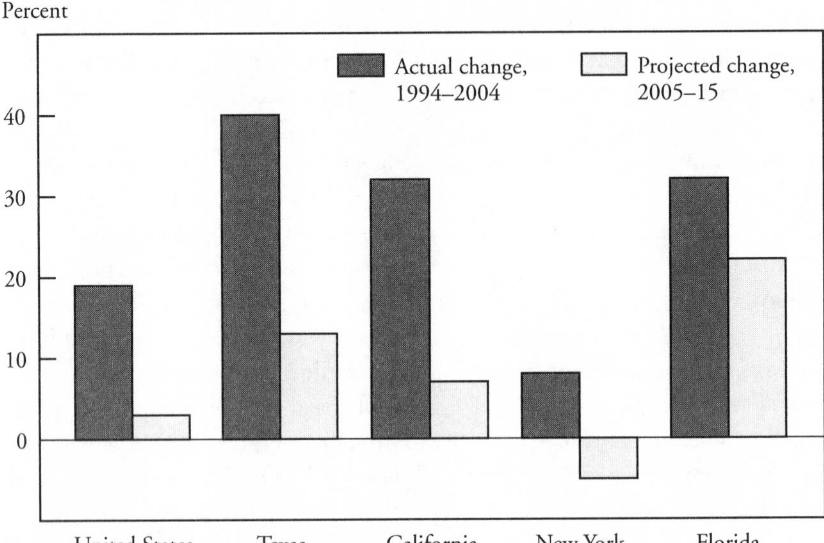

Source: Western Interstate Commission for Higher Education (2003).

through the educational pipeline. Nationally the number of high school graduates is projected to grow a meager 3 percent between 2005 and 2015, and many states will witness shrinking cohorts of high school graduates during that time. Three of the major immigrant-receiving states, California, Texas, and Florida, are notable exceptions (figure 3-6). On the basis of demographic projections and current completion rates, New York State is positioned for a decline in the number of high school graduates. This case attests that the window of opportunity to harness the demographic dividend by investing in youths will close soon, as the age structure stabilizes in line with the contours of stable population growth.

In fact, neither Texas nor California has made sufficient investments in postsecondary education to keep pace with growth in the college-eligible population. Given the changing composition of demographic growth, it is not surprising that opposition to affirmative action has been particularly vitriolic in these states. Texas's experience provides an apt illustration of the point. Although college enrollment in the state also increased as the number of high school graduates swelled, the expansion of postsecondary opportunities failed to keep up with growing demand, particularly at four-year institutions, which created a college squeeze for access to the most competitive institutions. Specifically, between 1994 and 2004, enrollment in Texas postsecondary institutions, both two- and four-year, rose 27 percent.[64] This is above the national trend but still well below the 40 percent increase in the number of high school graduates. The Texas college squeeze would have been even more intense if the state had not lost 25 to 50 percent of its high school students before graduation.

The diversification of Texas's college-age population added complexity to the college squeeze, which played out in public discourse as growing resistance to the use of race preferences in college admissions, but it was not a causal factor. Educational underinvestment is seldom invoked as the culprit for the rising number of applicants denied admission to a four-year institution in the state, yet it is the ultimate cause of the college squeeze and a source of economic vulnerability for the state in the future. Comptroller Carole Keeton Strayhorn estimated a 500 percent return on every dollar invested in the state's higher education system.[65] Put differently, underinvestment in higher education represents a formidable opportunity cost for the state.

Reaping the Demographic Bonus in an Aging White Society

With fertility declining throughout the world, even in large immigrant-sending nations such as Mexico, the opportunity to capitalize on the demographic bonus is time bound. The United States risks its future by not reaping the potential dividends of the current modest age bubble attributable to above-replacement immigrant fertility. The social and economic significance of changing population composition depends crucially on educational investments in today's school-age cohorts, which are far more diverse than the baby boom cohorts approaching retirement. Specifically, the next twenty-five years represent an opportunity unshared by America's industrialized peers to secure the future by capitalizing on a demographic bonus afforded by the modest bulge in the size of the school-age cohort. That bonus will fade as fertility decline shrinks the sizes of future cohorts.

Figure 3-7 maps diversification onto the changing age structure resulting from projected fertility decline and immigration retrenchment. In the year

64. Tienda (2006).
65. Strayhorn (2005).

Figure 3-7. *Population Pyramids for the United States, 2000 and 2030*[a]

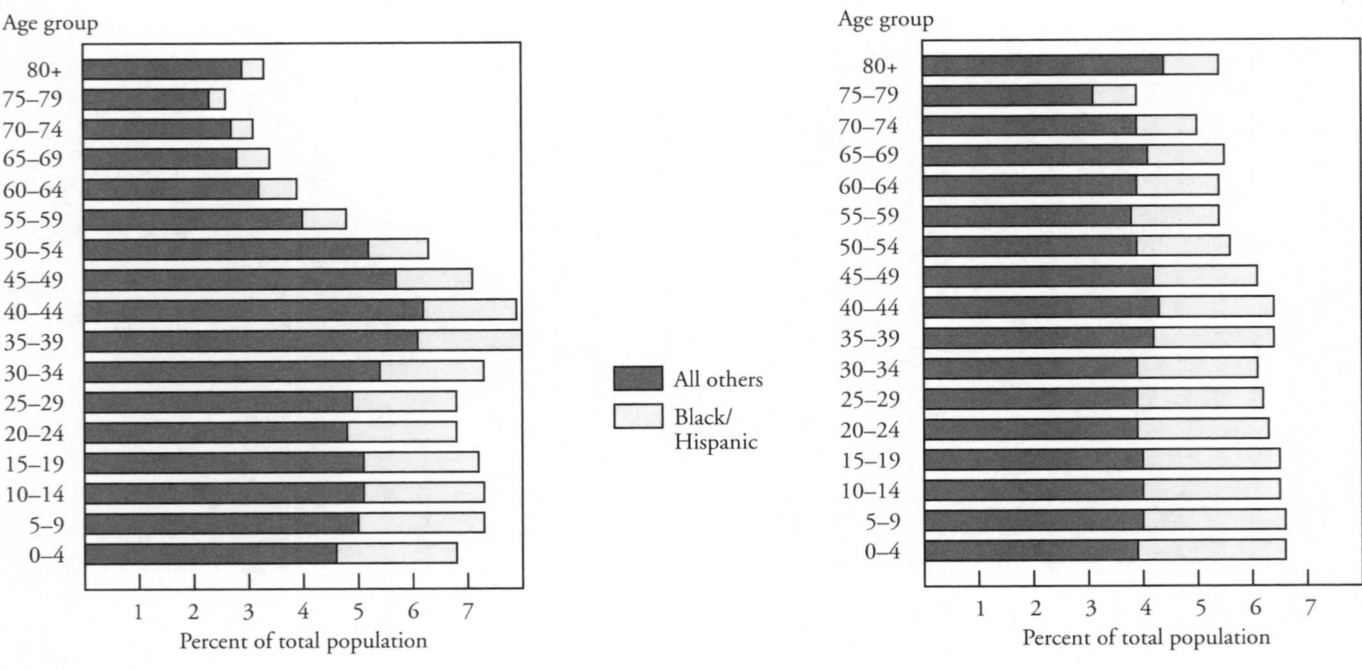

Source: Tienda (2006).

2000, just over half the U.S. population was between the working ages of 25 and 64, but whites outnumbered minorities by a ratio of 3.5 to 1. At the postretirement ages, the ratio of whites to minorities was 10 to 1.[66] Because of aging, the working-age population is projected to fall to 48 percent of the population by 2030, with the white-to-minority ratio falling to about 2 to 1. By that year, the retirement-age population will approach 20 percent, of which the vast majority will be white. For rapidly growing states such as Texas, California, and Florida, the potential demographic dividend is even greater and the time line a bit longer, but greater too is the risk of underinvestment.

Whether the growing youth population will contribute to economic productivity or become a drag on social resources hinges crucially on policy decisions to bolster educational investments, at both the preschool and postsecondary levels, particularly for economically disadvantaged youths. Improving educational outputs based on math and reading scores, high school graduation rates, and college graduation rates is imperative in order for the United States to prevent expected demographic shifts from deepening class divisions and eroding international competitiveness in math and science.[67] As Samuel Preston pointed out in his presidential address to the Population Association of America in 1984, declining fertility and population aging could produce a collision course in social investment priorities and dramatically alter the profile of economic well-being by age, especially if transfers to the elderly came at the expense of children.[68]

There are several mechanisms through which this last scenario can operate. One is the Social Security income transfer from workers to retirees. The economic future of retirees requires that new labor force entrants contribute the maximum to the Social Security system, which can best be achieved through human capital investments. Another mechanism is relative public expenditures for the young and the old. An analysis of trends in social spending from 1980 to 2000 revealed a growing gap between children and the elderly, partly because most programs serving the elderly were federal and universal, whereas most children's programs were state based and, with the exception of public

66. We combine blacks and Hispanics versus others for these calculations, both to provide more conservative estimates of the potential minority demographic dividend and because we wish to compare the two educationally disadvantaged groups with others. Not only are Asians not educationally disadvantaged, on average, but their average attainment exceeds that of whites by a considerable margin. Because their numbers are small, however, our inferences would not be altered if Asians were added to the minority population.

67. Kelly (2005).

68. Preston (1984).

education, means tested. Social benefits for the elderly averaged $15,400 per capita in 1980, in comparison with $4,400 for children; by 2000 these average expenditures rose to $19,700 and $6,400, respectively, with medical costs driving the public program costs for the elderly.[69] A recent estimate showed that per capita expenditures on health care for the elderly exceeded those for the population under age 65 by a factor approaching four; children, on the other hand, have the least spent on health care.[70] The ballot box is the ultimate resource available to the elderly, but not the young, to protect their interests.

Diversification adds complexity to the social tension between the old and the young, but this need not be so. On grounds of social justice and fairness, one can argue that increasing educational investment will serve broad democratic and social goals by promoting individual social mobility and economic development.[71] As shown throughout this volume, educational investment also makes good economic sense for individuals, for states, and for the nation. Yet as the recent affirmative action backlash attests, use of race-sensitive criteria to equalize higher educational opportunity meets with formidable resistance from opponents who claim that meritocratic principles are compromised in a mindless pursuit of proportionality.

Today, more than ever before, higher education is necessary to harness the demographic dividend afforded by the continued infusion of young people into an aging population. In a globalized world, population diversification represents a form of asset diversification, with dividends depending on investment portfolios. But continuing their current course, racial and ethnic differentials in educational attainment will undermine the social and economic integration prospects of recent immigrants and their children, and the nation will forgo the potential demographic dividend stemming from the baby boom echo and the above-replacement fertility rate of foreign-born women. Unless policy strategies are successful in weakening the link between group membership and pathways to social mobility, Americans risk reifying class divisions along race and ethnic lines, short-circuiting the nation's ability to maintain its international competitiveness.

There is no time for complacency if the United States is to retain its competitiveness in the face of rising challenges from a rapidly growing and developing China. The opportunity costs of not closing achievement and graduation gaps will continue to grow as global market integration continues apace. Rising to this monumental challenge requires a highly skilled labor force. The

69. Pati and others (2004).
70. Keehan and others (2004).
71. Cox and Alm (2004).

window of opportunity to harness the demographic dividend is closing, but unlike developing countries with high youth dependency rates, the United States has the economic resources to make the necessary investments. Whether it has sufficient political will is the real question.

References

Annie Casey Foundation. 2005. *Kids Count Pocket Guide.* Washington, D.C.: Population Reference Bureau.

Borjas, George J. 2006. "Making It in America: Social Mobility in the Immigrant Population." *Future of Children* 16, no. 2: 55–71.

Cox, W. Michael, and Richard Alm. 2001. *Taking Stock in America: Resiliency, Redundancy and Recovery in the U.S. Economy.* Dallas, Tex.: Annual Report of the Federal Reserve Bank of Dallas.

———. 2004. *What D'Ya Know?* Dallas, Tex.: Annual Report of the Federal Reserve Bank of Dallas.

Fischer, Mary J., and Marta Tienda. 2006. "Redrawing Spatial Color Lines: Hispanic Metropolitan Dispersal, Segregation, and Economic Opportunity." In *Hispanics and the Future of America,* edited by Marta Tienda and Faith Mitchell, pp. 100–37. Washington, D.C.: National Academies Press.

Fry, Rick. 2003. "Hispanic Youth Dropping Out of U.S. Schools: Measuring the Challenge." Washington, D.C.: Pew Hispanic Center (pewhispanic.org/reports/report.php?ReportID=19).

———. 2005. "The High Schools Hispanics Attend: Size and Other Key Characteristics." Washington, D.C.: Pew Hispanic Center (pewhispanic.org/files/reports/54.pdf).

Gibson, Campbell, and Kay Jung. 2006. "Historical Census Statistics on the Foreign-Born Population of the United States: 1850–2000." Bureau of the Census (www.census.gov/population/www.documentation/twps0081.html).

Haveman, Robert, and Timothy Smeeding. 2006. "The Role of Higher Education in Social Mobility." *Future of Children* 16, no. 2: 55–71.

Heckman, James J. 2006. "Skill Formation and the Economics of Investing in Disadvantaged Children." *Science* 312 (June 30): 1900–02.

Hirschman, Charles. 2006. "Immigration and the American Century." *Demography* 42, no. 4: 595–620.

Keehan, Sean P., and others. 2004. "Age Estimates in the National Health Accounts." *Health Care Financing Review (Web Exclusive)* 1, no. 1: 1–16 (www.cms.hhs.gov/NationalHealthExpendData/downloads/keehan-age-estimates.pdf).

Kelly, Patrick J. 2005. *As America Becomes More Diverse: The Impact of State Higher Education Inequality.* Boulder, Colo.: National Center for Higher Education Management Systems.

Knudsen, Eric I., and others. 2006. "Economic, Neurobiological, and Behavioral Perspectives on Building America's Future Workforce." *Proceedings of the National Academy of Sciences* 103, no. 27: 10155–62.

Landale, Nancy S., R. Salvador Oropesa, and Christina Bradatan. 2006. "Hispanic Families in the United States." In *Hispanics and the Future of America,* edited by Marta Tienda and Faith Mitchell, pp. 138–73. Washington, D.C.: National Academies Press.

Larsen, Luke J. 2004. "The Foreign-Born Population in the United States: 2003." *Current Population Reports* P20-551. Bureau of the Census.

McLanahan, Sara S., and Gary Sandefur. 1994. *Growing Up with a Single Parent: What Hurts, What Helps*. Harvard University Press.

McPherson, Michael S., and Morton Owen Shapiro. 2003. "Funding Roller Coaster for Public Higher Education." *Science* 302 (November): 1157.

———. 2004. "The Promise and Perils of Universal Higher Education." Ford Policy Forum, Forum on the Future of Higher Education.

Meissner, Doris, and others. 2006. *Immigration and America's Future: A New Chapter*. Report of the Independent Task Force on Immigration and America's Future. Washington, D.C.: Migration Policy Institute.

Migration Policy Institute. 2007. "Age Distribution of the Foreign Born as a Percentage of the Total Foreign-Born Population, for the United States: 1870–2000." Washington, D.C. (www.migrationinformation.org/datahub/charts/age.shtml).

National Center for Education Statistics. 2003. "Status and Trends in the Education of Hispanics." NCES 2003-008. Department of Education.

———. 2006. *Dropout Rates in the United States: 2002 and 2003*. NCES 2006-062. Department of Education.

Orfield, Gary, and Chungmei Lee. 2004. "Brown at Fifty: King's Dream or *Plessy's* Nightmare?" Civil Rights Project, Harvard University (www.civilrightsproject.harvard.edu/research/reseg04/brown50.pdf).

Organization for Economic Cooperation and Development. 2004. *Education at a Glance*. Paris (www.oecd.org/document/7).

Passel, Jeffrey S. 2004. "Methodology and Assumptions for Population Estimates and Projections by Race and Generation." Washington, D.C.: Urban Institute.

Pati, Susmita, and others. 2004. "Public Spending on Elders and Children: The Gap Is Growing." *Issue Brief* 10, no. 2. University of Pennsylvania, Leonard Davis Institute of Health Economics.

Preston, Samuel H. 1984. "Children and the Elderly: Divergent Paths for America's Dependents." *Demography* 21, no. 4: 435–56.

Prewitt, Kenneth. 2001. "Beyond Census 2000: As a Nation, We Are the World." *Carnegie Reporter* 1, no. 3: 3–11.

Reardon, Sean F., and John T. Yun. 2001. "Suburban Racial Change and Suburban School Segregation, 1987–95." *Sociology of Education* 74, no. 2: 79–101.

Rumbaut, Rubén G. 2006. "The Making of a People." In *Hispanics and the Future of America*, edited by Marta Tienda and Faith Mitchell, pp. 16–65. Washington, D.C.: National Academies Press.

Sacks, Peter. 2007. "How Colleges Perpetuate Inequality." *Chronicle of Higher Education* 53, no. 19: B9.

Schneider, Barbara, S. Martinez, and A. Owens. 2006. "Barriers to Educational Opportunities for Hispanics in the U.S." In *Hispanics and the Future of America*, edited by Marta Tienda and Faith Mitchell, pp. 179–221. Washington, D.C.: National Academies Press.

Shin, Hyon B. 2005. "School Enrollment: Social and Economic Characteristics of Students." *Current Population Reports* P20-554. Bureau of the Census.

Smith, James P. 2003. "Assimilation across Latino Generations." *American Economic Review* 93, no. 2: 315–19.

State Science and Technology Institute. 2005. "State Rankings of GSP per Capita: 1999–2003." Westerville, Ohio (www.ssti.org/Digest/2005/041805.htm).

Stier, Haya, and Marta Tienda. 2001. *The Color of Opportunity: Pathways to Family, Welfare, and Work*. University of Chicago Press.

Strayhorn, Carol Keeton. 2005. "The Impact of the State Higher Education System on the Texas Economy." Special Report, Texas Comptroller of Public Accounts (www.window.state.tx.us/specialrpt/highered05).

Swanson, Christopher. 2003. *Who Graduates? Who Doesn't? A Statistical Portrait of Public High School Graduation, Class of 2001*. Washington, D.C.: Urban Institute, Education Policy Center.

Taylor, Melissa, and others. 2002. "The Changing Population in the U.S.: Baby Boomers, Immigrants, and Their Effects on State Government." *Trends Alert*. Lexington, Ky.: Council for State Governments (www.csg.org/pubs/Documents/TA0412Population.pdf).

Tienda, Marta. 2002. "Demography and the Social Contract." *Demography* 39, no. 4: 587–616.

———. 2006. "Harnessing Diversity in Higher Education: Lessons from Texas." In *Ford Policy Forum, 2006: Exploring the Economics of Higher Education*, edited by Maureen Devlin, pp. 7–14. Washington, D.C.: NACUBO and Forum for the Future of Higher Education.

Tienda, Marta, and Faith Mitchell, eds. 2006. *Multiple Origins, Uncertain Destinies: Hispanics and the American Future*. Washington, D.C.: National Academies Press.

U.S. Bureau of the Census. 2001. "Nation's Median Age Highest Ever, but 65-and-Over Population's Growth Lags." Public Information Office (www.census.gov/Press-Release/www/2001/cb01 cn67.html).

———. 2005. "Texas Becomes Nation's Newest 'Majority-Minority' State." Public Information Office (www.census.gov/Press-Release/www/releases/archives/population/005514.html).

———. 2007. *Statistical Abstract of the United States: 2007*. Department of Commerce (www.census.gov/prod/2006pubs/07statab/pop.pdf).

Western Interstate Commission for Higher Education. 2003. *Knocking at the College Door: Projections of High School Graduates by State, Income, and Race/Ethnicity*. Boulder, Colo.: WICHE.

4 THOMAS BAILEY

Implications of Educational Inequality in a Global Economy

Education is a fundamental basis of productivity growth. Not only are educated workers more productive, but the technological changes that generate productivity are dependent on the availability of an educated workforce—both the scientists and engineers who directly generate innovations and the workers in many related occupations who support innovative work and create the economic and technical infrastructure on which innovation is based. In the past, the U.S. education system produced an educated workforce adequate to maintain a relatively high level of productivity growth, and at least the postsecondary education system was considered the best in the world. Reflecting what has been the generally accepted view of the superiority of U.S. postsecondary education, the 2006 report of the secretary of education's Commission on the Future of American Higher Education stated that "the American system has been the envy of the world for years."[1]

Although U.S. education levels rose dramatically during the twentieth century, the education system as a whole has continued to be highly inequitable with respect to race, ethnicity, and social class (see especially Rothstein and Wilder, this volume). Although the chapters in this book are focused primarily on elementary and secondary education, the higher education system is

1. U.S. Department of Education (2006, p. ix).

also profoundly inequitable in the sense that educational achievement is closely related to race, ethnicity, and socioeconomic status.[2] Moreover, economic, political, social, and demographic factors are changing in such a way that in the future the traditional educational inequality in the United States will increasingly stand in the way of the nation's ability to sustain productivity growth and compete successfully in international markets.

Marta Tienda and Sigal Alon, in their chapter in this book, argues that the current school-age population bulge, if its members can gain access to appropriate education, offers an opportunity to overcome some of the economic and demographic problems created by the aging of the baby boom generation. That bulge is made up disproportionately of African Americans and Hispanics, who have in the past had lower levels of educational attainment than whites. If this goes unchanged, integration of this bulge into the labor force may actually result in a drop in the overall level of education in the population, even as technological changes and developments in world markets call for greater education. Without improvements in educational opportunities for black and Hispanic students, the bulge may be a liability rather than an opportunity. In the past, educational inequality was a problem primarily for people who ended up with low levels of education; increasingly it will be a problem for everyone.

In the first section of this chapter I provide background on past discussions about the relationship between education and productivity. I then discuss the current political and economic environment as it relates to the development and expansion of higher education. Elementary and secondary schools provide the educational foundation for the U.S. economic system, but growth in productivity increasingly depends on the reach and quality of higher education. Next I discuss the growing racial and ethnic heterogeneity of the population and describe the growing gaps in educational attainment between higher-income and white students, on the one hand, and lower-income and black and Hispanic students, on the other. Finally, I report on forecasts of future overall educational levels based on Census Bureau population growth projections, showing that if the current distribution of education among racial and ethnic groups does not change, then the overall level of education in the country will fall just as technological and market forces are calling for a labor force with higher levels of education.

2. See Haveman and Smeeding (2006); Kane (2004); Tienda and Alon (this volume).

Education, Economic Growth, and Productivity

Reformers have linked education and economic growth for many years, predicting economic problems resulting from inadequate education. In the 1980s, education reform was motivated by a concern that the United States was falling behind some other advanced countries in its educational achievement and that this spelled trouble for the country's international competitiveness. The most famous example of this was the report *A Nation at Risk,* which raised alarms about the failing international competitiveness of the United States resulting from a scandalously deficient education system.[3] Many of these fears seemed to be realized in the late 1980s as Germany, Japan, and to some extent other growing Asian countries appeared to present formidable economic competition, especially in the manufacturing sector.

The focus of education reform during that decade was on elementary and high school education. Much less attention was paid to the higher education system. Indeed, it was widely believed that the U.S. university system was unchallenged, the best in the world. The potential economic problems lay with the middle levels of the occupational system, not the highest. Japan and Germany were believed to do a much better job of training the middle section of the skills distribution—the technical-level and skilled workers who formed the backbone of the advanced manufacturing sectors that appeared to be so successful. The German apprenticeship system and the extensive Japanese on-the-job training system spread up-to-date, sophisticated skills throughout the large center section of the skills distribution. Reports on the United States emphasized the declining quality of occupational and vocational training and the low level of private-sector investment in incumbent worker training. The conventional wisdom was that the United States continued to generate innovations and produce a highly skilled high-level workforce, but other countries, particularly Japan, relying on a broader base of middle-level skills, excelled at the application and development of those innovations.[4]

The U.S. economic boom of the 1990s, coupled with the economic troubles experienced by Japan and Germany, washed away much of the anxiety about competition from those countries by the middle to the late years of the decade. It was difficult to argue that the economic success of the country in the 1990s had been a product of reforms generated by the educational anxiety of the 1980s. Elementary students who might have benefited from the standards-based reform movement of that decade would hardly have entered the labor

3. National Commission on Excellence in Education (1983).

4. See, for example, National Center on Education and the Economy (1990).

force by the time the boom flourished. The federal reforms, such as the School-to-Work Opportunity Act and the National Skill Standards Board, were not even enacted until the middle of the decade and, in the end, amounted to little.[5] By 2005 these federal reforms had disappeared. But the passage of the No Child Left Behind Act made clear the continuing perception of failure in the K–12 system, despite the reforms of the previous decades.

Although changes in the quality of education might not provide a good explanation of fluctuations in the relative performances of different countries, a great deal of evidence exists about the labor market value of education and about the long-term relationship between education and economic growth. Moreover, evidence suggests that this relationship is growing stronger. A recent analysis of the link between education and growth, using county-level data for the United States, showed that the percentage of the population with less than a high school degree was negatively related to growth, and the percentages of the population with a high school degree and with at least a B.A. were positively related to growth.[6] Goldin and Katz have argued that historically the United States' international economic leadership was closely related to its huge lead in educational attainment.[7] Changes in education had a particularly strong effect on economic productivity and growth during periods of rapid educational expansion—during the "high school movement" between 1915 and 1940 and during the period of mass higher education between 1960 and 1980. According to them, productivity growth due to education has slowed since 1980, partly because of the slowdown in the growth of educational attainment, particularly for men.

An expanding economic literature analyzes the overall relationship between education and growth. Wage analyses since the mid-1980s have consistently shown a growing earnings premium for postsecondary education, particularly for bachelor's degrees. The average weekly earnings for men with no more than a high school degree who were employed full time fell by 12 percent in constant dollars between 1979 and 2002, but weekly earnings for men with bachelor's degrees grew by 20 percent. The equivalent earnings for women with only high school degrees grew by 8 percent while earnings for women with bachelor's degrees grew by one-third.[8] Research using longitudinal data from the National Center for Education Statistics (NCES) for the 1980s and 1990s

5. See Bailey and Morest (1998) for a discussion of the rise and fall of the school-to-work movement and its relationship to economic productivity. Neumark (2007) also discusses the demise of the school-to-work movement.

6. Young, Levy, and Higgins (2004).

7. Goldin and Katz (2001).

8. Bureau of Labor Statistics (2003); for the earlier decade, see Levy and Murnane (1992).

has revealed strong and large returns on earning a bachelor's degree, for both men and women.[9]

Thomas Kane has argued that although enrollments in higher education have grown in the last decades, this growth has been below the level that would have been expected given the increasing economic value of a college degree.[10] From an economic perspective, this suggests that there is underinvestment in education. The cause of this is difficult to determine. Kane suggested that some, although not definitive, evidence existed that the inability of low-income families to get financing for their education might be at fault. Poor quality K–12 education and various social problems faced by many students also prevent them from enrolling in and completing college, despite its potential economic benefits. Whatever the reason, Kane believed the data suggested that as a whole, the economy would benefit from more postsecondary education.

Technological change and growing international competition from increasingly educated foreign workforces suggest that in the future, the overall strength of the U.S. economy will be based on work that involves more advanced skills. Levy and Murnane, in their book on the effects of globalization and computerization on required skills, divided skills into five broad categories: expert thinking, complex communication, routine cognitive tasks, routine manual tasks, and nonroutine manual tasks.[11] On the basis of their categorization of occupations, they concluded that since about 1970, the use of expert thinking and complex communication had grown while the other, lower-skill functions had all declined. Certainly, many low-skill jobs remain, yet increasingly, individual well-being as well as collective economic progress will be based on the types of skills that higher education, at least in principle, is designed to teach.

Thus in the early twenty-first century, concerns about the effects of inadequate education on the international economic position of the United States returned as the boom of the late 1990s collapsed, trade deficits grew, and China, India, and other Asian countries emerged as potential competitors in higher-level technical occupations. In contrast to concerns about education and the workforce in earlier decades, anxiety in the current decade is based on the fear that other countries now threaten U.S. competitiveness at the higher levels of the occupational structure. Given the sizes of the populations in these countries, they potentially can produce many more highly educated engineers and technicians than the United States. And the perception is that

9. Marcotte and others (2005); see also Rouse (this volume).

10. Kane (2004).

11. Levy and Murnane (2004).

the quality of their engineering and technical education is growing rapidly. In the future, international competitiveness, according to this argument, will flow from imagination, innovation, and increased entrepreneurial activity founded in high skills and technical competence. If, in the 1980s, it was the multiskilled German apprentice graduate or the continuously trained Toyota worker who appeared to threaten the United States' international economic position, then in the new century it is the Indian software engineer and the Chinese entrepreneur.

The experience of the past two decades has shown that it is misguided to link international educational differences to short- and medium-term fluctuations. But we are confronted now with longer-term challenges to the United States' lead at the upper ends of the educational distribution. Although the 2007 U.S. trade deficit with China can hardly be blamed on deficiencies in the U.S. educational system, the long-term implications of the rapidly growing higher education systems in Asia and Europe raise challenges to this country's traditional leading role in technology and innovation. I look at developments in U.S. higher education in light of these challenges.

Developments in U.S. Postsecondary Education

Since the middle of the twentieth century, the United States has been the clear international leader in the share of its population enrolled in higher education. Its research universities have been recognized as the most effective in the world for educating a high-level workforce and generating innovations and scientific breakthroughs. U.S. higher education has been a successful export industry and has attracted the best students, professors, and researchers in the world.

But this dominance is weakening in terms of the share of the young population that has completed college. By 2004, according to the Organization for Economic Cooperation and Development (OECD), the share of the 45- to 54-year-old population that had "attained tertiary education" was higher in the United States (about 41 percent) than in any other OECD country, but the shares of the 25- to 34-year-old populations in Sweden, Japan, Korea, Belgium, Norway, Ireland, and Canada that had attained this level of education equaled or exceeded the share for that age group in the United States. Australia, Finland, Spain, and France were within three percentage points of the U.S. figure. Educational attainment in all these countries had grown faster than in the United States. Indeed, in the United States, the share of the younger population that had completed tertiary education (39 percent) was actually below that share for the 45- to 54-year-olds (41 percent). In every other OECD country, the younger age group was more highly educated than the older one.[12]

Moreover, many analysts have begun to question the quality of American higher education. The authors of a recent book titled *Declining by Degrees* called into question the quality of U.S. higher education.[13] While acknowledging that there are some excellent institutions, the authors (and the accompanying documentary of the same title that aired on the Public Broadcasting System in the summer of 2005) portrayed a very negative picture of public higher education (that is, the types of institutions attended by more than three-quarters of all college students). The institutions they described had large classes, underpaid and overworked professors who had little time to work closely with their students, and disaffected students. Many of the students were apparently more interested in partying than in serious studying, and others were overwhelmed by family commitments and their need to work to support themselves while studying. In 2006 the secretary of education's Commission on the Future of Higher Education emphasized what the commissioners saw as the dubious quality of the typical American college education. Citing data from the National Adult Literacy Survey, the commissioners concluded that "many students who do earn degrees have not actually mastered the reading, writing, and thinking skills we expect of college graduates. Over the past decade, literacy among college graduates has actually declined."[14]

The two studies just mentioned cannot be considered definitive analyses of trends in the quality of higher education in the United States. Changes in averages such as those cited may result from compositional changes in the types of students enrolled in college. Moreover, the commission itself pointed out that there were no reliable and comparable measures of college learning; therefore conclusions about changes in the quality of college remain speculative. Nevertheless, this discussion exposes a growing skepticism about the content of college education, whereas that quality had previously gone unquestioned.

Much of public policy concerning postsecondary education has been focused on access. Federal loans and financial aid and low tuition at community colleges and many public four-year institutions were designed to remove low income as an impediment to college access. In 2001 the congressional Advisory Committee on Student Financial Aid stated that "three decades ago, there was unanimous agreement on the nation's access goal: Low-income students who were academically prepared must have the same educational opportunity as their

12. Organization for Economic Cooperation and Development (2006).

13. Hirsh and Merrow (2005).

14. U.S. Department of Education (2006, p. x).

middle- and upper-income peers."[15] Certainly, college attendance has expanded, but there is still a long way to go. Data from the NCES for a representative sample of students followed from eighth grade in 1988 to 2000 revealed that almost one-quarter completed no postsecondary credits.[16] The NCES created an index to measure the socioeconomic status (SES) of the students in their data sets. This measure combines family income and the education and occupational status of the students' parents. Of those students who never completed postsecondary credits, half were from the lowest SES quartile.[17] As Marta Tienda and Sigal Alon show in their chapter in this volume, college enrollment is also skewed by race and ethnicity. So colleges have made progress on the access mission but remain far from the goal articulated in 2001 by the advisory committee.

Recently, increasing attention has been paid to college completion rates and other measures of success for students who do manage to enter college. In that regard, there is less to celebrate. Many students who start college never complete a degree. Indeed, the growth in enrollments over the last decades has not been matched by an equivalent growth in graduation.[18] For example, community colleges enroll close to half of all college students, yet fewer than half of those who initially enroll in a community college earn any degree or certificate within eight years of high school graduation. Almost one-fifth never complete ten credits.[19] And although the elite selective colleges may graduate 90 percent of their students within six years of enrollment, according to data from the NCES, many non-flagship, public, four-year institutions have six-year graduation rates well below 50 percent.[20] To be sure, there is economic value in a college education even if the student does not complete a degree.[21] But most studies reveal little measurable benefit to having a few credits or a certificate, a credential that typically takes a year or less of full-time study. And there is additional value in the degree itself, over and above the value of the courses that make up the degree program.[22]

Improving completion rates will probably require innovations in counseling, student and academic services, and pedagogy, as well as tuition and aid policies that remove financial barriers to low-income students. But progress on

15. U.S. Department of Education (2006, p. vi).

16. U.S. Department of Education (2003).

17. Calculations by the author from the National Education Longitudinal Survey (U.S. Department of Education [2003]).

18. Turner (2004).

19. Bailey and Morest (2006, chap. 1).

20. Scott, Bailey, and Kienzl (2006).

21. Kane and Rouse (1995).

22. Grubb (2002); Marcotte and others (2005).

these issues is thwarted by the growing pressure on higher education financing. Total public sector appropriations for higher education doubled from $31 billion (in 2000 dollars) in 1970 to $64 billion in 2001. But appropriations per student, which were at $5,409 in 2001, had fluctuated between $4,500 and $5,400 since 1970 ($5,227 in 1970). Appropriations as a proportion of GDP rose from 0.66 percent in 1970 to 0.79 percent in 1976 and fell to 0.64 percent in 2001.[23] State appropriations were under particular pressure during the first three or four years of the present century as states faced severe drops in revenues. The subsequent economic recovery restored some revenues, but higher education must compete for resources with the K–12 system, the prison system, and growing medical expenditures. Public colleges and universities will continue to find it difficult to increase revenues. Thus state appropriations for higher education per $1,000 of personal income fell from $7.81 in 2001 to $6.91 in 2005.[24]

As states have reduced their investments in higher education, students and families have taken on more of the costs. In 1981 net tuition (tuition minus financial aid) accounted for 21.5 percent of public higher education total educational revenues. By 2005 that share had risen to 36.7 percent. Almost one-half of that increase (47 percent) took place between 2001 and 2005.[25] Public investment in higher education remains substantial, but the boom of the late 1990s obscured the declining share of state budgets devoted to higher education. In general, students and their families are paying a larger share of the costs of college. Tuition has grown steadily, even at community colleges, and accounts for a larger portion of a typical family budget.

Over the past decades, the U.S. higher education system and indeed the country's labor force have benefited from the enrollment of hundreds of thousands of international students. These students have generated income for the colleges (many pay full tuition) and have helped sustain many graduate programs, especially technical and scientific programs. Moreover, many have stayed in the United States after graduation, adding to the educated workforce. But developments here and abroad, including restrictions on foreign students following the attacks on the Pentagon and World Trade Center on September 11, 2001, sharp increases in tuition, and increases in the quantity and quality of postsecondary education in other countries, led to a 2.4 percent decline in enrollment of foreign students in U.S. institutions of higher education in the 2003–04 academic year. This was the first such decline since the 1971–72 academic year. The decline slowed after that, but enrollments con-

23. National Center for Education Statistics (2005, pp. 200–01).

24. Mortenson (2005).

25. Lenth and others (2006, p. 26).

tinued to fall, by another 1.3 percent, between the 2003–04 and 2005–06 academic years.[26]

These developments expose the significant challenges facing the United States in the development of its workforce over the next decade. Evidence on the importance of high-level education to economic growth, research on the large and growing wage premium for a college education, and projections of the types of skills that will increasingly be needed all point to increasing demand for a college-educated workforce. Moreover, analysts see growing competition from abroad for high-skilled work, not just for low-wage, unskilled jobs. At the same time, the United States has lost its traditional lead in the share of its population with postsecondary education. More countries are close behind and gaining. In addition to these numerical issues, analysts are beginning to question the quality of U.S. higher education at the same time the public sector is reducing its commitment to funding such education. The shares of state budgets devoted to college and public expenditures per student have both declined. The share of college revenues that comes from students and their families has risen over the last decade, and slow economic growth, strong resistance to increased taxation, growing demands on state budgets, especially from medical expenses, and ballooning federal deficits all suggest that it will be difficult to increase the public investment in higher education. In many states, preventing further decline would be considered a positive outcome.

Inequality in Higher Education in the United States

As the country confronts the need to strengthen and expand its higher education, where are the students going to come from? In the future, it appears that the United States will be less able to rely on highly educated workers and students from abroad. To begin with, the baby boom generation is beginning to retire, which will result in the loss of millions of college-educated workers. As Tienda and Alon point out in chapter 3, the demographic bulge represented by the baby boom echo and continued high levels of immigration is one potential source of replacement workers. But for this source to provide the needed workforce, it must have an education level that not merely matches but exceeds that of the generation about to retire. As we have seen, OECD data indicate that by 2004 the college graduate share of the 25- to 34-year-old age group was slightly below that for the 45- to 54-year-old group.[27] Moreover,

26. Institute on International Education (2006).

27. Organization for Economic Cooperation and Development (2006, table A1.3a.).

many students still do not enter and succeed in college, and such students in the past have disproportionately come from demographic groups that are over-represented in the current population bulge.

According to the National Education Longitudinal Survey (NELS), about one-seventh of the students who were in eighth grade in 1988 had not earned a high school degree or General Educational Development (GED) credential by 2000. Another 12 percent never earned any postsecondary credits. Moreover, many students graduate from high school unprepared to be successful in college. Because they often lack adequate academic skills, many students must enroll in remedial education once they try to start college. Others arrive at college with little idea about what will be expected of them or what they need to do to manage their college careers. These deficiencies are to be found much more among low-income and minority students than among higher-income white students. Haveman and Smeeding have argued that low-income students face multiple barriers to college access—their schools do a poor job of preparing them, they are ill prepared to select and apply to college, they are poorly informed about the availability of financial aid, and they face greater financial barriers.[28] Strengthened high school academic preparation, financial aid reform, and programs to facilitate the transition into college are obvious responses to these problems.

Under any circumstances, these achievement levels need to be improved, but that objective is made more difficult because entrance into and achievement in college is closely related to income and race. Figure 4-1, which is based on data collected by the NCES through its National Educational Longitudinal Study of a representative sample of students who were eighth graders in 1988, displays high school outcomes and postsecondary educational enrollments for the four SES quartiles.[29] By 2000 almost one-fifth of the lowest SES group had not finished high school; another quarter had completed high school, some with GEDs, but had completed no postsecondary credits. Only about 15 percent had earned credits at four-year institutions. In contrast, 95 percent of the highest SES group graduated from high school and earned postsecondary credits, the large majority of them in four-year colleges. Moreover, over the last twenty years the differences in college enrollment between high- and low-income students have grown.[30] Certainly, there is great potential for expanding the high-level workforce by expanding educational opportunities for low-income students.

28. Haveman and Smeeding (2006).

29. U.S. Department of Education (2003).

30. Kane (2004).

Figure 4-1. *High School Completion and Initial Postsecondary Education by 2000 of Eighth Graders in 1988, by SES Quartile*

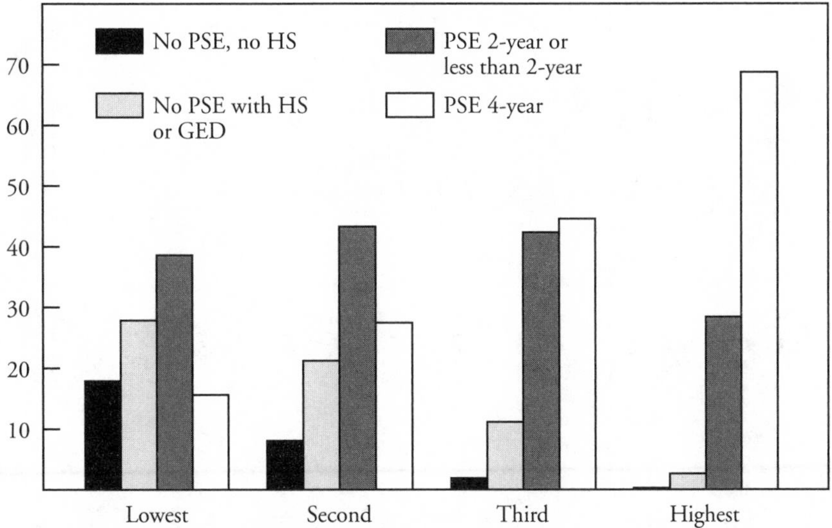

Source: U.S. Department of Education (2003).

In the past, much research has documented the stark differences in postsecondary enrollments and outcomes by race and socioeconomic status.[31] These differences are shown in table 4-1. Data for the table are based on all the students in the NELS sample who made it to twelfth grade by 1992.[32] Eighty percent of the white students in the sample earned at least one college credit by 2000, whereas only about 70 percent of Hispanic and African American students achieved that. The gaps between white and other students grew for students who had accumulated at least ten credits and those who had enrolled in a B.A.-granting institution. Finally, whereas almost 40 percent of the white students who reached twelfth grade had received a bachelor's degree by 2000, only 17 percent of the Hispanics and 21 percent of the African Americans had done so.

Moreover, these gaps have grown, not shrunk. According to the best longitudinal data available from the NCES, among high school seniors in the class of 1972, 47 percent of blacks, 47 percent of Hispanics, and 58 percent of

31. See, for example, Haveman and Smeeding (2006); Tienda and Alon (this volume).

32. U.S. Department of Education (2003).

Table 4-1. *Postsecondary Enrollments and Outcomes by Race or Ethnicity and Gender, 2000*[a]

Percent, except as indicated

	Participated in postsecondary education			*Earned at least a bachelor's degree*			
Group	*Entered at least one postsecondary institution*	*Earned more than 10 credits*	*Earned more than 10 credits and any credits from a 4-year institution*	*All 12th graders in sample*	*Earned more than 10 credits*	*Earned more than 10 credits and any credits from a 4-year institution*	*Average time to degree (years)*
All							
Total	78.2	68.8	52.2	35.1	51.0	67.2	4.58
Male	75.8	66.0	50.0	31.2	47.2	62.4	4.69
Female	80.7	71.6	54.3	39.0	54.4	71.7	4.49
Asian							
Total	91.8	82.3	68.5	47.7	58.0	69.6	4.64
Male	91.7	78.7	64.0	43.1	54.7	67.2	4.79
Female	91.9	86.8	74.1	53.6	61.7	72.3	4.49
Black							
Total	69.6	55.2	38.0	21.4	38.7	56.3	4.70
Male	63.7	48.0	29.9	14.6	30.4	48.8	4.93
Female	74.8	61.7	45.3	27.5	44.5	60.7	4.60
White							
Total	80.3	72.7	56.8	39.6	54.6	69.8	4.53
Male	78.0	70.1	54.9	35.6	50.8	64.8	4.63
Female	82.6	75.2	58.6	43.8	58.2	74.6	4.45
Hispanic							
Total	70.5	56.3	34.0	16.8	29.9	49.5	5.13
Male	68.8	55.9	35.0	15.7	28.1	44.9	5.36
Female	72.1	56.7	33.0	17.9	31.6	54.3	4.94

Source: National Education Longitudinal Study of 1988.

a. Figures are for 1992 twelfth graders who entered postsecondary education.

whites enrolled in at least one institution of higher education within 8.5 years of their senior year in high school. Two decades later, all groups of seniors in the high school class of 1992 had made substantial gains. The black college enrollment rate had increased by 23 percentage points, to 70 percent, the Hispanic rate by the same amount, also to 70 percent, and the white rate by 21 percentage points, to 79 percent. In absolute percentages, the gap was about the same, but the college enrollment rate had risen for all groups.

But if we examine the number of seniors from these classes who earned at least ten credits, then progress for blacks and Hispanics was less, and the gaps between these groups and whites in actual percentage points grew wider. Although all groups have made progress in enrollment in B.A.-granting institutions, gains by whites significantly exceed those by blacks and Hispanics. Fifty-six percent of the white seniors in the class of 1992 had earned at least ten credits and had earned some credits from B.A.-granting institutions, whereas only 38 percent of the black students in the class and 34 percent of the Hispanic students had done so (table 4-1). Thus, by 1992 blacks had achieved rates equivalent to the white rates in 1972. Hispanic students were still enrolling in B.A.-granting institutions at rates below those that whites had achieved two decades earlier.[33]

Thus, black and Hispanic students are less likely to get to twelfth grade; if they do, they are less likely to enroll in college; and if they do enroll, they are less likely to earn ten credits. Moreover, they are less likely to enroll in a B.A.-granting institution, and if they do, they are less likely to complete a degree. For the most part, there has been little or no progress in closing the various postsecondary components of these gaps in the educational pipeline. Some progress has been made in getting blacks and Hispanics into college, but the gaps between groups in post-enrollment success have not declined. Indeed, the overall gaps between Hispanics, blacks, and whites in B.A. attainment have clearly grown. Twenty-four percent of whites in the class of 1972 who entered postsecondary education earned bachelor's degrees within 8.5 years, and 39 percent from the class of 1992 did so. The equivalent numbers for the other groups were 12 and 21 percent, respectively, for blacks and 9 and 16 percent, respectively, for Hispanics. In terms of bachelor's degree attainment, by the 1990s blacks and particularly Hispanics were still well behind the point where whites had been in 1972.[34]

33. National Center for Education Statistics (2005, p. 159).

34. See National Center for Education Statistics (2005, p. 159). The table provides data on the percentage of those who participated in postsecondary education who completed more than ten credits and the percentage of those who completed more than ten credits who earned a bachelor's degree. The data presented here were derived by multiplying these two figures.

Figure 4-2. *Attainment of Bachelor's Degree or Higher, 1980, 1990, and 2000*

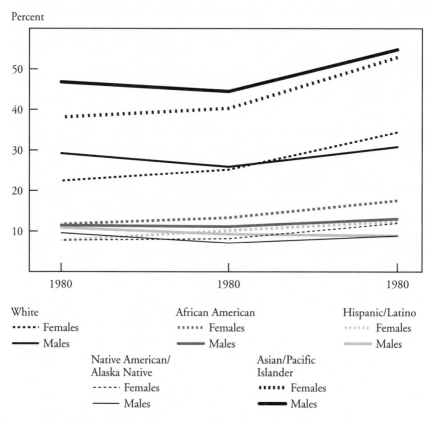

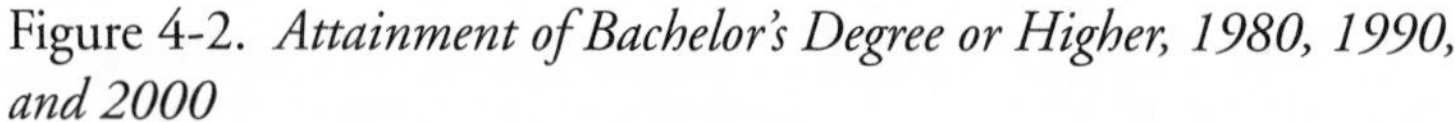

Source: Kelly (2005), based on U.S. Bureau of the Census, Public Use Microdata Samples based on 1980, 1990, and 2000 Census.

These longitudinal data are particularly revealing because they show the problems at each junction of the educational pipeline. Figure 4-2 displays cross-section data that show similar trends. According to the U.S. Census, in 2000 about 32 percent of the white 25- to 34-year-old population had bachelor's degrees, as did 16 percent of African Americans and 11 percent of Hispanics in that age range. For all three groups, the bachelor's-holding rates for women were about 2 percentage points higher than those for men. Comparing 1990 and 2000, the percentage point gap in the B.A. attainment rate between whites, on the one hand, and blacks and Hispanics, on the other, grew for the populations as a whole and for each gender group. The share of the young Hispanic male population that had bachelor's degrees or at least associate's degrees actually fell, possibly because of limited proficiency in English. In 1990 fewer than 10 percent of the young adult Hispanic males living in the United States had bachelor's degrees.[35]

Forecasts of Overall Levels of Educational Attainment

Given these growing gaps, demographic trends will make it difficult to increase overall educational attainment in the country. The U.S. population is growing increasingly heterogeneous. Several of the largest states in the country are becoming "majority minority." Hispanic populations particularly are growing. By 2020 the Census Bureau projects a 77 percent increase for the Hispanic population, a 32 percent increase for the African American, a 69 percent increase for the Asian population, and a less than 1 percent increase for the white population. These patterns present a mixed picture. The group with the lowest overall level of education, Hispanics, is growing the fastest, although the growth rate for Asians, the group with the highest level of education, is close behind. But overall, Hispanics and African Americans will account for more than 30 percent of the population in 2020, while the Asian share will still be about 6 percent.

Patrick Kelly used Census Bureau data and projections to calculate future overall educational levels. He took the Census projections for population growth by age group and race or ethnicity. Using those figures and assuming that the educational disparities between cohorts observed in the 2000 Census would remain the same, he projected changes in overall education levels for the population ages 25–64 by 2020.[36] The results are displayed in figure 4-3. These calculations suggest that the share of the population with less than a high school degree would increase from 16.1 to 18.5 percent. The share of the population at all other educational levels would fall slightly to make up for this 2.4 percentage point increase in the high school dropout population. Calculations for 25- to 34-year-olds produced similar conclusions. The low education levels and high growth rates of the Hispanic population are the most important factors that determine these negative results. Therefore, unless the educational level of African Americans and especially Hispanics can be raised over the next twenty years, when the economy will require an increasing number of workers with skills learned in college, the country will experience significant growth in the portion of the population that has not even graduated from high school.

35. Kelly (2005).

36. See Kelly (2005, appendix A) for a detailed description of the methodology.

Figure 4-3. *Projected Change in Overall U.S. Educational Attainment, 2000–20*

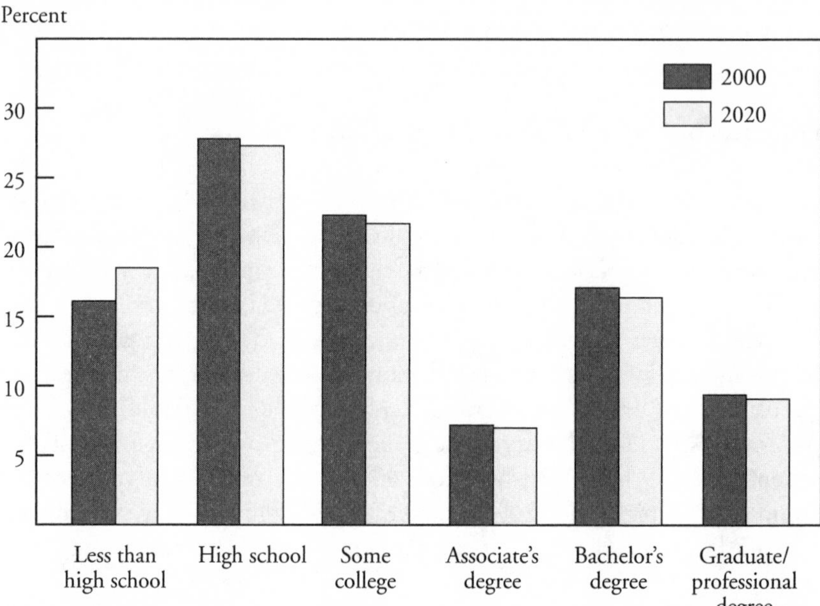

Source: Kelly (2005), based on U.S. Bureau of the Census, Public Use Microdata Samples based on 2000 Census and U.S. Population Projections.

Of course these projections assume that the current distribution of education for each ethnic group will remain the same. What factors might either alter the overall population projections or change the distribution of education within groups such that these projections would underestimate the changes in educational attainment?

The growth of the Asian population is one factor that increases the projected overall educational level. The growth of the Asian economies, however, may slow this source of population growth. Many highly educated Asians have stayed in the United States after studying here, but a slowdown in enrollments of foreign students may reduce this source of skilled labor. Without the effect of Asian population growth, the projections portrayed in figure 4-3 would imply an even greater relative shift toward lower education levels.

The most important factor that lowers the projected level of education is the current educational attainment levels of African Americans and Hispanics. Both groups are projected to grow much faster than the white population. As these groups encompass a larger proportion of the population, can we expect some economic or social processes to work toward diminishing the education gaps?

As we have seen, the gap in educational attainment between whites and African Americans and Hispanics has not declined. Population shifts and resultant labor market trends might reduce the earnings gap between whites and minorities, and this might give minorities a greater incentive to acquire more schooling. But researchers have not concluded that there are significant differences in the returns on schooling for different ethnic and racial groups.[37] Therefore, at least in the past, similar returns on schooling have not resulted in the equalization of educational attainment. Data on educational attainment for African American and Hispanic men are particularly discouraging. Educational levels of African American women will probably rise, but that may be offset by more negative trends for African American men.

Because the Hispanic population is heterogeneous and also in the process of change due to continued immigration, judging future educational trends for Hispanics is difficult. In 2000 about one quarter of the Hispanic population was foreign born. A majority of both the native and foreign-born Hispanic population was of Mexican origin. Very recent research indicates that although the flow of immigration declined between 2000 and 2005, within that flow the share of unauthorized immigrants rose. By 2004 more unauthorized migrants than authorized migrants were entering the country.[38] Thus the overall educational problems associated with the adjustment of immigrants to the United States are likely to grow.

Trends in educational achievement of second and higher generation Hispanics relative to immigrant Hispanics are mixed. James Smith, for example, showed that the educational gap between Hispanics and whites declined between the first (foreign-born) and second generation (the children of immigrants) of Hispanics.[39] Hagy and Staniec found that among high school graduates, foreign-born Hispanics were more likely than native-born Hispanics to attend a community college, and the children of foreign-born Hispanics (second generation)were more likely than third or higher generation Hispanics to attend a four-year college.[40] They also pointed out that Hispanics were particularly dependent on public higher education and therefore more likely to be negatively affected by a weakened public sector. Tienda and Alon, in this

37. Barrow and Rouse (2005).
38. Passel and Suro (2005).
39. Smith (2003).
40. Hagy and Staniec (2002).

volume, observes that much of the Hispanic population is concentrated in Texas and California and that neither state has made adequate educational investments to keep pace with the growth in their college-age populations.

Thus, despite overall gains in educational attainment, the gap between whites, on the one hand, and African Americans and Hispanics, on the other, has grown since the 1980s. African American women have made good progress, but minority men, particularly, have experienced little gain. Black and Hispanic students tend to come from lower-income families and have access to poorer quality schools. They tend to have lower levels of academic achievement in the K–12 system. All these factors are associated with lower enrollments in higher education and lower probabilities of completion once enrolled. But for African Americans in particular, achievement gaps persist even after controlling for these factors.

It is unclear whether, as these groups gain in population share, any market mechanism will work to eliminate these gaps. Therefore, just as the country needs to continue to strengthen its educational base, demographic trends are working against that goal. The United States has benefited over the last century from its relatively high levels of educational attainment. Productivity gains were driven by public commitment to the expansion of high school earlier in the twentieth century and the expansion of postsecondary education toward the end of the century. But that expansion has been threatened as expenditure on public higher education has met stiff resistance at the state level. Finally, in contrast to past decades, in the future the country may be unable to take advantage of highly skilled foreign workers—at least not for work that takes place within the United States.

Conclusion

Occupational forecasts, analyses of job content, trends in wages, and changes in international competition all point to an increasing need in the United States for workers with high-level skills. Achieving increases in skill levels will be difficult as long as current gaps in educational attainment based on income, race, and ethnicity remain. Those disparities will have a greater overall effect as Hispanics and African Americans account for a larger share of the population. Income is becoming more, not less, unequally distributed. Without a concerted effort to address this problem, it is unlikely that these gaps will fade away. The net cost of college has grown faster than overall increases in income, and differences in educational attainment between whites and Hispanics and African

Americans have grown since 1990. These developments are also taking place at a time of great resistance to increases in public investments in higher education.

Although I have focused primarily on higher education in this chapter, clearly the foundation for increases in college enrollment and, especially, college completion lies in the K–12 system. Many students who manage to enroll in college are already far behind. These circumstances blunt the effectiveness even of improved financial aid. In the short and medium run, colleges will continue to have to work with many students who arrive facing multiple academic, social, and economic problems. A comprehensive strategy to improve student outcomes will undoubtedly require a variety of measures including financial aid, programs to facilitate the transition from high school to college, improvements in remediation, and innovations in pedagogy. Colleges and states must also do better jobs of analyzing where the weaknesses in their systems are most pronounced. This is particularly true of the institutions in which lower-income students are most concentrated. Unfortunately, these are also likely to be the institutions that have the least money to pay for "discretionary" services such as institutional research.

In U.S. society, the extreme disparities in educational achievement based on income and the persistent gaps in educational outcomes between whites and African Americans and Hispanics should be reason enough to raise the educational attainment of low-income and minority students. Increasingly, the country as a whole has an economic stake in overcoming these inequities.

References

Bailey, Thomas, and Vanessa Smith Morest. 1998. "Preparing Youth for Employment." In *The Forgotten Half Revisited: American Youth and Young Families, 1988–2008*, edited by Samuel Halperin. Washington, D.C.: American Youth Policy Forum.

———, eds. 2006. *Defending the Community College Equity Agenda*. Johns Hopkins University Press.

Barrow, Lisa, and Cecilia E. Rouse. 2005. "Returns to Schooling by Race and Ethnicity." Working Paper WP-05-02. Federal Reserve Bank of Chicago.

Bureau of Labor Statistics. 2003. "Earnings by Educational Attainment and Sex, 1997 and 2002." *MLR: The Editors Desk* (October 23) (www.bls.gov/opub/ted/2003/oct/wk3/art04.htm).

Goldin, Claudia, and Lawrence F. Katz. 2001. "The Legacy of U.S. Educational Leadership: Notes on Distribution and Economic Growth in the Twentieth Century." *American Economic Review* 91, no. 2: 18–23.

Grubb, W. Norton. 2002. "Learning and Earning in the Middle, Part 1: National Studies of Pre-Baccalaureate Education." *Economics of Education Review* 21, no. 4: 229–31.

Hagy, Allison P., and J. Farley Ordovensky Staniec. 2002. "Immigrant Status, Race, and Institutional Choice in Higher Education." *Economics of Education Review* 21, no. 4: 381–92.

Haveman, Robert, and Timothy Smeeding. 2006. "The Role of Higher Education in Social Mobility." *Future of Children* 16, no. 2: 125–50.

Hirsh, Richard, and John Merrow, eds. 2005. *Declining by Degrees*. New York: Palgrave Macmillan.

Institute on International Education. 2006. *Open Doors 2006 Online: Report on International Educational Exchange*. New York (opendoors.iienetwork.org/?p=89192).

Kane, Thomas J. 2004. "College-Going and Inequality." In *Social Inequality*, edited by K. M. Neckerman, pp. 319–53. New York: Russell Sage Foundation.

Kane, Thomas J., and Cecilia Rouse. 1995. "Labor Market Returns to Two- and Four-Year Colleges." *American Economic Review* 85, no. 3: 600–14.

Kelly, Patrick. 2005. *As America Becomes More Diverse: The Impact of State Higher Education Inequality*. Boulder, Colo.: National Center for Higher Education Management Systems.

Lenth, Charlie, and others. 2006. "State Higher Education Finance FY 2005: A Report by State Higher Education Executive Officers (SHEEO)" (www.sheeo.org/finance/SHEF%20FY05%20full.pdf).

Levy, Frank, and Richard J. Murnane. 1992. "U.S. Earnings Levels and Earnings Inequality: A Review of Recent Trends and Proposed Explanations." *Journal of Economic Literature* 30, no. 3: 1333–82.

———. 2004. *The New Division of Labor: How Computers are Creating the Next Job Market*. Princeton University Press.

Marcotte, David, and others. 2005. "The Returns of a Community College Education: Evidence from the National Education Longitudinal Study." *Educational Evaluation and Policy Analysis* 27, no. 2: 157–75.

Mortenson, Thomas. 2005. "State Tax Fund Appropriations for Higher Education FY1961 to FY2005." *Postsecondary Education Opportunity* 151 (January): 1–7.

National Center for Education Statistics. 2005. *The Condition of Education 2005*. NCES 2005-094. Department of Education.

National Center on Education and the Economy. 1990. "America's Choice: High Skills or Low Wages." Washington, D.C.

National Commission on Excellence in Education. 1983. *A Nation at Risk: The Imperative for Educational Reform*. Government Printing Office.

Neumark, David. 2007. "Improving School-to-Work Transitions: Introduction." In *Improving School-to-Work Transitions,* edited by David Neumark, pp. 1–23. New York: Russell Sage Foundation.

Organization for Economic Cooperation and Development. 2006. "Education and Training: Education at a Glance" (www.oecd.org).

Passel, Jeffrey S., and Roberto Suro. 2005. *Rise, Peak, and Decline: Trends in U.S. Immigration 1992–2004*. Washington, D.C.: Pew Hispanic Center.

Scott, Marc, Thomas Bailey, and Greg Kienzl. 2006. "Relative Success? Determinants of College Graduation Rates in Public and Private Colleges in the U.S." *Research in Higher Education* 47, no. 3: 247–77.

Smith, James. 2003. "Assimilation across the Latino Generations." *American Economic Review* 93, no. 2: 315–19.

Turner, Sarah. 2004. "Going to College and Finishing College: Explaining Different Educational Outcomes." In *College Choices: The Economics of Where to Go, When to Go, and How to Pay for It,* edited by C. Hoxby, pp. 13–56. University of Chicago Press.

U.S. Department of Education. 2003. *NELS: 88/2000 Postsecondary Education Transcript Study (PETS: 2000).* NCES 2003-402 [data CD-ROM]. Washington D.C.: National Center for Education Statistics.

———. 2006. *A Test of Leadership: Charting the Future of U.S. Higher Education.* Government Printing Office.

Young, Andrew, Daniel Levy, and Mathew Higgins. 2004. "Many Types of Human Capital and Many Roles in U.S. Growth: Evidence from the County Level Educational Attainment Data." Paper presented at the CESifo/Harvard University–PEPG conference, Munich, Germany, September.

PART II

Quantifying the Costs of Inadequate Education

5 CECILIA ELENA ROUSE

Consequences for the Labor Market

Because of the strong relationship between years of completed education and annual earnings, education is the traditional route to upward mobility in the United States. The relationship is shown in figure 5-1. Although there is little increase in earnings for each year of completed schooling before the eleventh grade, a steep earnings gain accrues for each year beginning with high school completion. This relationship has increased dramatically since the mid-1960s. In 1964 a high school dropout earned 64 cents for every dollar earned by someone with at least a high school degree.[1] In 2004 the high school dropout earned only 37 cents for each dollar earned by someone with more education. High school graduation has been a necessary (but not sufficient) prerequisite for making it in America.

The labor market consequences of not graduating from high school are both private (in that they affect the individual in question) and public (in that they affect the whole of society). In this chapter I document the fact that if people do not complete high school, their incomes are lower, which also means they are less able to contribute to society—in this case as reflected in tax revenues. In this way I characterize a person as having "inadequate education" if he or she does not graduate, or has not graduated, from high school. Admittedly this is a narrow concept of the adequacy of education, because many people who graduate from high school nevertheless have very low skills. For example, according

1. I thank Lisa Barrow for calculating the earnings ratio in 1964.

Figure 5-1. *Average Annual Earnings, by Years of Completed Schooling*[a]

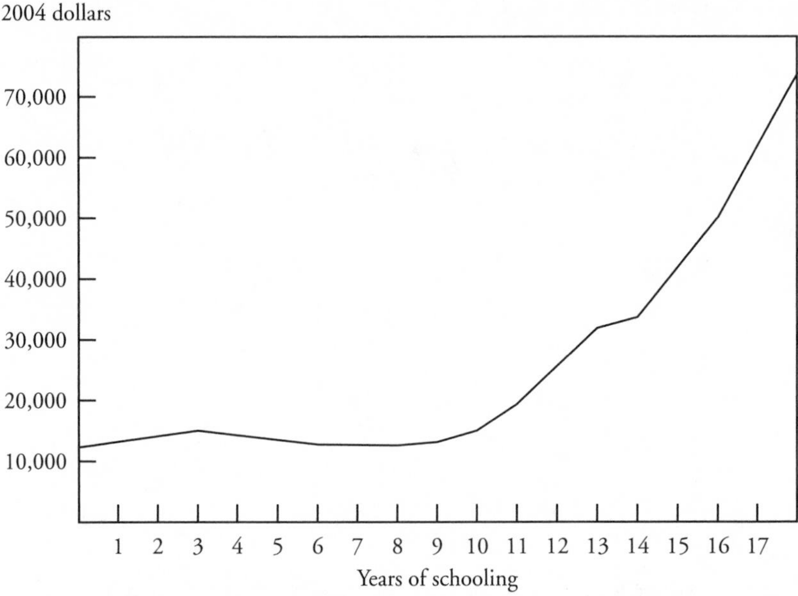

Source: Author's calculations using the March Current Population Survey, 2003 and 2004.
a. Includes persons aged 25–65.

to the National Assessment of Education Progress (NAEP), 26 percent of twelfth graders in 2002 scored below the basic level in reading, suggesting that they could not determine the basic meaning of a text. But although school quality is important, it is also extremely difficult to assess and quantify. I discuss issues related to school quality in a later section.

In the next section I review the "canonical" economic model of educational attainment, which (in theory) provides insights into why some people complete less schooling than others and into the empirical challenges of estimating the economic value of schooling. Subsequently, I review the literature in which researchers have attempted to estimate the causal effect of schooling on income and conclude that the basic "cross-sectional" relationship (the mean difference in income between those with and without high school degrees) is a fairly good approximation of the causal relationship. I discuss the data and methodology and then offer new estimates of the differences in income and tax payments between those with high school degrees and those without, in order to estimate the earnings and tax revenue losses associated with incomplete education. Because people who do not complete high school are less likely to be employed and have significantly lower annual earnings than those with at least a high school degree, they also contribute significantly less to tax revenues.

I calculate that, under plausible assumptions about income growth and the discount rate, the discounted present value of the lifetime difference in income between someone who graduates from high school but completes no further schooling and someone who does not graduate is likely about $260,000, and the lifetime difference in income tax payments is about $60,000.[2] Aggregated over one cohort of 18-year-olds who never complete high school, the combined losses of income and tax revenues are likely more than $156 billion, or 1.3 percent of GDP.

Why Does Schooling Improve Labor Market Outcomes?

According to the canonical economic model of schooling attainment, a person will choose to graduate from high school if he or she perceives that the lifetime benefits of doing so outweigh the lifetime costs of dropping out.[3] In the basic formulation of the model, this person has perfect information about future benefits and costs as well as access to adequate financial credit, if necessary. Indeed, this person will continue in school until the (marginal) benefit from the last year of schooling is equal to the (marginal) cost of that schooling.

When assessing costs and benefits, economists typically distinguish between *private* costs and benefits and *social* costs and benefits. Private costs and benefits are those borne uniquely by (or that accrue uniquely to) the individual. Social costs and benefits are those that are borne by (or accrue to) others. A classic example of a social cost is crime. Further, if additional education raises a person's income level, then the potential tax revenues for the government are increased, especially in a society such as the United States, which has a progressive income tax system. These tax revenues also form part of the social benefit of increased education. From the individual's perspective, however, these tax revenues lower the private benefit because of the income taxes required to raise them.[4]

2. I present the discounted lifetime difference in earnings and income taxes in order to account for the fact that a dollar earned fifty years from now is worth less than a dollar earned today. That is, by factoring in the discount rate I can place a present value on income earned and taxes paid in the future.

3. Becker (1967).

4. Further, because people with higher income consume more, they pay more in sales taxes, and because they are more likely to own property, they pay more in property taxes.

Left to their own devices, people deciding whether or not to pursue more education (or to graduate from high school, in my example) will care only about their private benefits and costs and not worry about whether social benefits or costs also exist. In the canonical model, if there are no social benefits or costs, then persons who choose not to complete high school are assumed to have made the "optimal" decision for themselves, such that neither they nor society would be better off if they were compelled to complete a high school degree.

Yet there are many reasons why the decision to drop out of high school may not in fact be individually or socially "optimal." First, the canonical model holds only under several important assumptions. For example, it assumes that people have perfect information about the costs and benefits of completing high school—that is, they understand what their lives would be like without a high school degree as well as with a degree. If people drop out of school not fully understanding the ramifications of their decision, then their action may be optimal neither for them nor for society (again, assuming no social benefits). Further, the model assumes that perfect credit markets exist. In some families the income a dropout might earn could make up a nontrivial proportion of the family income. If the family could instead borrow money to allow the child to graduate from high school, then the increase in earnings would allow the family to repay the loan (and then some), assuming that interest rates are lower than the return to schooling. But this requires access to credit markets with competitive interest rates. If credit markets do not function so smoothly, then a person's decision to drop out of high school may not be optimal.[5]

Importantly, in the presence of (net) positive social benefits that exceed (net) private benefits, it would be better, from society's point of view, if a person completed more schooling. In this case society has an incentive to encourage the person to attain more schooling through, for example, compulsory schooling laws.

Empirically, it is of interest to understand the magnitude of the benefit of completing high school in terms of wages and income. To fully understand why some people do not complete high school, however, one must also have a firm understanding of the perceived costs. Further, although there is a large literature estimating the private benefits of completing high school, the literature attempting to understand the social benefits is much smaller.[6]

5. Whether borrowing constraints explain differences in educational attainment, especially college attendance, by family background is an unresolved issue (see, for example, Ellwood and Kane [2000]; Heckman and Lochner [2000]). However, there is growing evidence from outside education that individuals, particularly teenagers, are credit constrained (see, for example, Gross and Souleles [2000]; Warner and Pleeter [2001]).

6. Using variation in compulsory school laws, Acemoglu and Angrist (2000) estimated surprisingly small social benefits to secondary school education in terms of wages.

In the economics literature it is conventional to define the average percentage difference in mean earnings for each additional year of schooling as the "return to schooling." As Jacob Mincer showed, if foregone earnings are the only cost of school attendance, then this is the private marginal benefit (or "return") on the investment in a year of schooling.[7] Estimates based on the Census Bureau's 2004 Current Population Survey (CPS) suggest that for each year of completed schooling, a person's earnings increase by about 11 percent.[8] Although the relationship between income and schooling has been well documented, the reason for its existence is more controversial. Some argue that education provides skills, or human capital, that raise a person's productivity.[9] If so, then because productivity is reflected in income, education is a key determinant of upward social mobility. It follows that much of the gap between the rich and the poor arises from a lack of skills among the poor, such that education and training should form the cornerstone of policies aimed at reducing income inequality.

Others argue that the documented relationship may not be causal, and education may not *generate* higher incomes.[10] It is possible that education and income are positively correlated because people with greater "ability" complete more schooling and likely would earn higher wages and salaries even if they had not received the additional schooling. In this case, the schooling-income connection may be a mirage—simply a reflection of the fact that higher-ability people command a premium for their (innate) skills in the labor market. The result is that empirical estimates of the return to schooling are too large ("upward biased," in statistical terms), because of "family background" or "ability" bias. In this view, increasing support for educational programs for the disadvantaged will have little or no effect on their labor market outcomes.

While much of this literature refers to the overall return to schooling, the same mechanics are at work when one considers the effect on income of completing high school. Do high school graduates earn more than dropouts because the education they received in high school is valuable in the labor market? Or are people who complete high school different from high school dropouts, and is it this difference (and not the schooling) that explains the higher income?

7. Mincer (1974). For higher education, a more detailed calculation of the "return" would incorporate the other costs of schooling, including tuition.

8. Based on a regression of the natural logarithm of hourly wages on years of completed education, a quadratic in potential experience, controls for sex, race or ethnicity, marital status, and nine regions, using the 2004 March Current Population Survey. The regression was weighted using the earnings weight.

9. See, for example, Becker (1967).

10. See, for example, Spence (1973).

In an effort to disentangle these two competing hypotheses, researchers have developed several methods to isolate the causal effect of education on income. Ideally one might conduct an experiment to determine definitively whether high school graduation (or schooling more generally) causes higher incomes. In such an experiment, one group of students would be randomly assigned to complete high school without regard to ability or general background; another group would be randomly assigned to drop out of high school. Years later we would compare the labor market outcomes of the two groups. On average, the only difference between the two would be whether they had graduated from high school. Contrasts of their earnings would, with a large enough sample, provide a credible estimate of the causal effect of high school completion on earnings.

The experiment just described has not been performed and probably never will be. As a result, researchers have looked elsewhere for convincing non-experimental evidence. Three broad approaches have been taken to estimate the causal effect of education on labor market outcomes. The first compares the wages of workers who have similar genetic and family backgrounds but who differ in educational levels. A systematic correlation between the educational differences and income differences of such workers is evidence of a link between income and schooling that cannot be a result of common family backgrounds. The second approach (so-called natural experiments) looks for a determinant of high school graduation, such as compulsory schooling laws, that is not also a determinant of incomes. By studying the relationship between this determinant and education and the relationship between this determinant and income, one can "back out" the causal relationship between education and income. The third approach uses randomized evaluations of programs designed to increase educational attainment to generate an experimental estimate of the effect of education on income. I next summarize the literature in which each of these approaches is used.

Empirical Estimates of the Return to Schooling

Many researchers have used sibling or twin pairs to construct estimates of the return to schooling. Because sibling and twin pairs share genetic material and were raised in similar household environments, their "ability" (and other, unobservable characteristics) is much more similar than that of random members of the population. As a result, when one relates differences in schooling between siblings to labor market outcomes, one implicitly accounts for these unobserved factors. Unfortunately, the measurement error in reported schooling poses an econometric challenge for these models. The reason is that classical measurement error is exacerbated in within-sibling (or within-twin) estimators, because sibling education levels are so highly correlated.[11] As a result, much of the more recent literature using this approach has focused on addressing the measurement error, as well as ability, bias.

Although the magnitude of the estimated return to schooling varies because of the widely different time periods covered, studies using siblings and twins indicate a significant relationship between schooling level and earnings. When adjustments for measurement error are possible, the resulting estimates typically differ insignificantly from the simpler cross-sectional (ordinary least squares) estimates of the return to schooling.[12]

"Natural Experiments" (Instrumental Variables) and Job Corps

Researchers have also attempted to find "natural experiments" that provide the kind of information an ideal experiment would provide. To do this they have attempted to locate exogenous events that might be expected to alter some people's schooling decisions but would not be expected to independently alter their income. The basic idea used in the application of this method is straightforward. Suppose we knew of an event that would increase a group's likelihood of graduating from high school. Suppose further that we were certain this event would have no direct effect on the group's earnings. We would then estimate the effect of high school graduation on earnings in two steps. In the first step we would estimate the effect of the event on the probability of high school graduation of the group. In the next step we would measure the effect of the same event on the earnings of the group. If we find that the earnings of the group have increased, then we can be sure that education was the cause of the earnings increase, because we were certain the event had no *direct* effect on earnings. The ratio of the income increase caused by the event to the increase in high school graduation caused by the event would be a straightforward estimate of the causal effect of high school graduation on earnings. This "instrumental variables" (IV)

11. Griliches (1977). Classical measurement error is measurement error that is uncorrelated with the error term in the outcome equation and with the true level of schooling.

12. See, for example, Altonji and Dunn (1996) and Ashenfelter and Zimmerman (1997) for studies using siblings. See Ashenfelter and Krueger (1994), Behrman, Rosenzweig, and Taubman (1994), and Rouse (1999) for studies using twins. Further, there is evidence from sibling studies that the return to schooling does not vary by family background (in Ashenfelter and Rouse [1998]) or by the race of the individual (in Barrow and Rouse [2005]).

estimator uses the "exogenous" event as the instrumental variable. Many studies using IV find that its estimate of the return to schooling is at least as large as that implied by conventional procedures.[13]

More recently, Philip Oreopoulos estimated the cost of dropping out of high school, using compulsory schooling laws in three countries as the exogenous event that affected schooling. He found remarkably consistent evidence across the three countries. Staying in school for one more year increased lifetime income by more than three times the peak income earned by those who dropped out before the end of high school.[14]

Experimental evaluations of job training programs provide yet another piece of evidence on the economic value of education. The most recent is an experimental evaluation of the Job Corps program conducted by Mathematica Policy Research.[15] Job Corps is a residential education and job training program aimed at disadvantaged youths without high school diplomas. A principal goal of the program is to encourage young people to complete their high school education or earn a General Educational Development (GED) credential. In the Mathematica evaluation, youths randomly assigned to Job Corps completed about one more year of schooling than those randomly assigned to the control group. After four years, those assigned to Job Corps had earnings about 12 percent higher than those assigned to the control group, generating an estimated return to one year of schooling of about 12 percent.[16]

Implications for Estimating Earnings Loss from Dropping Out of High School

The results of all these studies—those using family relationships, those using IV, and that from the Job Corps evaluation—are surprisingly consistent: they indicate that the return to schooling is not dominated by an omitted correlation between ability and schooling. As a result, this literature has led many to believe that the overall cross-sectional estimate of the economic value of education is likely quite close to the estimate one would generate from the ideal experiment. Indeed, Nobel Laureate James Heckman, with Pedro Carneiro,

13. Angrist and Krueger (1991) used a person's quarter of birth as the instrumental variable; Card (1995), Kane and Rouse (1993), and Kling (2001) used proximity to a two- or four-year college as the instrumental variable.

14. Oreopoulos (2003).

15. Burghardt and others (2001).

16. See Kane and Rouse (1999) for an estimate of the return to schooling using experimental evidence from the Job Training Partnership Act (JTPA) (which was replaced by the Workforce Investment Act in 1998). The estimated returns to schooling using the JTPA evaluation are also similar to others in the literature.

has written, "By now there is a firmly established consensus that the mean rate of return to a year of schooling, as of the 1990s, exceeds 10 percent and may be as high as 17 to 20 percent."[17] On this basis, I rely on survey data to estimate the difference in earnings between persons with and without high school degrees to get some idea of the earnings and tax revenue losses associated with not completing high school.

A Note about School Quality and Income

Before turning to these estimates, it is important to address the fact that whether or not a person has a high school degree is a limited measure of whether or not that person has received an "adequate education." Notably, the quality of the person's education is not explicitly part of this definition. The primary reason I do not calculate the social cost of a low *quality* education is that measures of school quality are imprecise and often difficult to achieve. For example, although there is good evidence that smaller classes result in higher student achievement, most data sets simply report the number of pupils per teacher.[18] In a one-room schoolhouse this is a good proxy for class size, but in larger schools with more heterogeneous class sizes it is not.[19] In addition, although many studies have assessed the effects of school quality on immediate student outcomes such as test scores, far fewer have assessed its effects on labor market wages, because of the long lag between the two measurements. That said, one study by Card and Krueger relating the quality of schooling received by people born between 1920 and 1949 and their earnings in 1979 found that a reduction in the pupil-teacher ratio of ten students increased average earnings by 4.2 percent.[20]

Part of the increase in earnings from improved school quality derives from an increase in educational attainment (including an increased likelihood of graduating from high school). For example, Card and Krueger also found that the ten-student reduction in the pupil-teacher ratio increased educational attainment by 0.6 years.[21] Evidence from the Tennessee class size reduction experiment (Project STAR) suggested that students placed randomly in smaller classes in grades K–3 performed better on standardized tests in the eighth grade and were more likely to take a college entrance exam such as the ACT or SAT—a sign that such students may have been more likely to attend college

17. Carneiro and Heckman (2003, pp. 148–49).
18. See, for example, Finn and Achilles (1990); Krueger (1999).
19. See, for example, Boozer and Rouse (2001).
20. Card and Krueger (1992).
21. Card and Krueger (1992, 1996).

as well.[22] Because of the likely effect of school quality on a person's level of schooling, I partially address issues of school quality by focusing on educational attainment.

Data and Methodology

To calculate the earnings and income tax revenue losses from not completing high school I use the Current Population Survey (CPS), a monthly labor market survey of approximately 50,000 households across the United States produced by the U.S. Bureau of the Census. The survey provides some of the most current information on income and wages for a national sample of households and individuals. I use the March CPS, which includes detailed information on labor market earnings and other income for the previous calendar year. One disadvantage of the March CPS is that it does not distinguish people who graduated from high school from those who received GEDs. Another is that it includes only the civilian non-institutionalized population. Thus it misses the potential effects of high school graduation that are realized through the military and the income gains or losses that accrue to the institutionalized population, such as people in jails and prisons. This limitation should be kept in mind when interpreting the results.[23]

These disadvantages are balanced, however, by the many advantages of the March CPS. First, it has individual reports of many kinds of income (such as that derived from wages and interest), in addition to social insurance (such as unemployment insurance) and transfer payments. Second, it has a measure of annual earnings. Annual earnings comprise a person's hourly wage, the number of hours worked per week, and the number of weeks worked per year. It therefore implicitly accounts for both the compensation a person receives for his or her time (which labor economists typically believe reflects the person's productivity or usefulness to the employer) and how much the person worked. If completing high school makes a person more "productive" because of the skills he or she has acquired, then this will be reflected in annual earnings. If

22. Krueger and Whitmore (2001). Others believe the evidence for the positive effect of school quality on subsequent educational attainment and earnings is not very strong. See, for example, the volume edited by Burtless (1996) for differing viewpoints.

23. I do not attempt to adjust the estimates in this chapter for the institutionalized population, because I would need to make assumptions about the likely earnings such persons would achieve if they were not incarcerated (or otherwise institutionalized), as well as estimate the fraction who would be incarcerated even if they had completed a high school degree. Further, I did not make adjustments for the military, because most of these people have high school diplomas. If their earnings are similar to those of people in the civilian labor market, then their omission likely has a negligible effect on the results.

completing high school provides people with access to more stable employment, such that they are employed for more hours per week and more weeks per year, then this, too, will be reflected in annual earnings.

I combined data from 2003 and 2004 to ensure a sufficient sample size. Further, I categorized people as having one of three levels of education: no high school degree, a high school diploma (including the GED), and at least a high school diploma (just over 60 percent of these people have completed at least some postsecondary education). The sample includes more than 300,000 persons ages 18 to 67. All figures are weighted using the sampling weights provided by the Bureau of Labor Statistics. And all monetary figures are inflated to 2004 dollars using the Chained Consumer Price Index for Urban Consumers (the CPI-U).

I estimated the income tax revenue gains associated with high school graduation using a computer program administered by the National Bureau of Economic Research, called the TAXSIM model.[24] TAXSIM is a set of programs and data sets that allow one to simulate a person's U.S. federal and state income taxes.[25] I used the tax calculator, a program that re-creates each year's federal and state tax law, and the March CPS to obtain a sample of people and their income sources. Because the income in the March CPS represents the previous calendar year, I simulated tax contributions using the tax laws for 2002 and 2003 (in other words, I calculated tax revenues on the basis of the tax law in effect at the time the income was earned).

Whereas the March CPS was designed to carefully account for a person's sources of income, it does not collect data on expenses. Thus the tax simulations do not adequately account for expenses such as rent, property taxes, child care, and mortgage interest that can be deducted from tax liabilities. Further, whereas capital gains and losses were reported in the March CPS in 2003, they were not reported in 2004. That said, the simulated tax revenues come close to the actual revenues reported by the Internal Revenue Service (IRS). For both the 2003 and 2004 CPS (tax years 2002 and 2003), the simulated federal tax revenues were only 1 percent lower than those reported by the IRS.[26]

A final note about methodology. In the United States, taxes are filed by the family, unless one is single or part of a married couple filing separately. In theory I could have grouped individuals in the CPS into "families," which are

24. I used TAXSIM version 6, documentation and programs for which can be accessed at www.nber.org/~taxsim/taxsim-cal6.

25. Feenberg and Coutts (1993).

26. The IRS data with which I compared the simulations were from the Internal Revenue Service Data Book, 2004, Publication 55B, Washington, D.C., issued March 2005 (table 7) (www.irs.gov/taxstats/article/0,,id=102174,00.html).

subunits of households. The problem is that once one has calculated the total taxes paid by a family, it is impossible then to back out the liability attributable to each individual, particularly because some aspects of the tax code are specific to the family unit. As a result, to calculate the difference in taxes paid by high school graduates and high school dropouts, I assumed that all individuals were "single" and did not live in families. (Thus I assumed that individuals were unmarried and had no children.) In this way I calculated the tax revenues to society on the basis of the *individual's* income alone. The degree to which this over- or understates the tax revenue benefits of high school graduation depends on the extent to which families receive benefits (such as food stamps) that depend on the size of the family, on the extent to which families take deductions (or credits) that rely on the family structure (for example, the child care credit), and on the size of the "marriage penalty," because people with high school degrees are more likely married.[27] The simulations based on individuals generated a total federal income tax slightly higher than that produced using families and 1 percent greater than that reported by the IRS.

Income and Tax Revenue Losses Resulting from Inadequate Education

An important social loss associated with people's receiving inadequate education is that they may not have acquired their "optimal" level of job market skills. They do not have the requisite skills to be employed to their fullest potential, which is reflected in their ability to find jobs as well as in their level of compensation once employed. The statistics in table 5-1 support this interpretation. In this sample, slightly more than 50 percent of high school dropouts were employed, in comparison with 69 percent of those whose highest level of education was a high school diploma and nearly 75 percent of those with at least a high school diploma. Similarly, high school dropouts were more likely to be unemployed, "discouraged workers," or out of the labor force.[28] They worked more than two fewer months per year than those whose highest level of education was a high school degree and nearly three fewer months per year than people with at least a high school diploma.

27. McLanahan (2004).

28. In order to be considered unemployed by the CPS, a person must not have a job and must be actively seeking employment. Discouraged workers would like a job but have given up looking for work, and those out of the labor force report not wanting a job at this time.

Table 5-1. *Average Labor Market Outcomes by Level of Educational Attainment*[a]
Units as indicated

Variable	*High school dropout*	*High school diploma*	*High school diploma or more*
Employed (percent)	53.0 (0.30)	69.0 (0.20)	74.4 (0.10)
Unemployed (percent)	7.2 (0.10)	5.3 (0.10)	4.2 (0.04)
Discouraged worker (percent)	0.5 (0.04)	0.3 (0.02)	0.2 (0.01)
Not in labor force—other (percent)	39.2 (0.30)	25.4 (0.10)	21.3 (0.10)
Number of weeks worked last year	26.9 (0.10)	35.7 (0.10)	38.1 (0.04)
Received any unemployment insurance last year (percent)	4.5 (0.10)	5.3 (0.10)	4.4 (0.04)
Unemployment insurance received during year (dollars)	171 (6)	225 (5)	210 (3)
Employer provides pension plan[b] (percent)	28.6 (0.30)	49.7 (0.20)	58.0 (0.10)
Covered by employer/union-provided health insurance[b] (percent)	20.9 (0.20)	41.2 (0.20)	48.5 (0.10)
Annual earnings (2004 dollars)	11,989 (261)	22,337 (210)	33,701 (202)

Source: March Current Population Survey, 2003, 2004.
a. Sample includes individuals ages 18–67. All means are weighted. Standard errors are in parentheses.
b. Among those with jobs.

Given that high school dropouts are more likely to be unemployed, it is natural to ask whether they are more likely to receive unemployment insurance (UI). In the sample described in table 5-1, only 4.5 percent of high school dropouts ever claimed UI during the previous year, in comparison with 5.3 percent of those whose highest degree was a high school diploma and 4.4 percent of those with at least a high school education. Although eligibility requirements differ across states, workers typically must have earnings that exceed a minimum threshold in several prior calendar quarters, must not have been fired for cause, and must be actively seeking work. Given their lower earnings and greater likelihood of not having a job, high school dropouts are less likely to be eligible for UI. Further, the amount of UI received is lower among high school dropouts, because the level of UI a person receives is based on earnings.[29]

Not only do high school dropouts work less than people with higher levels of education, but once they are working, the quality of their job benefits is lower as well. For example, high school dropouts are about one-half as likely to have pension plans or health insurance through their jobs as are people whose highest level of education is a high school diploma. And importantly, their earnings are lower. The average high school dropout in the table 5-1 sample earned about $12,000 per year, just over one-half the figure earned by those whose highest level of education was a high school diploma and one-third that earned by those with at least a high school education. These lower earnings were a function of dropouts' earning lower wages and working fewer hours and weeks per year.

Tax Revenue Losses

The lower annual earnings also mean that high school dropouts are less able to contribute to government revenues. Table 5-2 shows that on average, high school dropouts pay about $1,600 a year in federal and state income taxes and a total of $3,400 when Social Security taxes are included. This is one-half the contribution made by those who have completed only a high school degree and less than one-third the contribution of those with at least a high school degree.

From the social view, lost income and tax revenues are not only the losses that pertain to one person but the total losses for all high school dropouts. Over many individuals, these losses add up. Although one might think it is straightforward to calculate the number of high school dropouts accurately, in fact it is quite difficult. The CPS includes neither persons in the military nor those in institutional settings (and those in such settings are disproportionately high school dropouts).[30] Despite these disadvantages, I used the CPS to estimate the number of dropouts for purposes of this rough calculation. According to the CPS there were approximately 23 million persons ages 20–67 who had not completed high school in 2004.[31] This means that high school dropouts contributed more than $50 billion less in federal and state income

29. Because I use a tax simulator to calculate potential tax revenues, differences in unemployment compensation received (which is taxed) are implicitly factored into the later tax analysis.

30. Another potential source of information on dropouts is the Common Core of Data, administrative data gathered from school districts themselves. Unfortunately, school districts do not well track students who leave the district. Although some students leave school because they have decided to drop out, others simply move to another district and may complete high school there.

31. I use persons 20–67 years old because in March of each year, 18-year-olds have not yet completed the school year, so many of the seeming dropouts are simply students who are in the twelfth grade but

Table 5-2. *Estimated Average Taxes Paid, by Level of Educational Attainment*[a]
2004 dollars

Tax	*High school dropout*	*High school diploma*	*High school diploma or more*
Federal income tax	1,302	3,085	5,954
	(29)	(27)	(29)
State income tax	304	734	1,297
	(5)	(5)	(6)
Social Security tax (FICA)	1,769	3,221	4,497
	(12)	(11)	(9)
Total income taxes	3,374	7,040	11,747
	(43)	(41)	(41)

Source: Tax revenues simulated using TAXSIM, version 6, using data from the March Current Population Survey, 2001–04. Standard errors are in parentheses.
a. Sample includes individuals ages 18–67. All means are weighted.

tax payments annually than did those who had obtained a high school diploma (but attained no further schooling). The difference rises to $80 billion when one factors in Social Security contributions.

Before calculating lifetime differences in earnings and income tax revenues by educational attainment, it is worth considering the likely magnitude of losses in other taxes. I focus on property taxes, which are the major source of revenue for elementary and secondary education in the United States in most areas and for which information is available in the Decennial Census of the United States. Based on the 5 percent sample of the 2000 Census, I calculate that households headed by persons ages 18–67 who were high school dropouts contributed about $280 less in property taxes in 1999 (in 2004 dollars) than households headed by people who had completed a high school degree (but no further schooling), and about $800 less than those with at least a high school degree.[32] That there were approximately 13 million household heads ages 20–67 who were high school dropouts in the 2000 Census implies that high school dropouts contributed approximately $3.6 billion less in property taxes in 1999 than households headed by those whose highest degree was a high school diploma, approximately 7 percent of the losses due to federal and state income taxes.

have not yet graduated. And there is a significant decrease in the number of high school dropouts between ages 19 and 20 as people belatedly obtain diplomas.

32. Ruggles and others (2004). I extracted the data using the extracting program available at www.ipums.org.

One must exercise caution when interpreting these estimates regarding property taxes. First, although there is a literature establishing the causal relationship between education and earnings, I know of no research on the causal relationship between a person's education and property tax payments. These estimates may overstate the property tax revenue losses. Second, property taxes are based on the value of the housing unit, and therefore one can determine only payments made (jointly) by members of the housing unit and not payments made by a specific person.[33] Finally, although renters do not directly pay property taxes, they do so indirectly through the rent they pay, and these calculations do not include such contributions.[34] Nevertheless, property tax revenues likely form a nontrivial component of the social losses arising from inadequate education.

Lifetime Earnings and Income Tax Revenue Losses

One can calculate the lifetime earnings penalty for not completing a high school degree using information on income and taxes paid across the population. Figure 5-2, which plots average annual earnings by age and education, forms the basis for the calculation. The figure shows that earnings increase as people age (and are in the labor force longer), before reaching a peak in the early to mid-forties. Earnings growth increases with a person's educational attainment, which exacerbates the earnings losses associated with dropping out of high school observed among younger workers.

To use these data to calculate the lifetime earnings losses associated with inadequate education for an 18-year-old today, I assume that the age-earnings profiles observed here will continue for the person's working life (that is, for the next fifty years or so). Next I must make assumptions about how earnings will grow over the next fifty years and about the discount rate—the amount by which one must discount earnings in the future in order to place a value on such earnings today. In forecasting earnings growth, it is common to consider increases between 1 and 2 percent, which mirror prior real earnings and productivity growth and track assumptions about future productivity growth used in government forecasts. As for the discount rate, Moore and others recommend 3.5 percent.[35] A higher discount rate would reflect greater uncertainty.

33. In theory one could model each of the components that go into payments made when an individual lives with others and then "back out" the individual contribution. This estimate would be imprecise.

34. For example, in the 2000 Census, 51.3 percent of household heads who were high school dropouts reported owning their homes, in comparison with 64.7 percent of household heads who had high school degrees (and no further schooling) and 66.7 percent of household heads who had at least a high school degree.

35. Moore and others (2004).

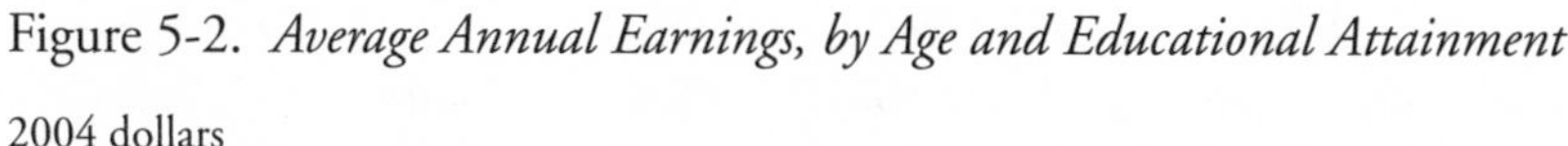

Figure 5-2. *Average Annual Earnings, by Age and Educational Attainment*

2004 dollars

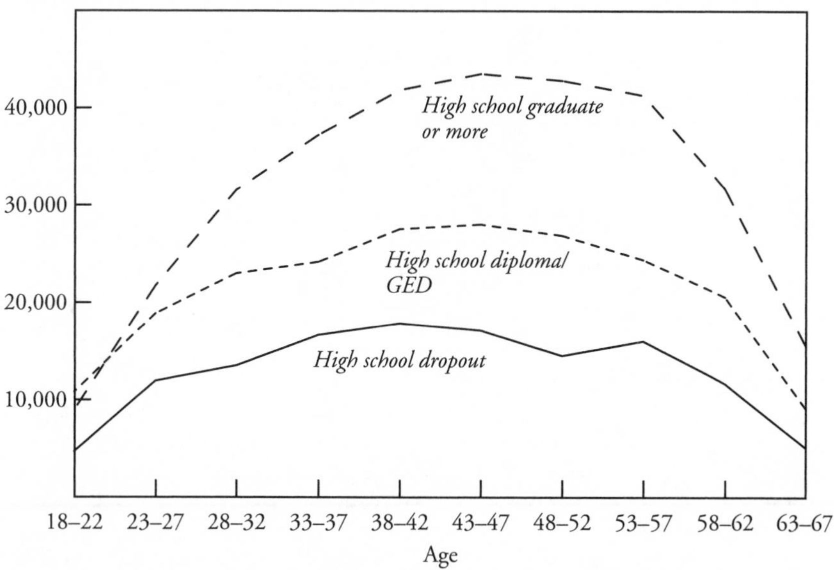

Source: Author's calculations using the March Current Population Survey, 2003 and 2004.

Table 5-3 shows the lifetime difference in the discounted present value of earnings between those whose highest level of educational attainment is a high school diploma and high school dropouts and between those with at least a high school diploma and high school dropouts. These differences are presented for a range of assumptions about future productivity growth and discount rates.[36] The table also shows lifetime differences in income taxes paid. Because Social Security is designed as a self-funding program in which benefits are paid for by contributions (such that one should not consider tax contributions as a net gain to society without also considering anticipated future benefits), the table also shows differences in taxes paid with and without Social Security contributions.

The lifetime earnings difference between dropouts and those with a high school diploma as the highest level of education ranges from $121,000, assuming 0 percent annual earnings growth and a 6 percent discount rate, to $294,000, assuming 2 percent annual earnings growth and a 3.5 percent discount rate. Given that the Social Security Trustees' intermediate forecast

36. Again, I present the lifetime earnings differences in discounted present-value terms (rather than using nominal dollars) in order to account for the fact that a dollar earned today is worth more than a dollar earned in fifty years.

Table 5-3. *Differences in Lifetime Earnings and Taxes Paid between High School Dropouts and High School Graduates and Graduates with Additional Schooling*
2004 dollars

	Annual productivity (earnings) growth (percent)					
	High school graduate			*High school graduate or more schooling*		
Discount rate (percent)	*0*	*1.5*	*2*	*0*	*1.5*	*2*
Earnings						
3.5	190,230	262,519	294,024	386,392	552,439	606,492
4.0	172,559	235,703	263,084	346,221	490,568	534,624
6.0	121,074	159,045	175,175	230,588	315,646	334,398
Non–Social Security income taxes paid						
3.5	41,683	59,210	66,946	104,209	152,691	174,253
4.0	37,456	52,669	59,349	92,623	134,528	153,076
6.0	25,311	34,242	38,080	59,709	83,852	94,331
Total income taxes paid						
3.5	69,527	97,494	109,771	155,254	224,969	247,702
4.0	62,743	87,083	97,713	138,511	198,907	217,359
6.0	43,135	57,572	63,746	90,688	125,808	133,513

Source: Author's calculations.

regarding productivity growth over the next seventy-five years is 1.6 percent, the estimates assuming a discount rate of 3.5 percent and productivity growth of 1.5 percent are sensible. In that case, the lifetime earnings losses associated with dropping out of high school are approximately $260,000. This figure underestimates the potential earnings loss, however, because it does not account for the fact that if some current high school dropouts were to complete high school, they would attend college. Upper-bound estimates of earnings losses are given by the figures for persons with at least a high school degree. In calculating these figures I assumed that if current dropouts were to attain their high school degrees, they would attend college at the same rate and complete the same distribution of years of schooling as current high school graduates. In this case, the estimated average lifetime earnings loss for an individual would be about $550,000.

I conducted a similar exercise for estimated income tax revenues (figure 5-3, table 5-3). Assuming a discount rate of 3.5 percent and a rate of growth of 1.5 percent, a high school dropout will contribute, on average, nearly $60,000 less in federal and state income taxes over his or her lifetime than someone

Figure 5-3. Average Annual Income Taxes Paid, by Age and Educational Attainment

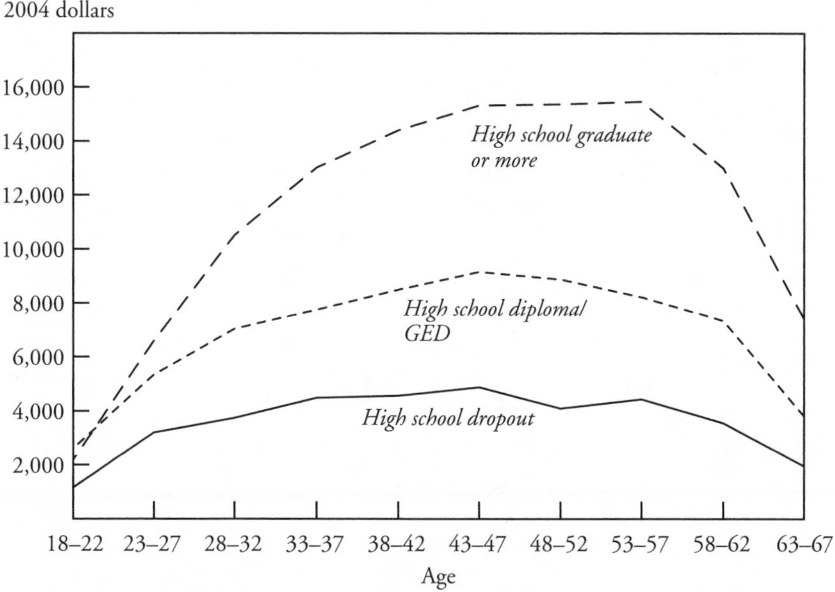

Source: Author's calculations using the March Current Population Survey, 2003 and 2004, and TAXSIM, version 6.

whose highest level of education is a high school diploma, and about $153,000 less than someone with at least a high school diploma. Including Social Security contributions, a high school dropout will contribute nearly $98,000 less in taxes than a high school graduate and about $225,000 less than someone with at least a high school degree.

Aggregating Income and Tax Revenue Costs

Again, these figures add up over a cohort. According to the March 2004 CPS, there were approximately 600,000 non-institutionalized persons age 20 who did not have high school degrees.[37] Thus, if I assume that there are currently approximately 600,000 18-year-olds who will choose to drop out of school and never complete a high school degree, then their aggregate lifetime earnings loss is more than $156 billion, resulting in an aggregate lifetime loss of about $36 billion in tax revenues (not including Social Security contributions) and

37. Again, I use 20-year-olds because many 18- and 19-year-olds will complete their high school education before turning 20.

$58 billion in total income tax revenues (or 4–6 percent of 2003 IRS income tax revenues). Upper-bound estimates for high school dropouts relative to persons with at least a high school diploma are about $330 billion in aggregate lifetime income, $92 billion in federal and state income taxes, and $135 billion in total income taxes when Social Security contributions are included.

Although these estimates imply large income and tax revenue losses due to a significant portion of the population's not having completed high school, they overstate potential gains to education and training programs designed to increase educational attainment. The reason is that nearly one-half of the 20-year-olds in the 2004 CPS who had not completed high school dropped out before the eleventh grade. On average they completed about ten years of schooling. Thus, it would require an unbelievably effective intervention to increase the high school graduation rate to 100 percent. To put the income and tax revenue gains into a metric on the same order of magnitude as a more realistic intervention, I also calculated the earnings and tax revenue gains that would result if all 20-year-old dropouts increased their educational attainment by one year.[38] The results are presented in table 5-4.

The estimated aggregate lifetime earnings gains on increasing educational attainment by one year for one cohort of high school dropouts range from nearly $34 billion (assuming no earnings growth and a discount rate of 6 percent) to more than $81 billion (assuming 2 percent annual earnings growth and a discount rate of 3.5 percent). The range of non–Social Security tax revenue gains is from $7 billion to $19 billion, and the range including Social Security is from $12 billion to $30 billion. Again, reasonable estimates to work with are a discount rate of 3.5 percent and an annual rate of earnings growth of 1.5 percent, suggesting aggregate lifetime earnings gains of $72 billion and lifetime federal and state income tax revenues of $16 billion ($27 billion including Social Security). Increasing the schooling of those without high school degrees by one year would generate an increase of $88 billion in lifetime income and income tax revenues (nearly $100 billion including Social Security contributions).

Summary and Policy Consequences

The empirical literature suggests that education has a causal effect on earnings. If a person is somehow able to complete another year of schooling, his or her

38. These gains are based on the assumption that no other changes would take place in the economy when this cohort increased its educational attainment. In theory, the wages of persons with high school degrees could fall because of the increased supply of such persons. However, the effect on wages of

Table 5-4. Differences in Aggregate Lifetime Earnings and Taxes Paid if All Dropouts Completed One More Year of Schooling
Thousands of 2004 dollars

	Annual productivity (earnings) growth (percent)		
Discount rate (percent)	*0*	*1.5*	*2*
Earnings			
3.5	52,757,175	72,480,056	81,069,711
4.0	47,932,717	65,166,199	72,634,256
6.0	33,868,550	44,242,401	48,647,072
Non–Social Security income taxes paid			
3.5	11,574,621	16,428,259	18,573,723
4.0	10,405,940	14,615,576	16,466,622
6.0	7,053,822	9,517,922	10,578,451
Total income taxes paid			
3.5	19,298,450	26,991,520	30,370,114
4.0	17,433,195	24,127,291	27,052,036
6.0	12,044,701	16,011,724	17,708,904

Source: Author's calculations.

income will rise by approximately 10 percent. This annual return aggregates to a relatively large benefit in return for high school completion for individuals and society. I estimate that people who do not complete high school are less likely to be employed, work fewer weeks per year, and make about one-half the earnings of those with high school diplomas but no further schooling. Further, these people contribute only 40 percent of the federal and state income tax revenues of those with high school diplomas. Aggregated over all high school dropouts ages 20–67, the annual losses in federal and state income taxes likely exceed $50 billion—enough to cover the annual discretionary expenditures of the U.S. Department of Education. These estimates do not include losses in terms of other tax revenues. As one example, households headed by high school dropouts ages 20–67 contributed approximately $3.3 billion less in property taxes in 1999 (in 2004 dollars) than did households headed by high school graduates (with no further schooling).

Over a lifetime, an 18-year-old who does not complete high school earns approximately $260,000 less than someone with a high school diploma and

increasing the number of 18-year-old high school graduates would likely be minimal, because they represent a very small fraction of the total labor force.

contributes about $60,000 less in lifetime federal and state income taxes. The combined income and tax losses aggregated over one cohort of 18-year-olds who do not complete high school is more than $156 billion, or 1.3 percent of GDP. If the educational attainment of that cohort of high school dropouts could be increased by one year, the United States would recoup nearly one-half of those losses.

These figures represent gross losses in terms of earnings and income taxes. The United States would need to make considerable investments in educational and other programs in order to improve educational attainment. Although I have not conducted such a cost-benefit analysis here, it is likely that the required investments would not equal the current losses—leading to net social gains. For example, one can compare these estimates of earnings and tax revenue losses with the cost of placing this entire cohort of 18-year-old high school dropouts in Job Corps, which would be $9 billion at a rate of approximately $15,000 per student. If 20 percent of these people increased their educational attainment by one year as a result of the program, then the total benefit would be about $18 billion. Again, I do not intend for this to be a proper cost-benefit analysis of Job Corps or of the net social gains resulting from unspecified educational interventions, but merely to put potential social gains into context.

There are reasons why these estimates may over- or understate the income and tax revenue losses associated with inadequate education. One is that I may not have assumed the proper discount rate or future rate of income growth. Similarly, if the shape of the relationship between earnings and the age of the person were to change, that would also change any estimated lifetime income and tax revenue estimates. Further, the tax simulations are rough approximations of true tax revenues, particularly given that the CPS provides no expenditure data and that in order to conduct analyses about individuals I had to ignore features of the tax code that affect families. These limitations likely inflate the tax revenue gains on high school completion. At the same time, the CPS undercounts the number of high school dropouts, leading to underestimates of losses.

In addition, the relationship I estimate between earnings and educational attainment using the CPS may overstate the expected benefits that would accrue as a result of policies that led to large numbers of dropouts' completing high school. One reason is that the cross-sectional estimates may partially reflect the fact that those who have completed high school are more "able" or "motivated" than those who did not and therefore would have earned more even if they had not completed high school. Although the academic literature suggests any such bias may be small, it may still exist.

One might also be concerned that the economic gains enjoyed by current high school graduates do not accurately represent the potential gains by current dropouts who would be encouraged to complete high school through interventions that increased their educational attainment. That is, persons who, in the current environment, found it not in their interest to complete their secondary schooling might benefit less (or perhaps more) from additional schooling than those who currently find it in their interest to do so. This is a theoretically important concern, yet the literature attempting to identify heterogeneity in the economic benefits of schooling is inconclusive. For example, some researchers estimate higher economic benefits of schooling for higher-ability individuals.[39] In contrast, studies analyzing twins and siblings have found that the economic gains of schooling do not vary by the educational attainment of the parents (which is strongly related to the wealth of the family), the "ability" and IQ of the individuals, and their race or ethnicity.[40] Importantly, there is some evidence that the economic gains of schooling may be higher for more disadvantaged persons, which would explain some of the empirical estimates of the economic benefit of schooling using instrumental variables techniques.[41] Given this lack of consensus in the literature, assuming that gains would remain relatively constant seems reasonable.

Another concern is that the marginal gains on a person's increasing his or her educational attainment may be much larger than those that would accrue if an entire cohort increased its educational attainment. Economic theory suggests that if the supply of high school graduates increases, then in order to employ all these newly skilled workers, employers will lower wages. Thus wages of high school graduates may decrease in the face of a large-scale increase in the proportion of high school graduates in the labor force. Although this is certainly a possibility, the demand for skilled workers continues to rise despite the increase in educational attainment that the U.S. labor market has observed since the mid-twentieth century.

Finally, it is worth reemphasizing that I have not carefully considered the magnitude of the loss of state sales and local property taxes attributable to inadequate education. Given that more than 90 percent of educational revenues come from state and local sources, the increased contributions to these taxes that would result from improved education are important as one considers the costs and benefits of educational improvements or interventions.

39. See, for example, Carneiro and Heckman (2003); Cawley and others (2000); Taber (2001).

40. See, for example, Altonji and Dunn (1996); Ashenfelter and Rouse (1998); Barrow and Rouse (2005).

41. Ashenfelter and Rouse (1998); Card (2001).

The income and tax revenue losses associated with a lack of high school completion are already large. As globalization of the labor market increases and U.S. workers—who are relatively skilled—compete with workers worldwide, so, too, will the costs of incomplete or inadequate education increase. Although it is difficult and expensive to improve educational attainment among those at risk of not completing high school, for the United States as a society it will also become increasingly costly not to.

References

Acemoglu, Daron, and Joshua Angrist. 2000. "How Large Are Human-Capital Externalities? Evidence from Compulsory-Schooling Laws." In *National Bureau of Economic Research Macroeconomics Annual 2000*, edited by Ben S. Bernanke and Kenneth Rogoff, pp. 9–59. MIT Press.

Altonji, Joseph, and Thomas Dunn. 1996. "The Effects of Family Characteristics on the Return to Education." *Review of Economics and Statistics* 78 (November): 692–704.

Angrist, Joshua D., and Alan B. Krueger. 1991. "Does Compulsory Schooling Affect Schooling and Earnings?" *Quarterly Journal of Economics* 106 (November): 979–1014.

Ashenfelter, Orley, and Alan Krueger. 1994. "Estimating the Returns to Schooling Using a New Sample of Twins." *American Economic Review* 84 (December): 1157–73.

Ashenfelter, Orley, and Cecilia Elena Rouse. 1998. "Income, Schooling, and Ability: Evidence from a New Sample of Identical Twins." *Quarterly Journal of Economics* 113 (February): 253–84.

Ashenfelter, Orley, and David J. Zimmerman. 1997. "Estimates of the Return to Schooling from Sibling Data: Fathers, Sons, and Brothers." *Review of Economics and Statistics* 79 (February): 1–9.

Barrow, Lisa, and Cecilia Elena Rouse. 2005. "Do Returns to Schooling Differ by Race and Ethnicity?" *American Economic Review* 95 (May): 83–87.

Becker, Gary S. 1967. *Human Capital: A Theoretical and Empirical Analysis, with Special Reference to Education.* Columbia University Press.

Behrman, Jere R., Mark R. Rosenzweig, and Paul Taubman. 1994. "Endowments and the Allocation of Schooling in the Family and in the Marriage Market: The Twins Experiment." *Journal of Political Economy* 102 (December): 1131–74.

Boozer, Michael A., and Cecilia Elena Rouse. 2001. "Intraschool Variation in Class Size: Patterns and Implications." *Journal of Urban Economics* 50 (July): 163–89.

Burghardt, John, and others. 2001. "Does Job Corps Work? Summary of the National Job Corps Study." Summary Report (June). Washington, D.C.: Mathematica Policy Research.

Burtless, Gary. 1996. *The Effect of School Resources on Student Achievement and Adult Success.* Brookings Institution Press.

Card, David. 1995. "Using Geographic Variation in College to Estimate the Returns to Schooling." In *Aspects of Labour Market Behaviour: Essays in Honour of John Vanderkamp*, edited by Louis N. Christofides, E. Kenneth Grant, and Robert Swidinsky, pp. 201–21. University of Toronto Press.

———. 2001. "Estimating the Return to Schooling: Progress on Some Persistent Econometric Problems." *Econometrica* 69 (September): 1127–60.

Card, David, and Alan B. Krueger. 1992. "Does School Quality Matter? Returns to Education and the Characteristics of Public Schools in the United States." *Journal of Political Economy* 100 (February): 1–40.

———. 1996. "Labor Market Effects of School Quality: Theory and Evidence." In *Does Money Matter?: The Effect of School Resources on Student Achievement and Adult Success*, edited by Gary Burtless, pp. 97–140. Brookings Institution Press.

Carneiro, Pedro, and James J. Heckman. 2003. "Human Capital Policy." In *Inequality in America: What Role for Human Capital Policies*, edited by Benjamin M. Friedman, pp. 77–239. MIT Press.

Cawley, John, and others. 2000. "Understanding the Role of Cognitive Ability in Accounting for the Recent Rise in the Economic Return to Education." In *Meritocracy and Economic Inequality*, edited by Kenneth Arrow, Samuel Bowles, and Steven Durlauf, pp. 230–65. Princeton University Press.

Ellwood, David T., and Thomas J. Kane. 2000. "Who Is Getting a College Education? Family Background and the Growing Gaps in Enrollment." In *Securing the Future: Investing in Children from Birth to College*, edited by Sheldon Danziger and Jane Waldfogel, pp. 283–324. New York: Russell Sage Foundation.

Feenberg, Daniel, and Elisabeth Coutts. 1993. "An Introduction to the TAXSIM Model." *Journal of Policy Analysis and Management* 12 (Winter): 189–94.

Finn, Jeremy D., and Charles M. Achilles. 1990. "Answers and Questions about Class Size: A Statewide Experiment." *American Educational Research Journal* 27 (Fall): 557–77.

Griliches, Zvi. 1977. "Estimating the Returns to Schooling: Some Econometric Problems." *Econometrica* 45 (January): 1–22.

Gross, David B., and Nicholas Souleles. 2000. "Consumer Response to Changes in Credit Supply: Evidence from Credit Card Data." University of Pennsylvania.

Heckman, James J., and Lance Lochner. 2000. "Rethinking Education and Training Policy: Understanding the Sources of Skill Formation in a Modern Economy." In *Securing the Future: Investing in Children from Birth to College*, edited by Sheldon Danziger and Jane Waldfogel, pp. 47–83. New York: Russell Sage Foundation.

Kane, Thomas J., and Cecilia Elena Rouse. 1993. "Labor Market Returns to Two- and Four-Year Colleges: Is a Credit a Credit and Do Degrees Matter?" Working Paper 4268. Cambridge, Mass.: National Bureau of Economic Research.

———. 1999. "The Community College: Educating Students at the Margin between College and Work." *Journal of Economic Perspectives* 13 (Winter): 63–84.

Kling, Jeffrey R. 2001. "Interpreting Instrumental Variables Estimates of the Returns to Schooling." *Journal of Business Economics and Statistics* 19 (July): 358–64.

Krueger, Alan B. 1999. "Experimental Estimates of Education Production Functions." *Quarterly Journal of Economics* 114 (May): 497–531.

Krueger, Alan B., and Diane M. Whitmore. 2001. "The Effect of Attending a Small Class in the Early Grades on College-Test Taking and Middle School Test Results: Evidence from Project STAR." *Economic Journal* 111 (January): 1–28.

McLanahan, Sara. 2004. "Diverging Destinies: How Children Fare under the Second Demographic Transition." *Demography* 41 (November): 607–27.

Mincer, Jacob. 1974. *Schooling, Experience, and Earnings.* Columbia University Press.

Moore, Mark A., and others. 2004. "'Just Give Me a Number!' Practical Values for the Social Discount Rate." *Journal of Policy Analysis and Management* 23 (Fall): 789–812.

Oreopoulos, Philip. 2003. "Do Dropouts Drop Out Too Soon? International Evidence from Changes in School-Leaving Laws." Working Paper 10155. Cambridge, Mass.: National Bureau of Economic Research.

Rouse, Cecilia Elena. 1999. "Further Estimates of the Economic Return to Schooling from a New Sample of Twins." *Economics of Education Review* 18 (April): 149–57.

Ruggles, Steven, and others. 2004. *Integrated Public Use Microdata Series: Version 3.0* [machine-readable database]. Minneapolis: Minnesota Population Center.

Spence, A. Michael. 1973. "Job Market Signaling." *Quarterly Journal of Economics* 87 (August): 355–74.

Taber, Christopher. 2001. "The Rising College Premium in the Eighties: Return to College or Return to Unobserved Ability?" *Review of Economic Studies* 68 (July): 665–91.

Warner, John T., and Saul Pleeter. 2001. "The Personal Discount Rate: Evidence from Military Downsizing Programs." *American Economic Review* 91 (March): 33–53.

6 PETER MUENNIG

Consequences in Health Status and Costs

PEOPLE WITH MORE education typically live longer and healthier lives. High school graduates, for example, live about six to nine years longer than high school dropouts.[1] They also are less likely to suffer from illness or disability in a variety of forms. In this chapter I seek to measure these benefits in dollar terms. I focus on the association between educational attainment and (1) reductions in morbidity and mortality and (2) reductions in government spending on health care. I examine these effects using a large, comprehensive health data set, the Medical Expenditure Panel Survey, covering the non-institutionalized civilian population in the United States. On the basis of conservative assumptions, I conclude that each additional high school graduate represents a health-related gain to the government of at least $39,000 in discounted lifetime medical expenditures. Monetized gains in health and longevity amount to an additional $183,000. I also discuss the limitations of this analysis.

Education-related gains in health and longevity have obvious benefits for the people who reap those gains. These benefits can be measured in quality-adjusted life years (QALYs), as I describe later, and monetized by applying

1. Link and Phelan (1995); Wong and others (2002). There is evidence that much of this difference in life expectancy can be attributed to educational attainment itself. Cutler and Lleras-Muney (2006); Groot and van den Brink (2004); Lleras-Muney (2004). It is possible that improving either educational attainment or educational quality leads to improvements in health, but here I focus on educational attainment alone because it is the best-studied outcome.

economists' estimates of the value of a statistical life. In addition, such gains can deliver savings in government health care programs such as Medicaid and Medicare.

Medicaid expenditures are the largest and fastest-growing state expense in an era of state budget shortfalls. Increasing educational attainment could reduce these expenses in two ways. First, because eligibility for Medicaid is based mostly on means-tested formulas, improving educational attainment is likely to reduce the number of people who are eligible for Medicaid.[2] Successful education interventions are thought to be causally associated with improvements in earnings, so education interventions would likely lower Medicaid enrollment regardless of the effect of educational attainment on health.[3]

Second, evidence suggests that improvements in educational attainment directly improve health outcomes.[4] Public-sector expenditures may therefore be further reduced if successful education interventions reduce the total amount of disability and disease among people who graduate from high school but nonetheless qualify for public programs.

This second pathway could also lead to reductions in Medicare spending. Although Medicare is best known as a program for retirees, it also covers low-income persons under the age of 65 who have qualifying disabilities, such as kidney disease.[5] Therefore, to the extent that education reduces the probability of disability, it should reduce Medicare enrollment and thereby further reduce public-sector costs. The financial effect could be significant, because persons with disabilities have per enrollee costs that are threefold those of non-disabled enrollees.[6]

Three countervailing effects, however, may limit the net public-sector savings attributable to increased education. First, people with more education are more likely to seek care than those with less education.[7] Second, less educated people may be more likely to die young, and the dead do not consume health care.[8] Therefore, even if improving educational attainment results in improvements in health, it may not greatly reduce expenditures among those who remain enrolled in Medicaid despite having graduated from high school.

2. Iglehart (1999a).

3. Carneiro and Heckman (2003).

4. Groot and van den Brink (2004); Lleras-Muney (2004).

5. Iglehart (1999b).

6. Iglehart (1999b); Keehan and others (2004). See also "A Profile of Medicaid," Centers for Medicare and Medicaid Services, Chartbook 2000.

7. Newhouse and Insurance Experiment Group (1993).

8. Rogot, Sorlie, and Johnson (1992); Sorlie, Backlund, and Keller (1995).

Third, more educated people are more likely to have jobs that offer private health insurance. As a result, they are less likely to fall into the category of the uninsured ill—a group whose care costs upward of $14 billion in tax revenue each year.[9] Employer expenditures on private health insurance plans, however, are tax deductible. In 1999 these deductions reduced federal tax revenues by approximately $76 billion.[10] Therefore, the net effect of increasing private insurance enrollment is to shift the burden of paying health costs from the states (which pay some of the costs associated with caring for the uninsured) to the federal government.

In sum, successful education interventions will almost certainly produce public-sector savings, but considerable uncertainty surrounds their extent. The most conservative approach to estimating the effects of education interventions on public expenditures is to calculate the associated reductions in expenditures on Medicaid, a means-tested program. A more complete estimate would also include potential reductions in Medicare and other public-sector program costs. This approach still omits some savings, such as those associated with reduced spending on the uninsured. But from the government perspective, savings associated with reducing the total number of uninsured persons are probably offset by tax deductions for employers.

Mechanisms through which Education Improves Health

Relative to people with high school diplomas, adults who do not graduate from high school are more likely to die prematurely from cardiovascular disease (35 percent of all deaths among high school dropouts), cancer (27 percent), infection (9 percent), injury (5 percent), lung disease (5 percent), and diabetes (4 percent).[11] The underlying risk factors for all these causes of death except injury are similar, and many are plausibly related to educational attainment. As figure 6-1 shows, cognitive ability, social standing, other psychological or emotional factors, behavioral risk factors, and health insurance form the core putative causal connections between educational attainment and many diseases, including cardiovascular disease, cancer, infection, and diabetes mellitus. Nonetheless, identifying the causal pathways linking education to health

9. Thorpe (2005).

10. Executive Office of the President, "Budget of the United States Government: Analytical Perspectives of the United States: Fiscal 1999."

11. Link and Phelan (1995); Wong and others (2002).

Figure 6-1. Selected Plausible Pathways through which Education Works to Improve Health

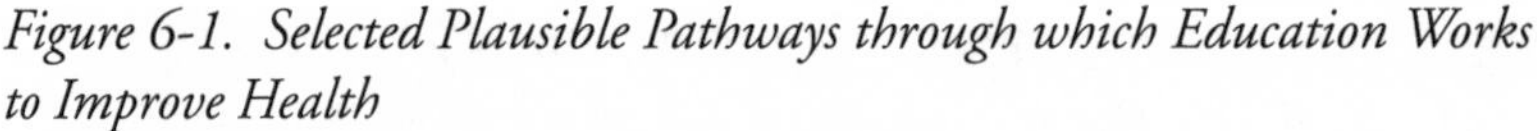

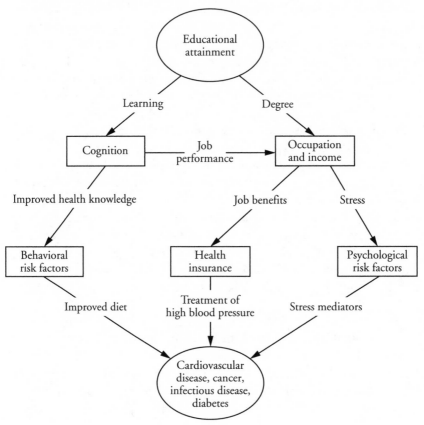

is not straightforward. In figure 6-1 I have eliminated many interconnections and examples for the sake of simplicity.

Effects of Improved Income and Occupation

One such pathway may lead from higher educational attainment through higher job quality and income, two factors that may reduce stress and thereby improve health outcomes. This pathway has not always been well understood. Early associations between "Type A" lifestyles and heart disease led to the popular misperception that affluence and education naturally led to stressful lifestyles.[12] Wealthier, more educated persons certainly have some stress in their lives, but this stress surrounds having "too many things to do." In contrast, those with less education report higher levels of stress associated with "too little money," "health problems," "little leisure time," a large amount of "environmental noise," and "problems with children."[13]

Although the evidence is not definitive, stress conceivably increases the risk of heart disease, infectious disease, diabetes mellitus, and possibly cancer, by profoundly altering the body's biochemical makeup. When faced with a predator, the body releases a cascade of chemicals associated with the "fight or flight" response system. These stress mediators are helpful when one is about to be attacked: they raise blood pressure to perfuse organs, increase blood sugar to give cells energy, and release a host of chemicals that can mitigate damage if the body is injured. When stress becomes chronic, however, these chemical mediators may lead to premature cell aging, DNA damage, blockages in the arteries supplying the heart and brain, and immunosuppression.[14] For instance, certain cells show telltale signs of premature aging: when we compare such cells in the most stressed and least stressed subjects, the gap in biological age may be as great as ten years.[15] Similarly, when subjects are randomly allocated to receive a live cold virus or a placebo, those with higher self-rated stress scores are more likely to become ill.[16]

In addition to reducing stressful living conditions, education may help mitigate the effects of stress by increasing access to social networks and other forms of support. Social networks may reduce loneliness and isolation as well as provide connections that can help people secure shelter or work when they are divorced or fired.[17] Higher levels of social support and lower levels of stress may also help reduce the initiation of risky health behaviors and foster their cessation.[18]

Conversely, social isolation or abuse may undermine both educational attainment and health. Studies on rodents, nonhuman primates, and humans all suggest that the social deprivations associated with poverty contribute to the incidence of adult social pathology and self-destructive behaviors, including those that raise the risk of injury or illness, such as smoking.[19] Depression,

12. Haynes and others (1978).

13. Taylor (2002).

14. McEwen (1998).

15. Epel and others (2004); Irie and others (2001).

16. Cohen and others (2003).

17. Cassel (1976).

18. Cassel (1976); Ross and Van Willigen (1997).

19. Clarke and Schneider (1997); Clarke and others (1994); Harlow and Suomi (1971); Higley and others (1993); Schneider, Coe, and Lubach (1992); Schneider and others (1999); Schneider and others (2002).

anger, and weak social networks also have strong associations with lower educational attainment and greater vulnerability to disease. These factors all fall under the heading "psychological risk factors" in figure 6-1.[20]

Education may also promote healthy behaviors and health outcomes by improving material living conditions. For example, people with little education are often forced to live in low-income neighborhoods that offer few opportunities for eating healthfully or exercising.[21] Studies based on the random assignment of housing vouchers have shown that the rate of obesity drops among subjects who move from such neighborhoods to more affluent areas.[22] To the extent that higher income removes people from poor neighborhoods, it also reduces their exposure to crime, poor housing conditions, and other environmental hazards, such as proximity to polluting industry. In addition, a better job translates directly into a higher probability of having a safe work environment.[23]

A final consideration is that by increasing income, successful educational interventions are likely to improve subjects' chances of enrollment in health insurance programs. Access to health insurance is widely believed to reduce the risk of premature death from cardiovascular disease (via cholesterol-lowering medications, anti-hypertensive medications, and blood sugar control in diabetics), infectious disease (via prompt treatment of life-threatening illness and the provision of anti-retroviral medications), and cancer (via early detection).[24] This relationship is depicted in the center of figure 6-1.

In short, by improving income and occupation, effective educational interventions may attenuate life stressors, improve social networks, reduce behavioral risk factors, and increase the likelihood of possessing health insurance. Other pathways exist as well. For instance, merely attending school can build self-esteem and promote healthier behavior.[25]

Effects of Greater Cognitive Ability

In addition to improving health by increasing income, education may also exert direct effects on health by improving cognitive ability.[26] People with greater cognitive ability are more likely to engage in healthy behavior (exercis-

20. Cohen and others (2003); Kubzansky and others (2001); Wilkinson (1999); Yan and others (2003).

21. Morland and others (2002).

22. Kling and others (2004).

23. DeNavas-Walt, Proctor, and Lee (2005).

24. Hadley (2003).

25. Link and Phelan (1995).

26. Adler and Ostrove (1999); Baker and others (2002); Barton and others (2003); Gottfredson (2004); Kiecolt-Glaser and others (2002); Mechanic (2002).

ing, for example); comprehend and comply with doctors' instructions (notably regarding medication); have the ability to negotiate complex bureaucracies such as health systems; develop effective coping mechanisms for dealing with stressors; meaningfully participate in health-promoting social activities; and, broadly, make good decisions. For example, better educated people may be better equipped to parse and resist harmful messages from industries that promote unhealthy products, such as cigarettes and junk food. People with more education and greater cognitive ability may also place more weight on the future, although in this case the causality is difficult to sort out because forward-looking persons are more likely to invest in education.[27]

Limits to the Effects of Education

There are limits, however, to what a "successful" education intervention can do for one's health. Often, when researchers speak of successful education interventions, they refer to improvements in schooling (for example, prekindergarten programs) that raise the high school graduation rate of a disadvantaged population. But even the most successful interventions are unlikely to produce new high school graduates who will be as prosperous and healthy as those who would have graduated without additional help. An effective educational intervention will increase the graduate's future income, occupational status, prestige, and access to social networks, all of which generate health.[28] Yet those who are born into relative affluence are not only born with many of these advantages in place but may also be exposed to consistently higher educational quality than can reasonably be realized through most educational interventions.

In addition, people born into relative affluence are also born into relative health. High-income children are less likely to have been exposed to tobacco and alcohol in utero, less likely to be exposed to toxins such as lead, and less likely to be victims of trauma through adolescence.[29] Abuse and toxic exposures not only affect physical health but also adversely affect cognitive development.[30] Finally, environmental stressors set off a harmful cascade of biochemical events related to psychological stress that begins in childhood.[31] For these reasons, disadvantaged children who later achieve economic success as a result of an educational intervention may, to varying degrees, be more likely to

27. Fuchs (2004).
28. Link and Phelan (1995).
29. Chen, Matthews, and Boyce (2002); Wilkinson (1999).
30. Canfield and others (2003); De Bellis and others (1999).
31. Brunner and others (1996).

have poor health and die prematurely in adulthood than others in their newly acquired social class.[32]

It is also important to keep in mind that children who do manage to overcome poor schooling, abuse, and other harsh environmental exposures and nonetheless respond to an educational intervention are either the most intellectually gifted or have been exposed to the least adverse circumstances. In other words, if ten students are exposed to an education intervention and one responds by graduating from high school, that student is probably better positioned to take full advantage of his or her high school diploma than the nine students who failed to respond.

Whereas poor children face many environmental obstacles, wealthy children who are coached, tutored, and pushed toward academic success face the fewest obstacles. Their success may therefore be more determined by genetic factors. Supporting this hypothesis, one twin study found that environmental factors primarily determined the IQs of poor children but genetic factors were the primary determinants of IQ among wealthy children.[33] This might explain why poor children assigned to small classes respond more vigorously to such interventions than nonpoor children.[34] If so, we would expect genetic factors to be less likely to confound the education-health association when measured among children raised in low-income families. Because the vast majority of high school dropouts come from this latter group, one would expect the measured health benefits of induced high school graduation to be less affected by genetic confounding.

Methods

In order to measure the health benefits associated with education interventions that increase the rate of high school graduation, I drew on the 2003 Medical Expenditure Panel Survey (MEPS). This survey, conducted by the Agency for Health Research and Quality, covers a nationally representative sample of more than 40,000 non-institutionalized civilian subjects. The 2003 MEPS oversampled African Americans and Hispanics. In addition to collecting detailed sociodemographic characteristics and medical expenditures, the MEPS contains an instrument capable of producing health-related quality of life scores.

32. Marmot and others (2001); Poulton and others (2002).

33. Turkheimer and others (2003).

34. Finn, Gerber, and Boyd-Zaharias (2005); Robinson (1990).

I used these scores to estimate health gains associated with increases in educational attainment. After I eliminated non-U.S.-born subjects, those younger than 25 and older than 65, subjects who required a proxy to answer questions, and subjects with missing values, 12,229 subjects remained in the analysis.

I used these data to estimate regression models identifying the relationship between educational attainment, on the one hand, and health-related quality of life scores and the probability of enrolling in public or private insurance, on the other. Each model included controls for age, race, ethnicity, and gender. Only nonmodifiable covariates (for example, race) were selected, because virtually all other demographic characteristics vary by educational attainment. For instance, income, employment status, marital status, family size, and most other predictors of insurance enrollment or health status vary by number of years of schooling completed. Because work and marriage often come after the completion of primary and secondary schooling, including these characteristics would artificially alter the effect size. Even effects associated with "fixed" characteristics may vary by educational attainment (for example, the racism experienced by a black professional will be different from that experienced by a black high school dropout).

To account for the fact that effective education interventions increase not only the number of high school graduates but also the number of students who go on to higher education, I built a Markov model that calculates outcomes for four groups: high school dropouts, high school graduates, those with some college, and college graduates.[35] In constructing this model I assumed that two-thirds of high school graduates receive no further education, one-sixth receive some college education, and one-sixth graduate from college. To obtain mortality rates for the four education categories, I multiplied the age-specific mortality rates by an education-specific, age-adjusted risk ratio.[36]

All analyses present data in constant 2005 U.S. dollars. Past public medical costs were inflated at a rate of 8 percent.[37] Future costs were discounted at a rate of 3.5 percent. Sensitivity analyses were conducted on the baseline discount rate, estimates of data error, and assumptions surrounding the effect of education on mortality rates. In addition, sensitivity analyses were conducted on the time before graduation that the intervention was administered.

35. High school dropouts are defined as persons with at least nine and fewer than twelve years of education. People in this group were assigned age-specific mortality rates for persons in the general U.S. population with less than a high school education. Kochanek and others (2004).

36. Backlund, Sorlie, and Johnson (1999).

37. Centers for Medicare and Medicaid Services, "Medicare: A Brief Summary" (cms.hhs.gov/publications/overview-medicare-medicaid/default3.asp [March 4, 2004]).

Reductions in Morbidity and Mortality

In health economics, changes in morbidity and mortality are measured in terms of a single outcome called the "quality-adjusted life year," or QALY. One QALY is a year of life lived in perfect health. The QALY comprises two components, health-related quality of life and years of life. Health-related quality of life is a measure of morbidity that varies from zero to one, with zero equal to a state of death and one equal to perfect health.[38] The health-related quality of life score is used to adjust life expectancy to reflect years of life in perfect health. For instance, a population with an average health-related quality of life of 0.8 and a life expectancy of 80 years would have a quality-adjusted life expectancy of 0.8 × 80 years = 64 QALYs.

For this analysis, I regressed health-related quality of life scores on relevant covariates and then predicted changes in health-related quality of life, measured in QALYs, by educational attainment. To assign an economic value to these changes, I multiplied them by a commonly used estimate for the dollar value of a statistical life.

Reductions in Government Spending on Health Care

To estimate the relationship between educational attainment and the probability of being enrolled in Medicaid, I used logistic regression. This approach requires two assumptions: first, that education produces an increase in wages, and second, that the magnitude of this increase in wages is similar to that predicted using logistic regression. To the extent that these assumptions hold, regression can be used to predict the percentage change in Medicaid enrollment by years of education completed. I then estimated overall program costs to the federal government and to each state by multiplying enrollment rates by per enrollee costs. The product of the probability of being insured by a public plan and the mean per enrollee cost is referred to as the per capita cost.

I performed a similar analysis for Medicare enrollment, using the assumptions that education reduces the incidence of conditions for which adults become eligible for Medicare and that regression produces a reasonable estimate of the magnitude of the effect of education on those conditions. Evidence from one very small randomized controlled trial and various instrumental variable analyses suggests that regression underestimates the extent to which education produces health, but these studies are far from conclusive.[39]

38. Gold and others (1996).

39. Lleras-Muney (2004); Schweinhart (2004).

Moreover, there is considerable variability in the association between educational attainment and the prevalence of specific diseases or conditions; a small number of conditions have a higher prevalence among the more educated.[40] None of these conditions, however, is related to the types of disability for which most Medicare recipients qualify. Therefore, the assumptions of the model seem reasonably likely to hold.

I obtained per enrollee costs for Medicaid and for all government health insurance programs together from the 2003 MEPS and inflated them to 2005 dollars. Because the MEPS does not capture all public investments, mean per enrollee costs were adjusted to account for costs out of range in the MEPS. Foremost, the MEPS excludes Medicaid payments to hospitals that serve a disproportionate share of the Medicaid population. These payments totaled $15.5 billion, or 11 percent of total Medicaid program costs, in 2001. Second, the in-range MEPS figures tend to be about 7 percent lower than similar costs from the National Health Accounts.[41] After adjusting for these two factors, the 2005 mean cost for all Medicaid adult (ages 25–64) enrollees was $7,696, and the mean cost for all public-sector users was $11,049.

Results

The health-related quality of life scores used in this study measure mobility, ability to perform usual activities, ability to take care of self, pain or discomfort, and anxiety or depression. By these measures, the health of the average 20-year-old high school dropout is comparable to that of the average 40-year-old college graduate.

Once one takes this difference and differences in life expectancy into account, each additional high school graduate produced by an education intervention is expected to gain a discounted 1.7 years of perfect health over his or her lifetime. This is a very conservative estimate; most models predict that high school graduation will produce six to nine years of additional (non-quality-adjusted) life expectancy.[42] Some, but not all, of the difference between the results of my analysis and those of previous studies is accounted for by discounting. The remainder is due to conservative assumptions surrounding the actual benefits realized by a high school graduate produced by an education intervention. In other words, the real world benefits realized by present-day

40. Cutler and Lleras-Muney (2006).
41. Selden and others (2001).
42. Wong and others (2002).

high school graduates relative to present-day high school dropouts are much greater than the numbers I present here.

Valuing this additional life conservatively at $110,000 per QALY gained measures the benefit of high school graduation at approximately $183,000 per person. The figure of $110,000 per QALY represents one of the lowest estimates in the medical literature and was used to ensure a conservative estimate. Some estimates exceed $350,000 per QALY gained.[43]

In addition, government health care costs drop with each additional high school graduate, because graduates are significantly less likely to be enrolled in Medicaid or Medicare (when considering only enrollees under the age of 65). Approximately 8 percent of high school graduates are enrolled in Medicaid, in comparison with 25 percent of high school dropouts and 1 percent of college graduates, when controlling for age, gender, race, and ethnicity. Similarly, whereas nearly 8 percent of adult high school dropouts are enrolled in Medicare before the age of 65, fewer than 4 percent of adult high school graduates and fewer than 1 percent of adult college graduates are enrolled in this program.

These differences in enrollment rates translate into large differences in annual public costs. The average high school dropout consumes $2,700 in public health insurance costs per year, the average high school graduate, $1,000, and the average college graduate, just $170. Over a lifetime, these annual costs add up. The average high school dropout consumes $59,000 in discounted public health insurance costs by the time he or she reaches age 65. In contrast, the average high school graduate with no further education consumes $23,000 in public health insurance costs over a lifetime, and the average college graduate, less than $4,000, I calculate that each additional high school graduate yields $39,000 of savings in lifetime government health insurance costs.

Finally, while the benefits are partly included in the foregoing numbers, it is informative to understand how insurance coverage varies with respect to educational attainment. Whereas 28 percent of high school dropouts are uninsured, 16 percent of high school graduates go uninsured. Just 6 percent of college graduates go uninsured.

Conclusion

Examining the health-related benefits of effective education interventions, I find that each additional high school graduate will gain 1.7 years of perfect

43. Hirth and others (2000).

health, valued at approximately $183,000. In addition, each new graduate will save the government approximately $39,000 in health care costs.

Certainly, it is unrealistic to expect that most of the 600,000 students who currently fail to graduate from high school in the United States each year can be converted into high school graduates. Nonetheless, it is informative to consider the net present value of the nationwide losses associated with social and school failures leading up to these large numbers of dropouts. Each and every annual cohort of high school dropouts represents a cost of $23 billion in public funds and $110 billion in forfeited health and longevity.

This study has a number of limitations beyond the necessary assumption that education increases income and life expectancy. First, the magnitudes of the effects of education on predicted Medicaid-Medicare enrollment and health-related quality of life were derived using cross-sectional data. This gradient may be artificially reduced or inflated by endogeneity or reverse causality. However, there is substantial evidence that linear regression does a good job of predicting the income increases seen in experimental settings, and fair evidence that it is conservative with respect to predicting mortality by educational attainment.[44]

Second, the overall cost savings are highly dependent on the predicted transition rates from high school to college. Real world progression rates are much higher than the ones I used. However, if an effective education intervention provides an opportunity for students to graduate from high school but almost none goes on to college, the estimated savings will be somewhat smaller than I have calculated.

Third, I generated public health insurance enrollment rates using logistic regression analysis. Although regression has been shown to be very good at predicting income gains associated with additional years of education, it may not be equally successful at capturing the relationship between educational attainment and public health insurance enrollment rates. For instance, additional years of education may improve a person's ability to navigate public bureaucracies, so those who receive an education intervention but remain within means-tested enrollment limits may be more likely to enroll than if they had not received the additional education.

Fourth, although very few model inputs were subject to random error (and those that were had very little), there are a number of important sources of nonrandom error. One-way sensitivity analyses and Monte Carlo simulations, however, produced relatively small effects on overall projected savings.

44. Carneiro and Heckman (2003); Lleras-Muney (2004).

References

Adler, Nancy E., and Joan M. Ostrove. 1999. "Socioeconomic Status and Health: What We Know and What We Don't." *Annals of the New York Academy of Sciences* 896: 3–15.

Backlund, Eric, Paul D. Sorlie, and Norman J. Johnson. 1999. "A Comparison of the Relationships of Education and Income with Mortality: The National Longitudinal Mortality Study." *Social Science and Medicine* 49, no. 10: 1373–84.

Baker, David W., and others. 2002. "Functional Health Literacy and the Risk of Hospital Admission among Medicare Managed Care Enrollees." *American Journal of Public Health* 92, no. 8: 1278–83.

Barton, Christopher, and others. 2003. "Coping as a Mediator of Psychosocial Impediments to Optimal Management and Control of Asthma." *Respiratory Medicine* 97, no. 7: 747–61.

Brunner, Eric J., and others. 1996. "Childhood Social Circumstances and Psychosocial and Behavioural Factors as Determinants of Plasma Fibrinogen." *Lancet* 347, no. 9007: 1008–13.

Canfield, Richard L., and others. 2003. "Intellectual Impairment in Children with Blood Lead Concentrations below 10 μg per Deciliter." *New England Journal of Medicine* 348, no. 16: 1517–26.

Carneiro, Pedro, and James J. Heckman. 2003. "Human Capital Policy." In *Inequality in America: What Role for Human Capital Policies*, edited by Benjamin M. Friedman, pp. 77–239. MIT Press.

Cassel, John C. 1976. "The Contribution of the Social Environment to Host Resistance: The Fourth Wade Hampton Frost Lecture." *American Journal of Epidemiology* 104, no. 2: 107–23.

Chen, Edith, Karen A. Matthews, and W. Thomas Boyce. 2002. "Socioeconomic Differences in Children's Health: How and Why Do These Relationships Change with Age?" *Psychological Bulletin* 128, no. 2: 295–329.

Clarke, A. Susan, and Mary L. Schneider. 1997. "Effects of Prenatal Stress on Behavior in Adolescent Rhesus Monkeys." *Annals of the New York Academy of Sciences* 807 (January 15): 490–91.

Clarke, A. Susan, and others. 1994. "Long-Term Effects of Prenatal Stress on HPA Axis Activity in Juvenile Rhesus Monkeys." *Developmental Psychobiology* 27, no. 5: 257–69.

Cohen, Sheldon, and others. 2003. "Emotional Style and Susceptibility to the Common Cold." *Psychosomatic Medicine* 65, no. 4: 652–57.

Cutler, David, and Adriana Lleras-Muney. 2006. "Education and Health: Evaluating Theories and Evidence." Paper prepared for the conference "Health Effects of Non-Health Policy," Bethesda, Md.

De Bellis, Michael D., and others. 1999. "Developmental Traumatology. Part 2: Brain Development." *Biological Psychiatry* 45, no. 10: 1271–84.

DeNavas-Walt, Carmen, Bernadette D. Proctor, and Cheryl Hill Lee. 2005. *Income, Poverty, and Health Insurance Coverage in the United States: 2004.* No. P60–229. U.S. Bureau of the Census.

Epel, Elissa S., and others. 2004. "Accelerated Telomere Shortening in Response to Life Stress." *Proceedings of the National Academy of Sciences of the United States of America* 101, no. 49: 17312–15.

Finn, J. D., S. B. Gerber, and J. Boyd-Zaharias. 2005. "Small Classes in the Early Grades, Academic Achievement, and Graduating from High School." *Journal of Educational Psycholog*, 97, no. 2: 214–23.

Fuchs, Victor. 2004. "Reflections on the Socio-Economic Correlates of Health." *Journal of Health Economics* 23, no. 4: 653–61.

Gold, Marthe R., and others. 1996. *Cost-effectiveness in Health and Medicine*. Oxford University Press.

Gottfredson, Linda S. 2004. "Intelligence: Is It the Epidemiologists' Elusive 'Fundamental Cause' of Social Class Inequalities in Health?" *Journal of Personality and Social Psychology* 86, no. 1: 174–99.

Groot, Wim, and Henriette Maasen van den Brink. 2004. "The Health Effects of Education: Survey and Meta-Analysis." University of Amsterdam.

Hadley, Jack. 2003. "Sicker and Poorer: The Consequences of Being Uninsured: A Review of the Research on the Relationship between Health Insurance, Medical Care Use, Health, Work, and Income." *Medical Care Research and Review* 60, no. 2, supp. (June): 3S–75S; discussion 76S–112S.

Harlow, Harry F., and Stephen J. Suomi. 1971. "Production of Depressive Behaviors in Young Monkeys." *Journal of Autism and Childhood Schizophrenia* 1, no. 3: 246–55.

Haynes, Suzanne G., and others. 1978. "The Relationship of Psychosocial Factors to Coronary Heart Disease in the Framingham Study, Part 1: Methods and Risk Factors." *American Journal of Epidemiology* 107, no. 5: 362–83.

Higley, J. Dee, and others. 1993. "Paternal and Maternal Genetic and Environmental Contributions to Cerebrospinal Fluid Monoamine Metabolites in Rhesus Monkeys (*Macaca mulatta*)." *Archives of General Psychiatry* 50, no. 8: 615–23.

Hirth, R. A., and others. 2000. "Willingness to Pay for a Quality-Adjusted Life Year: In Search of a Standard." *Medical Decision Making* 20, no. 3: 332–42.

Iglehart, John K. 1999a. "The American Health Care System: Expenditures." *New England Journal of Medicine* 340, no. 1: 70–76.

———. 1999b. "The American Health Care System: Medicare." *New England Journal of Medicine* 340, no. 4: 327–32.

Irie, Masahiro, and others. 2001. "Psychosocial Factors as a Potential Trigger of Oxidative DNA Damage in Human Leukocytes." *Japanese Journal of Cancer Research* 92, no. 3: 367–76.

Keehan, Sean P., and others. 2004. "Age Estimates in the National Health Accounts." *Health Care Financing Review* 1, no. 1: 1–16.

Kiecolt-Glaser, Janice K., and others. 2002. "Emotions, Morbidity, and Mortality: New Perspectives from Psychoneuroimmunology." *Annual Review of Psychology* 53: 83–107.

Kling, Jeffrey R., and others. 2004. "Moving to Opportunity and Tranquility: Neighborhood Effects on Adult Economic Self-Sufficiency and Health from a Randomized Housing Voucher Experiment." Working Paper RWP04-035. Cambridge, Mass.: National Bureau of Economic Research.

Kochanek, Kenneth D., and others 2004. "Deaths: Final Data for 2002." *National Vital Statistics Reports* 53, no. 5: 1–245.

Kubzansky, Laura D., and others. 2001. "Is the Glass Half Empty or Half Full? A Prospective Study of Optimism and Coronary Heart Disease in the Normative Aging Study." *Psychosomatic Medicine* 63, no. 6: 910–16.

Link, Bruce G., and Jo C. Phelan. 1995. "Social Conditions as Fundamental Causes of Disease." *Journal of Health and Social Behavior,* special number: 80–94.

Lleras-Muney, Adriana. 2004. "The Relationship between Education and Adult Mortality in the United States." Working Paper 8986. Cambridge, Mass.: National Bureau of Economic Research.

Marmot, Michael G., and others. 2001. "Relative Contribution of Early Life and Adult Socioeconomic Factors to Adult Morbidity in the Whitehall II Study." *Journal of Epidemiology and Community Health* 55, no. 5: 301–07.

McEwen, Bruce S. 1998. "Protective and Damaging Effects of Stress Mediators." *New England Journal of Medicine* 338, no. 3: 171–79.

Mechanic, David. 2002. "Disadvantage, Inequality, and Social Policy." *Health Affairs* (Project Hope) 21, no. 2: 48–55.

Morland, Kimberly, and others. 2002. "Neighborhood Characteristics Associated with the Location of Food Stores and Food Service Places." *American Journal of Preventive Medicine* 22, no. 1: 23–29.

Muennig, Peter, Peter Franks, and Marthe Gold. 2005. "The Cost Effectiveness of Health Insurance." *American Journal of Preventive Medicine* 28, no. 1: 59–64.

Newhouse, Joseph P., and the Insurance Experiment Group. 1993. *Free for All? Lessons from the Rand Health Insurance Experiment.* Harvard University Press.

Poulton, Richie, and others. 2002. "Association between Children's Experience of Socioeconomic Disadvantage and Adult Health: A Life-Course Study." *Lancet* 360, no. 9346: 1640–45.

Robinson, G. 1990. "Synthesis of Research on the Effects of Small Class Size." *Educational Leadership* 47, no. 7: 80–90.

Rogot, Eugene, Paul D. Sorlie, and Norman J. Johnson. 1992. "Life Expectancy by Employment Status, Income, and Education in the National Longitudinal Mortality Study." *Public Health Reports* 107, no. 4: 457–61.

Ross, Catherine E., and Marieke Van Willigen. 1997. "Education and the Subjective Quality of Life." *Journal of Health and Social Behavior* 38, no. 3: 275–97.

Schneider, Mary L., Christopher L. Coe, and Gabrielle R. Lubach. 1992. "Endocrine Activation Mimics the Adverse Effects of Prenatal Stress on the Neuromotor Development of the Infant Primate." *Developmental Psychobiology* 25, no. 6: 427–39.

Schneider, Mary L., and others. 1999. "Growth and Development following Prenatal Stress Exposure in Primates: An Examination of Ontogenetic Vulnerability." *Child Development* 70, no. 2: 263–74.

Schneider, Mary L., and others. 2002. "The Impact of Prenatal Stress, Fetal Alcohol Exposure, or Both on Development: Perspectives from a Primate Model." *Psychoneuroendocrinology* 27, no. 1–2: 285–98.

Schweinhart, Lawrence J. 2004. *The High/Scope Perry Preschool Study through Age Forty.* Ypsilanti, Mich.: High/Scope.

Selden, Thomas M., and others. 2001. "Reconciling Medical Expenditure Estimates from the MEPS and the NHA, 1996." *Health Care Financing Review* 23, no. 1: 161–78.

Sorlie, Paul D., Eric Backlund, and Jacob B. Keller. 1995. "U.S. Mortality by Economic, Demographic, and Social Characteristics: The National Longitudinal Mortality Study." *American Journal of Public Health* 85, no. 7: 949–56.

Taylor, Humphrey. 2002. *Poor People and African Americans Suffer the Most Stress from the Hassles of Daily Living.* J17677. Rochester, N.Y.: Harris Interactive.

Thorpe, Kenneth. 2005. "Paying a Premium: The Added Cost of Care for the Uninsured." Report 05-101. Washington, D.C.: Families USA.

Turkheimer, E., and others. 2003. "Socioeconomic Status Modifies Heritability of IQ in Young Children." *Psychological Science* 14, no. 6: 623–28.

Wilkinson, Richard G. 1999. "Health, Hierarchy, and Social Anxiety." *Annals of the New York Academy of Sciences* 896, no. 1: 48–63.

Wong, Mitchell, and others. 2002. "Contribution of Major Diseases to Disparities in Mortality." *New England Journal of Medicine* 347, no. 20: 1585–92.

Yan, Lijing L., and others. 2003. "Psychosocial Factors and Risk of Hypertension: The Coronary Artery Risk Development in Young Adults (CARDIA) Study." *Journal of the American Medical Association* 290, no. 16: 2138–48.

7

ENRICO MORETTI

Crime and the Costs of Criminal Justice

Criminologists and educators have long speculated that increasing the educational achievement of young males might lower the probability that they engage in criminal activities. There are several theoretical reasons for expecting a relationship between education and crime. First, and most important, schooling increases the economic returns on legitimate work. Second, education may directly increase the psychological cost of committing crime. Finally, schooling could alter preferences in indirect ways. For example, education might help teenagers better understand the consequences of their decisions and ultimately make them more farsighted, more risk adverse, or both.

From the policy point of view, what matters is the exact magnitude of the effect of education on criminal activity. Policymakers are presumably interested not only in whether it is theoretically possible to reduce crime rates by raising the education of potential criminals but also in whether doing so is cost effective with respect to other crime prevention measures.

Estimating the effect of education on criminal activity may also shed light on the magnitude of the social return on education. Economists interested in the benefits of schooling have traditionally focused on the private return on education. However, researchers have recently started to investigate whether schooling generates benefits beyond the private returns received by individuals. Crime is a negative externality with enormous social costs. If education reduces crime, then schooling will have social benefits that are not taken into account by individuals. In this case, the social return on education may exceed the private return. The exact magnitude of the social return on education is crucial in determining the efficient amount of public investment in education. Given the large social costs of crime, even small reductions in crime associated with education may be economically important.

Although there are good theoretical reasons to expect that increases in high school graduation rates may result in lower crime rates, quantifying this relationship is no easy task. The key difficulty in estimating the effect of education on criminal activity is that unobserved characteristics affecting schooling decisions are likely to be correlated with unobservables influencing the decision to engage in crime. For example, persons who grow up in poor, inner-city neighborhoods may be more likely to drop out of school and at the same time may be more likely to engage in criminal activities. As a result, one might observe a negative correlation between crime and education even if education has no causal effect on crime. In other words, the correlation between education and crime might not be causal but might simply reflect the influence of disadvantaged family background, bad peer influence, and poverty in general.

Determining whether or not the correlation between schooling and criminal activity is causal is crucial for policymakers. If the negative association is causal, then investing in public education will have important benefits not only for the persons who acquire the extra schooling but also for society at large, in the form of lower crime rates. If the negative association is spurious—for example, if it is driven only by the influence of family background or peer effects—then investing in public education will have little effect on crime rates. In this case it would be better for policymakers to try to address the root causes of criminal behavior rather than focus on education.

To address this problem, some researchers have focused on changes in state compulsory attendance laws across states and over time. Changes in state compulsory attendance laws can be used to isolate the causal effect of schooling on crime from all the other determinants of criminal behavior that might pollute a simple correlation. Furthermore, compulsory schooling laws are likely to be of direct interest for policy, because they represent one important tool available to policymakers to increase graduation rates.

Recent research shows that changes in these laws have a significant effect on educational achievement and do not simply reflect preexisting trends toward higher schooling levels in states that increase compulsory education. In the years preceding increases in compulsory schooling laws, there is no obvious trend in schooling achievement. Increases in education associated with increased compulsory schooling take place after changes in the law. In other words, it seems that increases in compulsory schooling raise education, not vice versa.

Notably, Lochner and Moretti found that states that raised high school graduation rates through increases in compulsory schooling experienced significant declines in incarceration rates. In particular, one extra year of schooling resulted in a 0.10 percentage point reduction in the probability of incarceration for whites, and a 0.37 percentage point reduction for blacks.[1] To help in interpreting the sizes of these effects, consider that differences in average education between blacks and whites can explain as much as 23 percent of the black-white gap in incarceration rates.

FBI data on arrests indicate that most types of crime are affected. In particular, estimates uncover a robust and significant effect of high school graduation on arrests for both violent and property crimes, an effect consistent with the magnitude of effects observed for incarceration data. When arrests are analyzed separately by crime, the greatest effects of graduation are associated with murder, assault, and motor vehicle theft.

Using these estimates, Lochner and Moretti calculated the social savings from crime reduction associated with high school completion. Their estimates suggest that a 1 percent increase in male high school graduation rates would save as much as $1.4 billion, or about $2,100 per additional male high school graduate.[2] (I review the methodology behind these estimates later in this chapter.) These social savings represent an important externality of education. The estimated externality from education ranges from 14 to 26 percent of the private return on high school graduation, suggesting that a significant part of the social return on education is in the form of externalities from crime reduction.

The Correlation between Education and Crime

Theory suggests several ways in which educational attainment may affect subsequent criminal decisions. First, schooling increases individual wage rates, thereby increasing the opportunity costs of crime. Second, punishment is likely to be more costly for the more educated. Incarceration implies time out of the labor market, which is more costly for high earners. Furthermore, previous studies estimate that the stigma of a criminal conviction is greater for white collar workers than for blue collar workers,[3] which implies that for more educated workers, the negative effect of a conviction on earnings extends beyond the time spent in prison.

1. Lochner and Moretti (2004).
2. Lochner and Moretti (2004).
3. See, for example, Kling (2002).

Third, schooling may alter individual rates of time preference or risk aversion. That is, schooling may increase the patience exhibited by individuals, as was shown in a study by Becker and Mulligan,[4] or their risk aversion. More patient and more risk-averse persons would place greater weight on the possibility of future punishments. Fourth, schooling may affect individual tastes for crime by directly affecting the psychological costs of breaking the law. For example, Kenneth Arrow, discussing the social benefits of education, argued that "like everything else interesting about human beings, preferences are a mixture of heredity and environment. Schools must surely have a major part, if only because they occupy a large part of a child's day. It is a traditional view that not only does education influence values but it ought to do so."[5]

Fifth, it is possible that criminal behavior is characterized by strong state dependence, so that the probability of committing a crime today depends on the amount of crime committed in the past. By keeping youths off the street and occupied during the day, school attendance may have long-lasting effects on criminal participation.[6]

These channels suggest that an increase in a person's schooling attainment should cause a decrease in his or her subsequent probability of engaging in crime. But it is also possible that schooling raises the direct marginal returns on crime. For example, certain white collar crimes are likely to require higher levels of education. Education may also lower the probability of detection and punishment or reduce the sentence lengths handed out by judges. David Mustard found little evidence of the latter.[7]

Irrespective of the reason, it is well known that persons with low levels of education are overrepresented in the criminal justice system. Table 7-1, based on data for men from the U.S. Census of Population, reports incarceration rates by race and educational attainment. It clearly shows that through 1980, the probability of imprisonment was substantially greater for blacks than for whites, and this was the case for all education categories. Incarceration rates for white men with fewer than twelve years of schooling were around 0.8 percent but averaged about 3.6 percent for blacks over the three decades. Incarceration rates declined with education for all years and for both races.

4. Becker and Mulligan (1997).

5. Arrow (1997).

6. Estimates by Jacob and Lefgren (2003) suggest that school attendance reduces contemporaneous juvenile property crime while increasing juvenile violent crime. Their results are consistent with an incapacitation effect of school that limits student capacities for engaging in property crime, but they also may suggest that the increased level of interaction among adolescents facilitated through schools raises the likelihood of violent conflicts.

7. Mustard (2001).

Table 7-1. *Incarceration Rates for Men, by Level of Education, 1960, 1970, and 1980*[a]
Percent

Category	*All Years*	*1960*	*1970*	*1980*
White men				
High school dropout	0.83	0.76	0.69	0.93
High school graduate	0.34	0.21	0.22	0.39
Some college	0.24	0.21	0.13	0.27
College +	0.07	0.03	0.02	0.08
Black men				
High school dropout	3.64	2.94	2.94	4.11
High school graduate	2.18	1.80	1.52	2.35
Some college	1.97	0.81	0.89	2.15
College +	0.66	0.00	0.26	0.75

Source: U.S. Census of Population.

a. High school dropouts are persons with fewer than 12 years of schooling or 12 years but no degree. High school graduates have exactly 12 years of schooling and a high school degree. Persons with some college have 13–15 years of schooling, and college graduates have at least 16 years of schooling and a college degree.

An important feature in table 7-1 is that the reduction in the probability of imprisonment associated with higher schooling is substantially greater for blacks than for whites. For example, in 1980 the difference between high school dropouts and college graduates was 0.8 percent for whites and 3.5 percent for blacks. Because high school dropouts are likely to differ in many respects from persons with more education, these differences do not necessarily represent the causal effect of education on the probability of incarceration. However, the patterns indicate that the effect may differ for blacks and whites.

This simple empirical regularity is difficult to interpret, because it does not control for the endogeneity of schooling. As I mentioned earlier, the most important difficulty in estimating the effect of education on criminal activity is that unobserved characteristics affecting schooling decisions may be correlated with unobservables influencing the decision to engage in crime. If persons from more disadvantaged backgrounds are more likely to drop out of school and to engage in criminal activities, then we might observe a negative correlation between crime and education, but that correlation might have nothing to do with education per se. And if the negative association is false, derived solely from the influence of family background, then increasing the educational attainment of males will not much affect crime rates.

The literature on this question is large. But despite the many theoretical reasons to expect a causal link between education and crime, quantifying this link empirically has proven difficult, probably because of the endogeneity in schooling. For example, Ann Dryden Witte concluded that "neither years of schooling completed nor receipt of a high school degree has a significant affect on an individual's level of criminal activity."[8] But this conclusion was based on only a few available studies, which found no significant link between education and crime after controlling for a number of individual characteristics.[9]

More recently, Lance Lochner estimated a significant and important link between high school graduation and crime using data from the National Longitudinal Survey of Youth (NLSY), produced by the Bureau of Labor Statistics.[10] Other research relevant to the link between education and crime has examined the correlation between crime and time spent in school.[11] These studies found that time spent in school significantly reduced criminal activity—more so than time spent at work—suggesting a contemporaneous link between school attendance and crime.

Jeff Grogger estimated a significant negative relationship between wage rates and crime, but he found no relationship between education and crime after controlling for wages.[12] Of course, increased wages are an important consequence of schooling. Several other researchers have also established a negative correlation between earnings levels (or wage rates) and criminal activity.[13] The relationship between crime and unemployment has been more tenuous,[14] but a number of recent studies that better address problems with endogeneity and unobserved correlates have found a sizable positive effect of unemployment on crime.[15] Education, then, may reduce crime by reducing unemployment.

The Causal Effect of Education on Crime

The estimates in table 7-1 are consistent with the hypothesis that education reduces the probability of imprisonment. If this is correct, then the effect appears to be statistically significant for both whites and blacks and quantitatively larger

8. Witte (1997).

9. Tauchen, Witte, and Griesinger (1994); Witte and Tauchen (1994).

10. Lochner (2003).

11. For example, Gottfredson (1985).

12. Grogger (1998).

13. Freeman (1996); Gould, Mustard, and Weinberg (2000); Machin and Meghir (2000); Viscusi (1986).

14. See Chiricos (1987) and Freeman (1983, 1995) for excellent surveys.

15. See Gould, Mustard, and Weinberg (2000); Raphael and Winter-Ebmer (2001).

for blacks. These estimates, however, are not easy to interpret. They may simply reflect the effects of unobserved individual characteristics that influence the probability of committing crime and dropping out of school. For example, persons with high discount rates or a taste for crime, presumably those from more disadvantaged backgrounds, are likely to commit more crimes and attend less school. To the extent that variation in unobserved discount rates and criminal proclivity across cohorts is important, these simple correlations could overestimate the effect of schooling on imprisonment.

It is also possible that juveniles who are arrested or confined to youth authorities while in high school face limited educational opportunities. Even though the data in the table include only men ages 20 and older, some are likely to have been incarcerated for a few years, and others may be repeat offenders. If their arrests were responsible for their dropout status, this should generate a negative correlation between education and crime. Fortunately, this does not appear to be an important empirical problem.

Is the relationship between schooling and imprisonment uncovered in table 7-1 causal? Lochner and Moretti provided evidence indicating that the relation is indeed causal and not spurious. Specifically, they used changes over time in the number of years of compulsory education that states mandate as an instrumental variable for education.[16] Compulsory schooling laws take different forms. They typically determine the earliest age at which a child is required to be in school, the latest age at which he or she is required to enroll, the minimum number of years he or she is required to stay in school, or all three. Lochner and Moretti assigned compulsory attendance laws to individuals on the basis of state of birth and the year when the person was 14 years old. They created four indicator variables, depending on whether years of compulsory attendance were 8 or fewer, 9, 10, or 11 or 12.

Table 7-2 quantifies the effect of compulsory attendance laws on different levels of educational achievement. These specifications include controls for the effects of age, year, state of birth, state of residence, and cohort of birth. To account for the effects of *Brown* v. *Board of Education* on the schooling achievement of Southern-born blacks, they also include an additional state of birth dummy for black cohorts born in the South who turned age 14 in 1958 or later. Identification of the estimates comes from changes over time in the number of years of compulsory education in any given state.

Looking at the estimates for whites, three points are worth making. First, the more stringent the compulsory attendance legislation, the lower the percentage of high school dropouts. In states or in years requiring 11 or more

16. Lochner and Moretti (2004).

Table 7-2. *Differences in Schooling Achievement between States with Eight Years of Compulsory Schooling and States with More Stringent Requirements*[a]
Percent

Years of compulsory attendance	*Dropout (1)*	*High school (2)*	*Some college (3)*	*College+ (4)*
Whites				
9	–3.25	3.27	–0.04	0.03
	(0.34)	(0.37)	(0.17)	(0.20)
10	–3.31	4.01	–0.30	–0.39
	(0.45)	(0.51)	(0.30)	(0.33)
≥11	–5.51	5.82	–0.68	0.36
	(0.47)	(0.52)	(0.26)	(0.32)
F-test [*p*]	47.91	45.47	3.05	1.67
	[0.000]	[0.000]	[0.027]	[0.171]
R^2	0.12	0.02	0.04	0.05
Blacks				
9	–2.36	3.09	–0.69	–0.03
	(0.46)	(0.41)	(0.23)	(0.16)
10	–1.76	4.06	–1.82	–0.47
	(0.65)	(0.64)	(0.39)	(0.23)
≥11	–2.96	5.02	–1.89	0.16
	(0.69)	(0.62)	(0.34)	(0.25)
F-test [*p*]	10.09	27.13	12.76	1.85
	[0.000]	[0.000]	[0.000]	[0.136]
R^2	0.19	0.07	0.06	0.02

a. Standard errors corrected for state of birth and year of birth clustering are in parentheses. The excluded variable is the case in which compulsory attendance is 8 years or fewer. The dependent variable in column 1 is a dummy equal to 1 if the respondent is a high school dropout. Coefficient estimates multiplied by 100. The dependent variables in columns 2–4 are dummies for high school, some college, and college, respectively. Sample for whites includes white males ages 20–60 in 1960, 1970, and 1980 Censuses; N = 3,209,138. Sample for blacks includes black males ages 20–60 in 1960, 1970, and 1980 Censuses; N = 410,529. Age effects are 14 dummies (20–22, 23–25, and so forth). State of birth effects are 49 dummies for state of birth (Alaska and Hawaii are excluded). Year effects are 3 dummies for 1960, 1970, and 1980. State of residence effects are 51 dummies for state of residence. Cohort of birth effects are dummies for decade of birth (1914–23, 1924–33, and so forth). *F*-tests are for whether the coefficients on the excluded instruments are jointly equal to zero, conditional on all the controls (3 degrees of freedom).

years of compulsory attendance, the number of high school dropouts is 5.5 percent lower than that in states or in years requiring 8 years or fewer (the excluded case). Second, the percentages in columns 1 and 2 are roughly equal, but with opposite signs. For example, in states or years requiring 9 years of schooling, the share of high school dropouts is 3.3 percentage points lower than in states or years requiring 8 years or less of schooling; the share of high

Table 7-3. *Differences in Imprisonment Rates between High School Graduates and High School Dropouts*[a]
Percent

	OLS estimate		2SLS estimate	
Group	*(1)*	*(2)*	*(3)*	*(4)*
Whites	–0.77 (0.02)	–0.77 (0.02)	–0.61 (0.35)	–0.89 (0.37)
Blacks	–3.39 (0.01)	–3.39 (0.01)	–7.32 (3.66)	–8.00 (3.78)
Additional controls:				
state of residence × year effects		*y*		*y*

a. Standard errors corrected for state of birth and year of birth clustering are in parentheses. The dependent variable is a dummy equal to 1 if the respondent is in prison. All coefficient estimates multiplied by 100. All specifications control for age, year, state of birth, cohort of birth, and state of residence. Sample for whites includes males ages 20–60 in 1960, 1970, and 1980 Censuses; $N = 3{,}209{,}138$. Sample for blacks includes males ages 20–60 in 1960, 1970, and 1980 Censuses; $N = 410{,}529$. Age effects include 14 dummies (20–22, 23–25, and so forth). State of birth effects are 49 dummies for state of birth (Alaska and Hawaii excluded). Year effects are 3 dummies for 1960, 1970, and 1980. State of residence effects are 51 dummies for state of residence. Cohort of birth effects are dummies for decade of birth (1914–23, 1924–33, and so forth).

school graduates is 3.3 percentage points higher. This suggests that compulsory attendance legislation does reduce the number of high school dropouts by "forcing" students to stay in school. Third, the effects of compulsory attendance are smaller and, in most cases, not significantly different from zero in columns 3 and 4.

The estimates for blacks shown in table 7-2 are also generally consistent with the hypothesis that higher compulsory schooling levels reduce high school dropout rates, although the coefficients in column 1 are not monotonic as they are for whites.

Having shown that compulsory schooling laws provided a plausible exogenous variation in graduation rates, Lochner and Moretti used this variation to estimate the causal effect of high school graduation on crime. Compulsory schooling laws are also directly interesting for policymakers, because they represent a key policy tool for raising educational achievement.

Estimates of the effects of high school completion using ordinary least squares (OLS) and two stages least squares (2SLS) are reported in table 7-3. In column 1, covariates include year dummies, age, state of birth, and state of current residence, which are all likely to be important determinants of criminal behavior and incarceration. To account for the many changes that affected Southern-born blacks after *Brown* v. *Board of Education,* they also include a state of birth dummy for black men born in the South who turned age 14 in 1958 or later.

The OLS estimates indicate that white high school graduates have a probability of incarceration 0.77 percentage points lower than that of white dropouts. The estimates made using 2SLS are similar. Incarceration rates among black graduates are 3.4 percentage points lower than among black dropouts according, to the OLS estimates. The 2SLS estimates are larger, ranging from –7 to –8 percentage points.

To gauge the size of these effects on incarceration, one can use these estimates to calculate how much of the black-white gap in incarceration rates is due to differences in educational attainment. In 1980 the difference in incarceration rates for whites and blacks was about 2.4 percent. Using the estimates for blacks, I conclude that 23 percent of the difference in incarceration rates between blacks and whites could be eliminated by raising the average education levels of blacks to the same level as that of whites.

Causal Estimates of the Effect of Education on Arrest Rates

One limitation of the estimates presented so far is that they do not differentiate among types of criminal offenses. Lochner and Moretti used arrest data collected by the FBI Uniform Crime Reports (UCR) by state, criminal offense, and age for 1960, 1970, 1980, and 1990. For each year and reporting agency, arrests were reported by age group, gender, and type of offense.

The estimated effects of education on arrest rates, by type of crime, are reported in table 7-4. The first two rows show similar effects across the broad categories of violent and property crime. The subsequent figures suggest that the effects vary considerably within these categories. A one-year increase in average years of schooling reduces murder and assault by almost 30 percent, motor vehicle theft by 20 percent, arson by 13 percent, and burglary and larceny by about 6 percent. Estimated effects on robbery are negligible, whereas those for rape are significantly positive. This final result is surprising and not easily explained by standard economic models of crime.

Lochner and Moretti found similar patterns when they looked at the relationship between high school graduation rates and arrest rates, reported in columns 3 and 4. The estimates for detailed arrests imply that a 10 percentage point increase in graduation rates would reduce murder and assault arrest rates by about 20 percent, motor vehicle theft by about 13 percent, and arson by 8 percent.

As a whole, these results suggest that schooling is negatively correlated with many types of crime, even after controlling for a rich set of covariates that absorb

Table 7-4. *OLS Estimates for Arrest Rates, by Type of Crime*[a]
Effect sizes

	Average education[b]		*High school graduation status*[c]	
Type of crime	*(1)*	*(2)*	*(3)*	*(4)*
Broad category				
Violent crime	–0.121	–0.116	–0.751	–0.793
	(.025)	(.044)	(.198)	(.291)
Property crime	–0.111	–0.105	–0.593	–0.621
	(.026)	(.044)	(.208)	(.304)
Narrow category				
Murder	–0.276	–0.274	–2.062	–2.133
	(.041)	(.058)	(.403)	(.403)
Rape	0.113	0.118	1.094	1.049
	(.037)	(.048)	(.307)	(.353)
Robbery	–0.007	–0.005	0.184	0.113
	(.031)	(.047)	(.253)	(.333)
Assault	–0.297	–0.292	–2.136	–2.179
	(.028)	(.048)	(.226)	(.326)
Burglary	–0.057	–0.052	–0.202	–0.250
	(.032)	(.048)	(.268)	(.347)
Larceny	–0.058	–0.052	–0.235	–0.277
	(.027)	(.045)	(.209)	(.311)
Vehicle theft	–0.201	–0.197	–1.227	–1.271
	(.030)	(.048)	(.251)	(.346)
Arson	–0.133	–0.127	–0.745	–0.784
	(.044)	(.053)	(.358)	(.408)
Additional controls:				
state × year		*y*		*y*

a. Standard errors corrected for state, year, and age clustering are in parentheses. Violent crimes include murder, rape, robbery, and assault. Property crimes include burglary, larceny, vehicle theft, and arson. Average schooling and high school graduation rate are by age group, state, and year. All specifications control for percentage black, age × offense effects, offense × year effects, age × year effects, state × age effects, and state × offense effects. There are eight age groups, eight offenses, fifty states, and four years. All models are weighted by cell size.

b. Effect of increasing a person's education by one year on his probability of being arrested.

c. Difference in arrest rates between high school graduates and high school dropouts.

heterogeneity at the state, year, crime, and age levels. Both 2SLS and OLS estimates are similar, again suggesting that endogeneity problems are empirically unimportant.

One might also expect effects of this magnitude based on the estimated effect of increased wage rates on crime and arrest rates. For example, Grogger estimated an elasticity of criminal participation with respect to wages of around

1.0 to 1.2, using self-report data from the NLSY.[17] Gould, Mustard, and Weinberg estimated the drop in arrests following a 1 percent increase in local wage rates for unskilled workers to be in the neighborhood of 1 to 2 percent.[18] When using March Current Population Survey (CPS) data from 1964 to 1990, a standard log wage regression controlling for race, experience, experience-squared, year effects, and college attendance yields an estimated coefficient on high school graduation of 0.49. Combining this estimate of the effect of schooling on wages with the elasticity of arrests with respect to wages estimated by Gould and colleagues produces an effect of 0.5 to 1.0. That is, a 10 percent increase in high school graduation rates should reduce arrest rates by 5 to 10 percent through increased wages alone. This covers Lochner and Moretti's range of estimates and confirms that an important explanation for the effect of high school graduation on crime resides in the higher wage rates associated with finishing high school.[19]

Policy Implications: Social Savings from Crime Reduction

Given the estimated effects of education on crime, it is possible to determine the social savings associated with increasing education levels. Because the social costs of crime differ substantially across crimes, Lochner and Moretti used estimates based on the effect of schooling on arrests by offense type to determine the social benefits of increased education. Recognizing the inherent limitations of the exercise, they nonetheless provided a rough estimate of the social savings from crime reduction resulting from a 1 percent increase in high school graduation rates.

Columns 1–4 of table 7-5 report the costs per crime associated with murder, rape, robbery, assault, burglary, larceny or theft, motor vehicle theft, and arson. Victim costs and property losses are taken from Miller, Cohen, and Wiersema.[20] Victim costs reflect an estimate of productivity and wage losses, medical costs, and quality of life reductions based on jury awards in civil suits. Incarceration costs per crime equal the incarceration cost per inmate (approximately $17,000 multiplied by the incarceration rate for that crime). Total costs are computed by summing incarceration costs and victim costs less 80 percent of property losses, which are already included in victim costs and

17. Grogger (1998).
18. Gould, Mustard, and Weinberg (2000).
19. Lochner and Moretti (2004).
20. Miller, Cohen, and Wiersema (1996).

Table 7-5. *Social Costs per Crime and Social Benefits of Increasing High School Completion Rates by One Percent*[a]

1993 dollars, except as indicated

Crime	*Victim costs per crime (1)*	*Property loss per crime (2)*	*Incarceration cost per crime (3)*	*Total cost per crime (4)*	*Estimated change in arrests (number) (5)*	*Estimated change in crimes (number) (6)*	*Social benefit (4) × (6) (7)*
Violent crime							
Murder	2,940,000	120	845,455	3,024,359	–373	–373	1,128,085,907
Rape	87,000	100	2,301	89,221	347	1,559	139,095,539
Robbery	8,000	750	1,985	9,385	134	918	8,615,430
Assault	9,400	26	538	9,917	–7,798	–37,135	368,267,795
Property crime							
Burglary	1,400	970	363	987	–653	–9,467	9,343,929
Larceny/theft	370	270	44	198	–1,983	–35,105	6,950,790
Motor vehicle theft	3,700	3,300	185	1,245	–1,355	–14,238	17,726,310
Arson	37,500	15,500	1,542	39,042	–69	–469	18,310,698
Total					–11,750	–94,310	1,696,396,398

Source: Lochner and Moretti (2004).

a. Victim costs and property losses are from Miller, Cohen, and Wiersema (1996). Total costs for arson are the sum of victim costs and incarceration costs. Estimated change in arrests is calculated from column 4 of table 7-4 and the total number of arrests in 1990 Uniform Crime Reports. Estimated changes in crimes adjusts the arrest effect by the number of crimes per arrest. The social benefit is the estimated change in crimes in column 6 times the total cost per crime in column 4.

may be considered a partial transfer to the criminal.[21] The table reveals substantial variation in costs across crimes. Violent crimes such as murder and rape impose enormous costs on victims and their family members, whereas property crimes such as burglary and larceny serve more to transfer resources from the victim to the criminal.

It is important to recognize that many costs of crime are not included in this table. For example, the steps people take each day to avoid becoming victimized—from their choice of neighborhood to leaving the lights on when they are away from home—are extremely difficult to quantify. Nor are more obvious costs such as private security measures included in table 7-5. Even law enforcement (other than costs directly incurred when officers pursue or solve a particular crime) and judicial costs are absent here, mostly because they are difficult to attribute to any particular crime. Finally, the costs of other crimes not in the table may be sizable. Nearly 25 percent of all prisoners in 1991 were incarcerated for drug offenses, amounting to more than $5 billion in jail and prison costs alone.

Column 5 reports the predicted change in total arrests in the United States based on the arrest estimates reported in column 4 of table 7-4 and the total number of arrests in the Uniform Crime Reports. The estimates imply that nearly 400 fewer murders and 8,000 fewer assaults would have taken place in 1990 if high school graduation rates had been 1 percentage point higher. Column 6 adjusts the arrest effect in column 5 by the number of crimes per arrest. In total, nearly 100,000 fewer crimes would take place. The implied social savings from reduced crime are obtained by multiplying column 4 by column 6 and are shown in column 7. Savings from murder alone are as high as $1.1 billion. Savings from reduced assaults amount to nearly $370 million. Because the estimates suggest that graduation increases rape and robbery offenses, they partially offset the benefits from reductions in other crimes. The final row reports the total savings from reductions in all eight types of crime. These estimates suggest that the social benefits of a 1 percent increase in male U.S. high school graduation rates, from reduced crime alone, would amount to $1.6 billion. And these calculations leave out many of the costs associated with crime and include only a partial list of all crimes. Given these omissions, $1.4 billion should be viewed as an underestimate of the true social benefit.

One might worry that the large estimated effects for murder, combined with the high social costs of murder, account for most of the benefits. When Lochner and Moretti instead used the estimated effects for violent and property crimes

21. For the crime of arson, total costs equal victim costs plus incarceration costs, because it is assumed that none of the property loss is transferred to the criminal.

(table 7-4), the resulting total social benefits from crime were reduced to $782 million. (An overconservative estimate that considered only savings from reductions in incarceration costs would yield a savings of around $50 million.)

The social benefit per additional male graduate amounts to around $1,170–$2,100, depending on whether estimates in the first or second group in table 7-4 are used. To put these amounts into perspective, it is useful to compare the private and social benefits of completing high school. Completing high school would raise average annual earnings by about $8,040. Therefore, the positive externality in crime reduction generated by an extra male high school graduate is between 14 and 26 percent of the private return on high school graduation. The externalities from increasing high school graduation rates among black males are likely to be even greater, given the larger estimated effects on incarceration and arrest rates among blacks. On the other hand, the fact that women commit much less crime than men, on average, suggests that the education externality stemming from reduced crime is likely to be substantially smaller for them.

For another interesting comparison, consider what a 1 percent increase in male graduation rates entails. The direct costs of one year of secondary school were about $6,000 per student in 1990. Comparing this initial cost with $1,170–$2,100 in social benefits per year thereafter reveals the tremendous upside of completing high school.[22]

How do these figures compare with the deterrent effects of hiring additional police? Steven Levitt argued that an additional sworn police officer in large U.S. cities would reduce annual costs associated with crime by about $200,000, at a public cost of roughly $80,000 per year.[23] To generate an equivalent social savings from crime reduction would require graduating 100 additional high school students, for a one-time public cost of around $600,000 in schooling expenditures (and a private expense of nearly three times that amount in terms of earnings forgone by the new graduates while they are in school). Of course such a policy would also raise human capital and annual productivity levels of the new graduates by more than 40 percent, or $800,000, based on my estimates using standard log wage regressions. So although increasing police forces is a cost-effective policy proposal for reducing crime, increasing high school graduation

22. Because the arrest estimates reflect the average difference between all high school graduates and all dropouts (rather than comparing those with 12 versus 11 years of schooling), the estimated benefits are likely to be greater than the benefits that result from simply increasing the schooling of those with 11 years by one additional year. However, as table 7-3 reveals, 70 percent of the reductions seem to be associated with finishing the final year of high school.

23. Levitt (1997).

rates offers far greater benefits when both crime reductions and productivity increases are considered.

Conclusion

There are many theoretical reasons to expect that education reduces crime. By raising earnings, education raises the opportunity cost of crime and of time spent in prison. Education may also make people less impatient or more risk averse, further reducing the propensity to commit crime. To empirically explore the importance of the relationship between schooling and criminal participation, Lochner and Moretti used three data sources: individual-level data on incarceration from the U.S. Census, state-level data on arrests from the Uniform Crime Reports, and self-report data on crime and incarceration from the National Longitudinal Survey of Youth.

All three data sources produced similar conclusions: schooling significantly reduces criminal activity. This finding is robust to different identification strategies and measures of criminal activity. The estimated effect of schooling on imprisonment is consistent with its estimated effect on both arrests and self-reported crime. Different estimators produce similar conclusions about the quantitative effects of schooling on incarceration and arrest. Lochner and Moretti found similar estimates when using aggregated, state-level UCR data and when using individual-level data on incarceration and self-reported crime in the Census or NLSY.

Given the consistency of their findings, it is reasonable to conclude that the estimated effects of education on crime cannot easily be explained away by unobserved characteristics of criminals, unobserved state policies that affect both crime and schooling, or educational differences in the conditional probability of arrest and imprisonment given crime. Evidence from other studies regarding the elasticity of crime with respect to wage rates suggests that a significant part of the measured effect of education on crime can be attributed to the increase in wages associated with schooling.

The effect of education on crime implies that there are benefits to education not taken into account by individuals themselves, so the social return on schooling is larger than the private return. The estimated social externalities from reduced crime are sizable. A 1 percent increase in the high school completion rate of all men ages 20–60 would save the United States as much as $1.4 billion per year in reduced costs from crime incurred by victims and by society at large. Such externalities from education amount to $1,170–2,100 per additional high school graduate, or 14–26 percent of the private return to schooling. It is difficult to imagine a better reason to develop policies that prevent people from dropping out of high school.

References

Arrow, Kenneth. 1997. "The Benefit of Education and the Formation of Preferences." In *The Social Benefits of Education,* edited by Jere R. Behrman and Nevzer Stacey, pp. 10–45. University of Michigan Press.

Becker, Gary S., and Casey B. Mulligan. 1997. "The Endogenous Determination of Time Preference." *Quarterly Journal of Economics* 112, no. 3: 729–58.

Chiricos, Ted G. 1987. "Rates of Crime and Unemployment: An Analysis of Aggregate Research." *Social Problems* 34, no. 2: 187–211.

Freeman, Richard B. 1983. "Crime and Unemployment." In *Crime and Public Policy,* edited by James Q. Wilson, pp. 87–101. San Francisco: ICS Press.

———. 1995. "The Labor Market." In *Crime,* edited by James Q. Wilson and Joan Petersilia, pp. 167–98. San Francisco: ICS Press.

———. 1996. "Why Do So Many Young American Men Commit Crimes and What Might We Do About It?" *Journal of Economic Perspectives* 10, no. 1: 25–42.

Gottfredson, Linda. 1985. "Youth Employment, Crime and Schooling." *Developmental Psycology* 21: 419–32.

Gould, Eric, David Mustard, and Bruce Weinberg. 2000. "Crime Rates and Local Labor Market Opportunities in the United States: 1979–1997." Working paper. Ohio State University.

Grogger, Jeff. 1998. "Market Wages and Youth Crime." *Journal of Labor Economics* 16, no. 4: 756–91.

Jacob, Brian, and Lars Lefgren. 2003. "Are Idle Hands the Devil's Workshop? Incapacitation, Concentration, and Juvenile Crime." Working Paper 9653. Cambridge, Mass.: National Bureau of Economic Research.

Kling, Jeffrey R. 2002. "The Effect of Prison Sentence Length on the Subsequent Employment and Earnings of Criminal Defendants." Working paper. Princeton University.

Levitt, Steven D. 1997. "Using Electoral Cycles in Police Hiring to Estimate the Effect of Police on Crime." *American Economic Review* 87, no. 3: 270–90.

Lochner, Lance. 2003. "Education, Work, and Crime: A Human Capital Approach." University of Rochester.

Lochner, Lance, and Enrico Moretti. 2004. "The Effect of Education on Crime: Evidence from Prison Inmates, Arrests, and Self-Reports." *American Economic Review* 94, no. 1: 155–89.

Machin, Stephen, and Costas Meghir. 2000. "Crime and Economic Incentives." Working paper. London: Institute for Fiscal Studies.

Miller, Ted R., Mark A. Cohen, and Brian Wiersema. 1996. "Victim Costs and Consequences: A New Look." Final Summary Report. Washington, D.C.: National Institute of Justice.

Mustard, David. 2001. "Racial, Ethnic, and Gender Disparities in Sentencing: Evidence from the US Federal Courts." *Journal of Law and Economics* 44, no. 1: 34–56.

Raphael, Steven, and Rudolf Winter-Ebmer. 2001. "Identifying the Effect of Unemployment on Crime." *Journal of Law and Economics* 44, no. 1: 57–78.

Tauchen, Helen, Ann Dryden Witte, and Harriet Griesinger. 1994. "Criminal Deterrence: Revisiting the Issue with a Birth Cohort." *Review of Economics and Statistics* 76, no. 3: 399–412.

Viscusi, W. Kip. 1986. "Market Incentives for Criminal Behavior." In *The Black Youth Employment Crisis*, edited by Richard B. Freeman and Harry J. Holzer, pp. 104–35. University of Chicago Press.

Witte, Ann Dryden. 1997. "Crime." In *The Social Benefits of Education*, edited by Jere R. Behrman and Nevzer Stacey, pp. 101–23. University of Michigan Press.

Witte, Ann Dryden, and Helen Tauchen. 1994. "Work and Crime: An Exploration Using Panel Data." Working Paper 4794. Cambridge, Mass.: National Bureau of Economic Research.

8

JANE WALDFOGEL
IRWIN GARFINKEL
BRENDAN KELLY

Welfare and the Costs of Public Assistance

In modern economies, adequate education is a prerequisite for full participation in the labor market and for the achievement of a basic standard of living. People who fail to achieve sufficient educational attainment are put at greater risk for reliance on income-tested safety-net programs. Although there are people who complete high school but still need public assistance, a basic premise in this chapter is that ensuring that all Americans are educated to at least the level of a high school degree will lead to significant reductions in reliance on income-tested safety-net programs.

In this chapter we explore how three major programs of the safety-net portion of the welfare state—cash assistance, food assistance, and housing assistance—are affected by the failure to educate future citizens so that they can adequately participate in society. We begin by describing the basic methodology we use to calculate our estimates and then apply this methodology to each of the areas of public assistance. We then present a series of cost estimates and comparative statistics that illustrate the magnitude of the savings that could be generated by making sure that every student obtains at least a high school degree.

We are grateful to Ji Young Yoo for her help with estimates from the March 2003 Current Population Survey and to the volume editors for their comments and suggestions.

Background and Methodology

It is well established that adults who lack a high school degree are at elevated risk of being on some form of public assistance.[1] Less educated adults are less likely to be employed and earn lower wages when they are employed, and those who lack a high school degree are at greatest risk (see Rouse, this volume). The problems of low levels of employment and low earnings are particularly stark for single mothers, who cannot rely on a second earner to boost family income. Thus it is not surprising that less educated adults, particularly less educated single mothers, are more likely to use public assistance than are members of other groups. Much of the literature pertains to "welfare," that is, cash assistance provided to (primarily) single mothers through what used to be the Aid to Families with Dependent Children (AFDC) program and is now the Temporary Assistance to Needy Families (TANF) program. We use the welfare example to present our methodology.

Program data for TANF, shown in table 8-1, confirm that women who are high school dropouts are much more likely to be on welfare than women who have a high school degree or more. Of the approximately 1.2 million single mothers on TANF in 2002 (the latest year for which detailed program data are available), more than 500,000 (nearly half) were high school dropouts. When we consider participants as a share of all high school dropout single mothers, we can see that this group is participating in TANF at a rate much higher than the rates of other education groups. Twenty-seven percent of all single mothers who were high school dropouts were on TANF, in comparison with only 17 percent of those with a high school degree and fewer than 1 percent of those with more than a high school education.

However, we need to be cautious in concluding on the basis of this evidence that the lack of a high school degree accounts for *all* the differences in welfare use between high school dropouts and more educated mothers. Women who lack a high school degree might differ from more highly educated women in other ways, and those other differences might predispose them to have higher levels of welfare receipt even if they received more education. Thus a naïve comparison of women with and without high school degrees might lead us to overestimate the effect of education on welfare receipt. At the same time, it is possible that such a comparison might be biased in the other direction. High school graduates who go on to become single mothers presumably differ from other high school graduates. It might be that interventions that promote

1. See, for example, Bane and Ellwood (1994).

Table 8-1. *Welfare Use by Single Mothers, by Level of Education*
Number except as indicated

Education level	*Single-mother TANF recipients*	*Single mothers as percent of all single-mother TANF recipients*	*Single mothers in United States*	*TANF participation rate (percent)*[a]
Less than high school	531,688	45.2	1,966,000	27.0
High school	605,795	51.5	3,577,000	16.9
Greater than high school	38,818	3.3	4,599,000	0.8
Total	1,176,300	100.0	10,142,000	11.6

Sources: Number of single-mother families on TANF is from U.S. Department of Health and Human Services, *TANF Annual Report* (2002). Number of single mothers in the United States is from U.S. Bureau of the Census, *America's Family and Living Arrangements* (2003).

a. TANF participation rates are calculated by dividing the number of single-mother families on TANF in a given education group by the total number of single-mother families in that education group in the United States.

higher rates of high school graduation also lower single parenthood. If so, then naïve estimates of the effect of a high school education on reducing public assistance use would be too low.

In a scientifically ideal world, the basis for our estimates of the effect of being a high school dropout on welfare receipt would be derived from randomized experiments in which children were assigned to either complete high school or drop out of high school. Because we cannot, ethically or practically, conduct such an experiment, we must rely on second best estimates from multivariate regression models that control for as many confounding characteristics as possible, in an attempt to yield the *ceteris paribus* (all else equal) effect of being a high school dropout. We use these regression estimates to calculate *ceteris paribus* differences in the probability of a woman's utilizing each of three forms of public assistance—cash welfare, food stamps, and housing assistance—associated with whether the woman has less than a high school education, a high school degree, or more than a high school degree. As we discuss in detail later, we use regression estimates from the literature where available, but in most instances current estimates are unavailable, and therefore we calculate our own estimates using data from the March 2003 Current Population Survey (CPS).

We begin with projections of the effect of moving high school dropouts to high school graduates. After computing the probability of welfare receipt for persons with high school degrees relative to high school dropouts, we apply this probability to the total population of high school dropouts in order to determine the estimated effect on public assistance receipt of providing the target population—high school dropouts—with a high school education. The reasoning for this is best illustrated by considering an extreme case. Assume that the entire TANF population consists of persons with less than a high school education and that the probability that someone with a high school degree is on TANF is zero. If the entire population were to receive a high school education, then the expected reduction in TANF participation would be 100 percent, because the risk of being on welfare would fall from the baseline probability to zero. In reality, the distribution is not so extreme; some high school graduates are on public assistance, but their risk of being on assistance is less than that of high school dropouts.

The estimates just described will understate the effects of increased education if some current high school dropouts who benefit from improved education and graduate from high school then go on to obtain more education. Thus we also calculate some estimates for which we assume that some current high school dropouts go on to obtain more than high school degrees. Among the current U.S. population of single mothers (the main group on which we focus in this chapter), 56 percent of those with high school degrees have at least some college or indeed a college degree or more, whereas only 44 percent have no more than a high school degree (see table 8-1). Thus it is reasonable to assume that some single mothers who were given the chance to graduate from high school might go on to obtain more education. At the same time, it is likely that those who currently are dropping out of high school have on average less inclination to go on in school than those currently graduating. Thus, in our estimates that move high school dropouts to high school or beyond, we conservatively estimate that the majority of the dropouts (roughly two-thirds) who benefit from improved education will obtain no more than a high school degree, and only one-third will go on to obtain more than a high school education.

The expected effect of increased education on the target population will not eliminate all the participants in each public assistance program. Therefore, to calculate a percentage reduction in the participation rate for each program, we multiply the new participation rate by the total target group to compute the overall reduction in each program area.

Once a reduction in a program's caseload is estimated, program savings are determined on the basis of per participant costs. Using program administrative data, we calculate a per participant cost for each program by dividing the total cost of the program by the number of beneficiaries. Multiplying the participant cost by the reduction in the number of beneficiaries provides a bottom-line estimate of the total program savings.[2]

Unless otherwise noted, all our program, participation, and cost data are from 2002 (the most current year for which detailed information was available). When we use the March CPS, we use data from the 2003 survey, which collects information about public assistance receipt in the prior year, 2002. All our estimates refer to annual costs.

Reduction in Welfare (TANF) Costs Associated with Increased Education

The first program we examine is cash assistance, often referred to simply as welfare. Since the mid-1990s, participation in welfare in the United States has declined dramatically. From its historic high in 1994, the total number of participants on welfare has dropped by 60 percent.[3] Thousands of people have left welfare or not enrolled, motivated by a combination of changes in federal and state welfare, increases in the earned income tax credit, in child care, and in child support enforcement, improvements in the economy, and possibly changes in cultural norms regarding work, motherhood, family obligations, and personal responsibility.[4] Many of the people who have left welfare or were diverted from the program were less disadvantaged than those who remain on welfare, because better educated parents are more likely than their less educated counterparts to find employment, retain their positions, advance in the labor market, and receive child support.[5]

Despite changes in welfare over the past decade, thousands of families and children continue to rely on the program for assistance. Improvements in the educational attainments of American students hold the potential to sustain the declines in welfare use and produce significant savings to the public.

We begin by determining the probability of a person's participating in welfare in the first place. We offer two sets of estimates. For the first, we turn to the literature and use results presented by Jayakody, Danziger, and Pollock from analyses of a sample of 2,728 single mothers from the 1994–95 National Household Survey of Drug Abuse, an annual, national, cross-sectional survey of

2. We treat all cases as having the same average cost. If single-mother family cases receive more benefits than child-only or two-parent family cases, then we will underestimate the savings associated with moving the single mothers off benefits, and the reverse for the others.

3. U.S. Department of Health and Human Services (2004).

4. Blank (2002); Grogger (2004); Grogger and Karoly (2006).

5. Miller (2002); Seefeldt (2004).

the civilian, non-institutionalized population conducted by the U.S. Department of Health and Human Services. Employing a logistic (logit) regression model that controls for mother's age, number of children under 12, mother's marital status, race or ethnicity, residence in an urban area, and region of the country, as well as mother's health, mental health, and use of substances including cocaine, alcohol, and cigarettes, Jayakody, Danziger, and Pollock found that single mothers with a high school education were 55 percent less likely to be on welfare than those who were high school dropouts.[6] These results provide us with an estimate of the change in welfare use that would result if women who are high school dropouts had high school degrees instead.

A drawback of this estimate is that it is taken from the period before the implementation of the Personal Responsibility and Work Opportunity Reconciliation Act (PRWORA) of 1996. A primary purpose of PRWORA was to reduce the dependence of single mothers on welfare by encouraging employment. Theory does not necessarily predict how PRWORA may have affected differential rates of welfare participation among women with different levels of education. On the one hand, less educated women could be more likely than more educated women to respond to welfare reform by reducing their participation in welfare, whether through increased employment or fertility-related behavioral changes. On the other hand, if welfare reform results in "creaming off" the more educated welfare recipients, then people with less education may be at a statistically greater risk of being on welfare than they were in the past.

For this reason we take the results calculated using Jayakody, Danziger, and Pollock's figures as a baseline approximation and compare them with a second set of estimates that we produced using post–welfare reform data. Specifically, we constructed a sample consisting of all single mothers from the March 2003 CPS, a large, nationally representative survey that includes detailed data on both family demographics and public assistance use. We estimated logit models for TANF participation and used these to determine the effect of being a high school dropout versus having a high school degree. The results indicate that persons with high school degrees are 24 percent less likely to be on welfare than those who are high school dropouts. This is a much smaller differential than that found by Jayakody, Danziger, and Pollock, which suggests that perhaps welfare reform has disproportionately affected the least educated and reduced the elevated risk of welfare use by high school dropouts.[7] Nevertheless,

6. Jayakody, Danziger, and Pollock (2000).

7. It is unlikely that differences across the two models account for the difference in estimated effects of being a high school dropout. Although we control for the same set of demographic and background variables, Jayakody, Danziger, and Pollock controlled for several health-related factors that we do not observe in the March 2003 CPS (use of substances including cocaine, alcohol, and cigarettes, mental

a sizable differential remains, so there is still scope for welfare savings if high school dropouts are educated to high school degree level.

With these two figures in hand for the extent to which improved educational attainment might reduce TANF participation, we proceed to the next step in our analysis, which is to project the reduction in TANF use that would result if all women who were high school dropouts instead had high school degrees. Applying the estimates of Jayakody, Danziger, and Pollock, who found that TANF participation rates of high school graduates were only 45 percent as high as those of high school dropouts, reduces the welfare participation rate of single mothers who are high school dropouts from 27 percent to 12 percent.[8] This is a large reduction (indeed, larger than we would have obtained if we had simply used the unadjusted percentages in the raw data and assumed that giving high school dropouts a high school education would equate their odds of welfare receipt with those of high school graduates). Reducing the participation rate for high school dropouts from 27 percent to 12 percent removes more than 292,000 women from the welfare rolls.

What does this mean in terms of reduced welfare costs? Our estimates indicate that moving high school dropouts to high school graduates would result in a substantial reduction in welfare costs—a savings of nearly $3.5 billion per year, or roughly 25 percent of what the United States currently spends on TANF cash assistance for single-mother families.

When we conducted our own post-PRWORA regression analysis using data from the March 2003 CPS, we found a smaller differential in the welfare participation of high school dropouts relative to high school graduates. Using the same methodology, but now with the estimate from our regression with March CPS data, the number of high school dropout women on TANF drops by about 125,000, for a savings of $1.5 billion. This is a much smaller figure than the one we obtained using the estimate from the previous literature, and we are unable to say which figure is closer to the truth. The safest conclusion is that increasing high school dropouts' education to the level of a high school degree would result in $1.5 billion to $3.5 billion in savings in TANF costs per year.

As noted earlier, both these estimates may understate the savings that might be associated with increased education, if some of the dropouts who obtain a high school degree go on to obtain more than a high school education. Therefore, we repeated these estimates assuming that increased education led two-thirds of the dropouts to obtain a high school degree and one-third to obtain

health, and health). Thus, if anything, omitted variable bias should lead us to find larger effects of being a high school dropout in the March CPS models, not smaller ones.

8. Jayakody, Danziger, and Pollock (2000).

more than a high school education. We conducted these estimates using results from Jayakody, Danziger, and Pollock and our own post-PRWORA estimates from the March 2003 CPS. Because women with more than a high school education have even lower odds of being on TANF than those with just high school education, these new estimates result in larger caseload reductions and greater cost savings. Using the Jayokody, Danziger, and Pollock figures, we find that more than 322,000 single mothers are removed from TANF, for a savings of $3.8 billion per year. Using our own figures from the March 2003 CPS, we find that 177,000 single mothers are removed from TANF, for a savings of $2.2 billion per year.

Before moving on to the other public assistance programs, it is important to note that even these latter estimates may still understate the savings that might be associated with increased education. There are three major concerns here. The first is that we have assumed that gaining more education would have no effects on other behavioral outcomes. Yet it is possible, as we discussed earlier, that as women gained more education, they would make other changes (for example, be more likely to marry or to have fewer children) that would make them less likely to be on welfare. Modeling these behavioral effects properly is beyond the scope of this chapter, but future work should take these possible effects into account.

A second omission is that we have focused only on women in these estimates. It is plausible that increases in men's education could also lead to reductions in the welfare use of low-income women. Men with more education would be in a better position to marry or, if they remained unmarried, to contribute child support. Again, this is an issue that should be taken into account in future work.

Third, we have considered an important but incomplete portion of the cash assistance caseload. Our estimates refer to single mothers receiving federally funded TANF. But our estimates do not include single mothers or others who receive assistance through "child-only" TANF benefits, state-funded cash assistance programs such as general relief or general assistance, or means-tested programs for people with disabilities, such as Supplemental Security Income (SSI). If we considered a broader range of cash assistance programs and recipients other than single mothers, we could find additional savings. Because data on which to produce such estimates are lacking, we prefer to focus on TANF single-mother cases here, although we do briefly consider other recipients of our three main public assistance programs at the end of the chapter. Further work on these programs and participants should be included in a future research agenda.

Finally, there is one important reason why our estimates might overstate the savings associated with increased education. As discussed earlier, it is likely that high school graduates differ from high school dropouts in ways other than whether or not they have high school degrees. That is the rationale for controlling for race or ethnicity, age, location, and other demographic characteristics. But it is likely that even after controlling for these differences there are unmeasured differences, such as ambition, motivation, and talent, that lead to variations in both high school completion and utilization of welfare programs. Future research should make use of data sets that have such measures and thereby allow us to get purer estimates of the net effect of high school completion.

Reduction in Food Stamp Costs Associated with Increased Education

We made a similar set of estimates for the Food Stamp Program, again focusing on single mothers, who make up a large proportion of the caseload. Although participation in the Food Stamp Program has declined in recent years, it remains one of the largest safety-net programs in the United States, serving 8.2 million low-income households in 2002, the most recent program year for which detailed data are available. Families with children make up 54 percent of the caseload, and of those, more than 60 percent are headed by single mothers.

As is the case with TANF, less educated single mothers are at greater likelihood of food stamp receipt than more educated single mothers. But the relative overrepresentation of high school dropout single mothers is less pronounced than it is for TANF. As shown in table 8-2, program data indicate that 38 percent of high school dropout single mothers in the United States participate in the Food Stamp Program, in comparison with 31 percent of high school graduate single mothers and 18 percent of more than high school educated single mothers.

We were unable to locate a recent published study that estimated the effects of education on food stamp receipt among single mothers, so we produced our own regression estimates from the March 2003 CPS and applied them to simulate the effects of increasing education to high school or to high school and beyond, using the methods described earlier.

We first estimated the effect of moving high school dropouts to high school graduates. This scenario reduces the food stamp participation rate of single-mother dropouts from 38 percent to 31 percent, just about even with the baseline rate for high school graduates. It results in removing more than 140,000 recipients from food stamps, for a savings of $353 million per year—about 5 percent of current program expenditures on single-mother families.

Table 8-2. *Food Stamp Use by Single Mothers, by Level of Education*
Number except as indicated

Education level	*Single-mother households receiving food stamps*[a]	*Single mothers as percent of all single-mother food stamp recipients*	*Single mothers in United States*	*Food stamp participation rate (percent)*[b]
Less than high school	754,179	28.0	1,966,000	38.4
High school	1,103,441	41.0	3,577,000	30.8
Greater than high school	832,380	30.9	4,599,000	18.1
Total	2,690,000	100.0	10,142,000	26.5

a. Number of single-mother households is from U.S. Department of Agriculture (2003, table 3.3).

b. Number of single-mother households receiving food stamps divided by total number of single mothers in the United States.

We then estimated the results from a more ambitious education improvement that moves two-thirds of dropout single mothers to high school graduates and one-third to more than high school. This scenario reduces the caseload by more than 228,000 recipients, for a savings of $655 million per year, 9 percent of current program expenditures on single-mother families.

Thus the savings in food stamp costs associated with increased education for single mothers, although sizable, are less substantial than the savings in TANF costs. In large part this is because the discrepancy in participation rates by education level is much more pronounced for TANF than it is for the Food Stamp Program. This is seen most clearly in the figures for single mothers with more than a high school education. Fewer than 1 percent of this group participate in TANF, in comparison with 18 percent who participate in the Food Stamp Program. But even among those with just a high school degree, the participation rate in food stamps is markedly higher than that for TANF (31 vs. 17 percent). Thus, increasing the education of single mothers to high school or even to high school and beyond does not make as substantial a dent in food stamp receipt as it does in TANF receipt.

It is important to note that our estimates for food stamps are subject to the same potential biases as our estimates for TANF. A further weakness of our estimates for food stamps is that we have to rely on survey data to estimate participation rates by level of education. This is problematic because receipt rates are underreported in survey data such as those of the CPS, and the degree of underreporting may vary by income or education.

Reductions in Housing Assistance Costs Associated with Increased Education

The final program area we examine is housing assistance. We focus on two major housing assistance programs, public housing and Section 8 vouchers and certificates. Together these programs offset housing costs for just over 2 million single-mother families in the United States. Published program data do not indicate the breakdown of these single mothers by educational status, but we are able to use survey data from the March 2003 CPS to project the shares of program recipients from our three education groups.[9] As shown in table 8-3, the resulting figures indicate that the share of single mothers receiving housing assistance is 26.5 percent for high school dropouts, 24 percent for high school graduates, and 15 percent for those with more than a high school education. As was the case for food stamps, the differential in participation in housing assistance by education status is not as sharp as the differential for TANF.

We were unable to find a recent published estimate of the effects of education on housing assistance receipt among single mothers, so we carried out our own analysis using the March 2003 CPS and then used the results to estimate the effects of improved education, using the methods described earlier. We first estimated the results from the scenario in which high school dropout single mothers are moved to high school education, which removes approximately 3,600 single-mother families from housing assistance, for a savings of about $18 million per year. We then estimated the results from the "high school and beyond" scenario, which has a more substantial effect, removing 63,000 single-mother families from housing assistance and saving nearly $313 million per year. As was the case with food stamps, these savings are quite a bit less than those from TANF reductions, again reflecting the higher take-up of housing assistance than of TANF among more educated single mothers.

Other Potential Savings Associated with Increased Education

That we have focused on single-mother participation in TANF, the Food Stamp Program, and housing assistance means that we have not taken into account potential savings due to reductions in single-mother participation in other programs or reductions in other groups' participation in TANF, the Food

9. Receipt of housing assistance, like other public assistance programs, is underreported in the CPS, so we prefer to use program data for our total caseload numbers. But because program data do not provide a breakdown by education, we use CPS data (on the share of reported participants who come from each education group) to divide the total caseload numbers into education groups. Therefore, our esti-

Table 8-3. *Housing Assistance Use by Single Mothers, by Level of Education*
Number except as indicated

Education level	*Single-mother families receiving housing assistance*[a]	*Single mothers as percent of all single-mother housing assistance recipients*	*Single mothers in United States*	*Housing assistance participation rate (percent)*[b]
Less than high school	521,942	25.3	1,966,000	26.5
High school	850,716	41.6	3,577,000	23.8
Greater than high school	674,072	32.9	4,599,000	14.7
Total	2,046,730	100.0	10,142,000	20.2

a. Authors' calculations using administrative data (totals for the Public Housing and Section 8 Certificate and Voucher Programs, reported in U.S. Department of Housing and Urban Development [1998]) multiplied by the percentage of Section 8 and public housing households headed by a female (*A Picture of Subsidized Housing in 1998*, Social Conditions Table, p. 18). Educational distribution calculated by multiplying total number of households assisted by the proportion by educational status as reported in the March 2003 CPS.

b. Number of single-mother households receiving housing assistance divided by total number of single mothers in the United States.

Stamp Program, housing assistance, or other public assistance programs. Although modeling such cost reductions in detail is beyond the scope of this chapter, it is of interest to include some illustrative figures for what the scope of such savings might be. Without including them, we are surely underestimating the total savings in public assistance costs that could be generated through improved education.

Therefore we made some back-of-the-envelope estimates in which we assumed that the effects of improved education on the participation of groups other than single mothers would be comparable in magnitude to those for single mothers. Thus, if single mothers constitute 60 percent of the caseload of TANF, we assumed that our estimates accounted for only 60 percent of the total reduction in costs that would result from improving education. In fact, single mothers account for 57 percent of the total TANF caseload, 18 percent of the total food stamp caseload, and 80 percent of the total non-elderly housing assistance caseload.

Table 8-4 summarizes our previous estimates for single mothers in addition to presenting our crude estimates for the total savings that could be gained from

mates here, as was the case for the Food Stamp Program, are limited in that receipt of housing assistance, like receipt of food stamps, is underreported in the CPS.

Table 8-4. *Estimated Cost Savings for TANF, Food Stamps, and Housing Assistance from Improving Educational Attainment*

2002 dollars[a]

	Assuming all dropouts obtain at least a high school degree		*Assuming one-third of dropouts go on to more than high school*		*Total estimated savings*	
Program	*Lower odds ratio for TANF*	*Higher odds ratio for TANF*	*Lower odds ratio for TANF*	*Higher odds ratio for TANF*	*Lower odds ratio for TANF*	*Higher odds ratio for TANF*
TANF	1,540,379,209	3,483,504,743	2,184,935,048	3,842,411,292	3,833,219,382	6,741,072,442
Food stamps	353,091,318	353,091,318	655,473,627	655,473,627	3,703,240,831	3,703,240,831
Housing assistance	18,084,493	18,084,493	312,603,631	312,603,631	389,294,684	389,294,684
Total	1,911,555,020	3,854,680,554	3,153,012,306	4,810,488,550	7,925,754,897	10,833,607,956

a. The figures for TANF vary depending on whether the lower or higher odds ratio is used. The figures for Food Stamps and Housing Assistance do not vary.

increased education. The first two columns show the estimated savings if all single mothers had at least a high school education, and the next two columns show the estimated savings if one-third of those without a high school education went on to obtain more than a high school education. The last two columns present our estimates of total cost savings: $3.8 billion to $6.7 billion for TANF, $3.7 billion for food stamps, and $0.4 billion for housing assistance. Total cost savings for all three programs amount to $7.9 billion to $10.8 billion.

Conclusion

Our estimates indicate that the potential savings in public assistance costs that might be produced through improved education are substantial. When we add up all the savings we have identified, the total ranges from $7.9 billion to $10.8 billion. The estimates rely upon a number of simplifying assumptions and are cruder than would be ideal. Some of the assumptions are likely to lead to underestimates, whereas others are likely to lead to overestimates. Future research should address the limitations we have identified. It is unlikely, however, that future research will overturn our central conclusion that improved education will result in substantial savings in the costs of public assistance.

References

Bane, Mary Jo, and David T. Ellwood. 1994. *Welfare Realities: From Rhetoric to Reform.* Harvard University Press.

Blank, Rebecca M. 2002. "Evaluating Welfare Reform in the United States." *Journal of Economic Literature* 40, no. 4: 1105–66.

Grogger, Jeffrey. 2004. "Welfare Transitions in the 1990s: The Economy, Welfare Policy, and the EITC." *Journal of Policy Analysis and Management* 23, no. 4: 671–95.

Grogger, Jeffrey, and Lynn Karoly. 2006. *Welfare Reform: Effects of a Decade of Change.* Harvard University Press.

Jayakody, Rukmalie, Sheldon Danziger, and Harold Pollock. 2000. "Welfare Reform, Substance Abuse and Mental Health." *Journal of Health Politics, Policy and Law* 25, no. 4: 623–51.

Miller, Cynthia. 2002. "Leavers, Stayers, and Cyclers: An Analysis of the Welfare Caseload." New York: Manpower Demonstration Research Corporation.

Seefeldt, Kristin. 2004. "After PRWORA: Barriers to Employment, Work, and Well-Being among Current and Former Welfare Recipients." *Poverty Research Insights* (Fall). National Center for Poverty, University of Michigan.

U.S. Department of Agriculture. 2003. *Characteristics of Food Stamp Households: Fiscal Year 2002.* FSP-03-CHAR02. Food and Nutrition Service, Office of Analysis, Nutrition, and Evaluation. Alexandria, Va.

U.S. Department of Health and Human Services, Administration for Children and Families. 2004. *TANF Sixth Annual Report to Congress.* Government Printing Office.

U.S. Department of Housing and Urban Development. 1998. *A Picture of Subsidized Housing in 1998: United States Summaries.* Office of Policy Development and Research. Government Printing Office.

PART III

Directions for Reform

9 HENRY M. LEVIN
CLIVE R. BELFIELD

Educational Interventions to Raise High School Graduation Rates

GIVEN THE SUBSTANTIAL economic benefits of more education, the challenge becomes that of finding educational interventions that would help children attain high school graduation and other educational goals at a reasonable cost. This challenge is harder than it sounds. Although many children live in circumstances that facilitate learning, many others are in families that have low incomes, poor housing, inadequate nutrition, and insufficient dental and health care, which undermine educational progress and limit the benefits derived from good instruction.[1] Additionally, only about 10 percent of a person's waking hours from birth to age 18 are spent in school, which highlights how much learning is achieved outside of school.[2] Furthermore, educational strategies to improve learning cannot capitalize on a highly predictable science that gives assurances about what children from different backgrounds will learn. Although researchers generally agree on what makes for a good school environment, not all children will succeed from exposure to the same conditions. Educational strategies and reforms may benefit students differentially according to gender, race, or other factors. Therefore, although the economic benefits of high school graduation appear substantial, the costs of achieving graduation may be sizable as well.

1. See Rothstein (2004); Rothstein and Wilder (this volume).
2. Levin and Belfield (2002).

In order to identify effective interventions for increasing high school graduation rates, we undertook a search of the overall literature on high school completion. This included searches of journal articles in databases such as JSTOR and ERIC, as well as the use of Internet search engines and library resources. Of particular interest were evaluation studies of interventions that had been used to increase high school graduation for students in at-risk situations.

Of the hundreds of articles and reports that emerged, very few met our criterion of showing, through a rigorous and systematic evaluation, that an intervention increased high school graduation rates. We were especially interested in studies based on experimental or quasi-experimental methodologies or on a credible econometric design. We found few experimental designs with random assignment, few quasi-experimental studies with strong design to ensure equivalent groups for comparison, and few rigorous statistical and econometric methods to identify effects of interventions.[3] Some evaluations suggested that the examined intervention had little educational effect. Five studies met our criteria of using a credible evaluation design and yielding demonstrable improvements in the rates of high school graduation. We describe these interventions in what follows and provide estimates of their costs per new high school graduate.

Next, we use the economic analyses from part 2 of this volume to calculate the public savings per new high school graduate. That is, we add up the extra taxes graduates pay, the savings in government health costs (Medicaid and Medicare), the savings to the criminal justice system, and reductions in welfare payments. We use a consistent accounting framework, considering the perspective of a person age 20 in 2005. This framework allows us to fully calculate the public returns on investment in reducing the incidence of inadequate education. That is, we can compare the public investment costs for interventions to raise the graduation rate with the public savings from having more graduates.

Interventions that Raise the Rate of High School Graduation

The five interventions whose effectiveness is supported by research studies are summarized in table 9-1. Two of the interventions take place in preschool, one takes place in elementary school, one takes place in high school, and one is implemented across the K–12 years.

3. In some cases, evaluations of interventions were nonexistent or were of very poor quality. Although proponents of many educational interventions claim to show positive results, few such claims are based on careful and rigorous evaluations. Many evaluators look at changes in outcomes over time without adjusting for changes in student characteristics, attrition, and other factors that may influence outcomes. Oth-

Table 9-1. *Interventions that Demonstrably Raise the High School Graduation Rate*

Intervention	*Details*	*Extra high school graduates if intervention is given to 100 students*
Perry Preschool Program (PPP)	1.8 years of a center-based program for 2.5 hours per weekday, child:teacher ratio of 5:1; home visits; group meetings of parents.	19
First Things First (FTF)	Comprehensive school reform based on small learning communities with dedicated teachers, family advocates, and instructional improvement efforts.	16
Chicago Child-Parent Center program (CPC)	Center-based preschool program: parental involvement, outreach and health/nutrition services. Based in public schools.	11
Project STAR: class size reduction (CSR)	4 years of schooling (grades K–3) with class size reduced from 25 to 15.	11
Teacher salary increase (TSI)	10 percent increase in teacher salaries for all years, K–12.	5

Sources: Belfield and others (2006); Finn, Gerber, and Boyd-Zaharias (2005); Loeb and Page (2000); Quint and others (2005); Reynolds and others (2001).

The Perry Preschool Program (PPP) is a high quality program that was the focus of an experimental study using random assignment of applicants to the program or to a control group.[4] Participants were 3 or 4 years of age. The program was in session from October to May in 1963 and 1964 and involved three components: a center-based program for 2.5 hours each weekday morning, with a child-to-teacher ratio of from 5:1 to 6.25:1 and teachers trained in special education and early childhood development; home visits by teachers for 1.5 hours a week to work with parents; and parent group meetings. Participants in the program were followed up through their school years and beyond. The experimental participants showed superior educational and other outcomes along many dimensions, including graduation rates.

The Chicago Child-Parent Centers (CPC) provide early childhood education and family support services, emphasizing mathematics and reading skills

ers use a comparison school without adjusting for differences in student demography. For an overview, see Levin and McEwan (2001, pp. 115–29); for a full explanation, see Shadish, Cook, and Campbell (2002).

4. Belfield and others (2006).

and using high staff-to-student ratios and parental education.[5] The evaluation strategy used a quasi-experimental design to compare the performance of CPC participants with a matched control group of nonparticipants and employed covariate adjustments to ensure comparability of groups. Members of both groups were followed to age 20.[6] High school graduation rates and other educational performance measures of CPC participants exceeded those of the control group.

Class size reduction (CSR) is a popular strategy that has traditionally been used to improve educational outcomes. However, rigorous evaluations of class size reductions are rare. Fortunately, a large-scale study experiment of reductions in class size was mounted in Tennessee, the so-called Project STAR.[7] This intervention is modeled here as one example of class size reduction strategies. The methods and results of Project STAR have been examined and largely endorsed by two independent studies.[8] Students were randomly assigned to larger classes, which averaged 24–25 students, or to smaller ones, which averaged 14–15 students, for up to four years, from kindergarten to third grade. Longitudinal follow-up of students found that those in smaller classes for more years had higher test scores and were more likely to graduate from high school than students assigned to larger classes. The largest effects were found for students from the lowest socioeconomic backgrounds (free-lunch eligible).[9]

It has long been argued that schools can attract better teachers at higher salaries and that such teachers will improve student educational results. Presumably the higher salaries generate a more talented teaching force over time. The teacher salary increase (TSI) study by Loeb and Page estimated the effects of raising teacher salaries using state data with a ten-year time lag.[10] Although the research design was not experimental, this was a high quality, controlled observational study showing the benefits of high quality teaching in raising high school graduation.

First Things First (FTF) is the only high school reform among the interventions that has demonstrated an effect on high school graduation rates.[11] It is a particularly important case because it reflects closely the present wave of urban high school reform, with its emphasis on small learning communities, instructional

5. The CPC program includes both a preschool and a school-age program, but we focus on the element with the most powerful effects, the preschool experience.

6. Reynolds and others (2001).

7. Finn and Achilles (1999).

8. Krueger (1999); Mosteller (1995).

9. Finn and Achilles (1999); Finn, Gerber, and Boyd-Zaharias (2005).

10. Loeb and Page (2000).

11. Quint and others (2005).

improvement, and teacher advocacy for each student.[12] For FTF, small learning communities require that schools or subunits of schools with which students and faculty are affiliated be limited to no more than 350 students. Key teachers remain together for several years. Each student is matched with a staff member, who meets with the student regularly, monitors his or her progress, and works with parents to support student success. Instructional improvement results from high expectations and rigor in the curriculum as well as engaging approaches focused on state standards. The research design was an interrupted time-series on data from Kansas City, Kansas, the site that had accumulated the most extensive FTF experience, and comparison schools in other parts of the state. The evaluation showed higher graduation rates as well as benefits in terms of greater student attendance and higher test scores in mathematics and reading.[13]

Table 9-1 shows the number of new high school graduates that each intervention would yield if the intervention was delivered to 100 students. The Perry Preschool Program is the most effective, with 19 new graduates. First Things First would yield 16 new graduates, class-size reduction and the Chicago Child-Parent Centers program 11 each, and increasing teacher salaries would yield 5 new graduates. These interventions have shown larger effects for minorities and low-income families, who are most at risk of dropping out, although they may not apply to all students equally.[14] Nevertheless, these are significant increases in the rates of graduation.

Other interventions might have even more powerful effects than the ones we have described, but we lack the systematic evaluations needed to establish and verify their results. On the basis of a general review of the evidence, we see a convergence of agreement on a common set of features that lead to increased high school graduation rates and educational success. These features are (1) small school size, (2) high levels of personalization, (3) high academic expectations, (4) strong counseling, (5) parental engagement, (6) extended-time school sessions, and (7) competent and appropriate personnel.

Small size describes a small school or a small program within a school in which students and staff are known to each other and accountable to each other.

12. Another example of small learning communities at the high school level is the Institute for Student Achievement. See www.studentachievement.org for further details. As such reforms develop, they are more likely to be formally evaluated in relation to changes in high school graduation rates.

13. One caution here is that implementation in Kansas City showed a high level of commitment to the reform. Schools in other districts that were evaluated did not have this level of commitment or implementation, and their results were much weaker. Replication of results for this reform therefore requires a high degree of commitment to implementation.

14. In the case of PPP and CPC, almost all the participants were African American. In the case of CSR, we use the mean effect across the experimental group. The TSI figures are for all groups. For FTF, about half the students were African American and another 39 percent were Hispanic.

Personalization refers to a caring environment in which every student is perceived as an important member of the community by both staff and other students and in which an individual's personal and academic needs are addressed. High academic expectations call for a demanding level of academic work that each student is expected to meet if given appropriate assistance. Strong counseling refers to the ready availability of personnel who can provide guidance and advice to students facing considerable personal challenges. Parental engagement enlists the efforts of parents in support of the educational aspirations and accomplishments of their children and the school. Extended time refers to longer school days, weeks (Saturday classes), and school years, to allow sufficient time for instruction and other activities designed to enable students to succeed. Competent and appropriate personnel refers not only to the teaching qualifications of personnel but also to their commitment to the mission of the school.

Current thinking suggests that these interventions be done in combination to constitute a different school and schooling experience.[15] For example, although there is a vigorous "small school" movement in the United States, the evidence suggests that shrinking school size is unlikely to be adequate to improve educational outcomes in the absence of other changes. It is also necessary to have institutional support so that interventions are implemented properly.

Of course not all educational interventions need to be initiated in the schools. A substantial amount of the variance in educational performance is associated with influences in the home and community.[16] Studies of high school dropouts also confirm the importance of differences in conditions outside of school. These findings suggest that the strongest programs for increasing high school graduation rates and subsequent college participation will combine interventions in schools with those in families, neighborhoods, and communities. Absent detailed information about the effectiveness of these new interventions, however, we restrict our focus to those that have demonstrated effectiveness.

Public Costs of the Selected Interventions

Each of the five interventions has overall costs that must be considered in a benefit-cost analysis. First we estimate the input costs of delivering the interventions, on the basis of the resources used. Because our overall analysis is designed to compare the public benefits of additional high school graduates

15. Quint (2006).
16. Rothstein (2004).

with the public costs, we need to calculate the public cost per additional graduate. Obviously, the cost of an additional graduate will be much greater than the average cost per student receiving the intervention, because some students receiving the intervention would have graduated without it. We focus on how many additional students will graduate as a consequence of the intervention and the costs associated with producing each additional graduate.

The costs of the intervention per additional graduate are not the only public costs of higher graduation rates. Each additional graduate obtains more years of high school than do dropouts. Thus we must consider the additional public costs for the extra years of high school for each additional graduate, as well as the costs of progression to college for the share of students who proceed.

The three components of public cost per additional high school graduate, then, are (1) the public cost per additional graduate of the intervention; (2) the public cost of additional years of high school for each additional graduate; and (3) the public cost of postsecondary education for each additional graduate who continues beyond high school. We calculate the total public cost for each intervention using present values for a person age 20 in 2004. Present values signify the cumulative value of costs (or benefits) adjusted for their timing. In this study they are calculated using a discount rate of 3.5 percent, as recommended by Moore and others.[17] To reflect greater uncertainty and the lower valuation of future benefits, we also apply a discount rate of 5 percent for sensitivity testing.

Cost per Intervention

The direct program costs for each intervention are summarized in table 9-2. These figures were obtained either from the primary sources or from our own calculations based on the program ingredients.

For the Chicago Child-Parent Centers program we use the cost estimates reported by Temple and Reynolds.[18] This program has a powerful effect on reducing special education and grade retention during school years. The associated cost saving is deducted from the overall program cost. Therefore, the total program cost per participant is $2,726 in 2004 dollars. Accounting for inflation and expressed as a present value, the cost per student is $4,728.

For the Perry Preschool Program we use cost estimates reported by Belfield and others.[19] This program, too, has powerful effects on special education and

17. Moore and others (2004). For an explanation of discounting and present value, see Levin and McEwan (2001, pp. 90–94).

18. Temple and Reynolds (2007).

19. Belfield and others (2006).

Table 9-2. *Direct Program Costs per Student for Each Intervention*[a]
2004 dollars except as indicated

Year	*Chronology* *Time period (years)*	*Grade*	*Age*	*Cost per student* *Chicago Parent-Child Centers*	*Perry Preschool Program*	*Teacher salary increase*	*Class size reduction*	*First Things First*
1988	–16	pre-K	4	2,726	7,227	. . .	. . .	. . .
1989	–15	K	5	. . .	. . .	178	2,019	. . .
1990	–14	1	6	. . .	. . .	174	2,093	. . .
1991	–13	2	7	. . .	. . .	170	2,172	. . .
1992	–12	3	8	. . .	. . .	168	2,227	. . .
1993	–11	4	9	. . .	. . .	166	. . .	. . .
1994	–10	5	10	. . .	. . .	163	. . .	. . .
1995	–9	6	11	. . .	. . .	160	. . .	. . .
1996	–8	7	12	. . .	. . .	157	. . .	. . .
1997	–7	8	13	. . .	. . .	154	. . .	. . .
1998	–6	9	14	. . .	. . .	150	. . .	1,158
1999	–5	10	15	. . .	. . .	147	. . .	1,167
2000	–4	11	16	. . .	. . .	141	. . .	1,179
2001	–3	12	17	. . .	. . .	136	. . .	1,200
2002	–2	College	18	. . .	. . .	. . .	. . .	. . .
2003	–1	College	19	. . .	. . .	. . .	. . .	. . .
2004	0	College	20	. . .	. . .	. . .	. . .	. . .
Present value at age 20				4,728	12,532	2,865	13,075	5,493

a. CPC and PPP costs are net of the cost savings to the education system from reduced grade retention and special education (Belfield and others [2006]; Temple and Reynolds [2006]). Discount rate is 3.5 percent.

grade retention, and we deduct these cost savings. The annual cost per student is $7,227, assuming that the program is delivered to a person of preschool age. Taking a present value by the time that person reaches age 20, the program cost per student is $12,532.

For the intervention of increasing teacher salaries, there are no reported costs. Our cost calculations are based on the average teacher salary in 2004 of $46,597 and on a class size of 25.[20] Each teacher receives a 10 percent increase in pay. In nominal dollars, increasing teacher salaries will cost $140–$180 per year per student. The total present value cost of this intervention calculated at age 20 for the K–12 school years is therefore $2,865.

20. Bureau of Labor Statistics (www.bls.gov). This assumes no additional fringe benefit costs.

For the intervention to reduce class size, there are no reported costs of the ingredients used in Project STAR, the intervention on which we base our class size effects. A national study puts the annual instructional cost of reducing class size to 15 at approximately $1,400 per student.[21] In the Project STAR experiment, the median class size was reduced from 24 pupils to 15.[22] In order to ascertain the cost, the additional teachers and classrooms necessary were calculated for every 100 students, and national cost averages were applied. For classrooms, construction costs were obtained for 2004 and amortized over thirty years at 5 percent interest to obtain an annual cost. Teacher salaries and benefits for 2004 were used for teacher costs. In present value at age 20, the per student cost is $13,075.

Finally, First Things First is a bit more complex, because it requires a range of additional resources. Data were obtained from a report for Kansas City, Kansas, the most important application of the FTF intervention.[23] The following changes took place to provide the FTF intervention. First, class sizes were reduced from 26 to 20 students. For every 350 students, additional personnel included a counselor, a technical assistant, and a special education teacher. Costs for the additional personnel were derived from the Bureau of Labor Statistics.[24] Additional classrooms were required to accommodate the reductions in class size, along with additional common facilities space for serving such classrooms. The construction costs were amortized over thirty years at 5 percent to obtain annual costs.[25] Assuming a high school size of 2,600 students, delivering FTF would require the following additional ingredients: 12.22 additional math and language arts teachers; 11.8 small learning communities served by a counselor, an assistant, and a special education instructor; and 12.2 additional classrooms. The cost per year per student is $1,160–$1,200 in nominal dollars, and it is necessary to deliver the program for four years across grades 9–12.[26] In total, the present value cost of the program calculated at age 20 is $5,493 per student.

21. Brewer and others (1999) estimated the instructional costs (excluding facilities costs) of reducing class size to 15 students. They estimated that 45 percent more classes would be needed, at a cost of $1,400 per student per year. State-level estimates for Wisconsin, Michigan, and California have ranged from $435 to $2,000 per student per year (Harris and Plank [2000]; Molnar and others [1999]; Ogawa, Huston, and Stine [1999]). Krueger (1999) estimated the costs of Project STAR to be 47 percent of annual per student expenditures in public schools. The intervention is assumed to be delivered for four years, from kindergarten through third grade.

22. Finn and Achilles (1999).

23. Quint and others (2005).

24. Bureau of Labor Statistics (www.bls.gov).

25. McGraw Hill School Construction Data (www.edfacilities.org/cd/dodge0507.pdf).

26. The cost assumptions are as follows: Each teacher salary (with fringe benefits) is $56,009 annually. Each small learning community requires a counselor, a technical assistant, and a special education instructor. Their respective annual salaries (with fringe benefits) are $61,494, $36,962, and $54,931. In

Table 9-3. *Costs per Student of Additional Educational Attainment*
2004 dollars except as indicated

	Chronology			*Cost per student*		
Year	*Time period (years)*	*Grade*	*Age*	*School costs*	*Two-year college*	*Four-year college*
2000	–4	11	16	8,589	. . .	. . .
2001	–3	12	17	8,781	. . .	. . .
2002	–2	College	18	. . .	7,502	7,502
2003	–1	College	19	. . .	7,624	7,624
2004	0	College	20	. . .	. . .	10,941
2005	1	College	21	. . .	. . .	11,269
Present value at age 20				19,592	15,927	37,756
Present value cost per additional high school graduate at age 20[a]				. . .	24,735	. . .

a. Assumes that each high school graduate incurs expected costs that total two additional years of school for completion. On the basis of the data on college participation of low achievers used to assess the probable postsecondary paths of additional high school graduates, the following probabilities of additional attainment are used: one-twelfth of 0.5 years of two-year college; one-twelfth of two-year college; one-twelfth of 0.5 years of four-year college; and one-twelfth of four-year college. Gender- and race-specific progression rates are calculated (see chapter 1). Discount rate is 3.5 percent.

Costs of Additional Attainment

Additional attainment costs, reported in table 9-3, are taken from the *Digest of Education Statistics.* Public expenditure for a year of high school in 2000 was $8,589. For persons who become high school graduates, two additional years of high school are assumed. In present value and accounting for inflation, the additional cost per high school graduate is therefore $19,592. Public expenditure per year in two-year colleges (net of tuition and fees payable by students) in 2000 was $7,203.[27] In present value and accounting for inflation, the additional cost per two-year (associate's) degree is therefore $15,927.

Public expenditure per year in four-year colleges (net of tuition and fees payable by students) in 2000 was $10,203.[28] It is assumed that college degree holders spend two years in the two-year college system and then progress for the next two years to the four-year college system. In present value and ac-

addition, each 20-student classroom costs $29,292 (amortized over 30 years at 5 percent). This total cost must then be divided by 2,600 (the number of students in the school) to derive the per participant cost.

27. National Center for Education Statistics (2002, tables 312, 314, and 334, nominal dollars; 2003, table 168, nominal dollars).

28. National Center for Education Statistics (2002, tables 312, 314, and 334, nominal dollars).

Table 9-4. *Total Present Value Cost of Programs per Student and Per Additional High School Graduate*[a]
2004 dollars

	Chicago Parent-Child Centers	*Perry Preschool Program*	*Teacher salary increase*	*Class size reduction*	*First Things First*
Intervention cost per student	4,728	12,532	2,865	13,075	5,493
Cost per new graduate[b]					
Intervention cost	42,979	65,959	57,301	118,862	34,331
Attainment cost[c]	24,735	24,735	24,735	24,735	24,735
Total cost	67,714	90,694	82,036	143,597	59,066

a. Present values are expressed from the perspective of a person age 20 in 2005. Discount rate is 3.5 percent.

b. Assumes that each intervention must be delivered to 100 persons to yield new graduates. Number of new graduates varies per intervention.

c. Assumes that each high school graduate incurs expected costs that are the total of two years of school and of college fees. For gender- and race-specific college progression rates, see chapter 1.

counting for inflation, the additional cost per four-year college (B.A.) degree is therefore $37,756.

Each additional high school graduate has an expected probability of progression to higher education based on the calculations in chapter 1. This will result in costs to the state via subsidies for college. The cost in terms of attainment for each additional graduate is approximately $24,735, although the exact figure depends on gender and race because of differences in who goes to college.[29]

Total Public Costs per Intervention

The total public costs are the sum of the program costs and the additional attainment costs resulting from the effect of each intervention in raising graduation rates.[30] Table 9-4 provides estimates of the total public costs per student served by each intervention and for each additional high school graduate. The costs per student refer to all students who benefit from the intervention. Some

29. See table 1-5, this volume.

30. We have not included any deadweight losses from raising tax revenues to pay for these interventions. Deadweight losses are incurred to raise tax revenues to pay for services that are needed because of inadequate education. Therefore, including deadweight losses in the costs of the interventions would require inclusion of such losses on the benefits side, too.

of these would have graduated without the intervention. Costs per additional graduate refer to public costs divided only by the additional graduates produced, as listed in table 9-1. The costs vary significantly across the interventions, from $59,000 to $144,000. The lowest cost per additional graduate is found for First Things First, the only intervention implemented at the high school level and the one least affected by adjusting to present value at age 20, because of the brief duration from high school to that age. The Chicago program shows the second lowest cost, followed by policies to increase teacher salaries and the Perry Preschool Program.

These costs per new high school graduate are not trivial, particularly if interventions must be delivered to all children regardless of their likelihood of dropping out. However, they must be weighed against the benefits of producing additional high school graduates in order to ascertain the value of the investment.

The Public Benefits of High School Graduation

On the basis of the analyses and evidence in part 2, we now calculate the public benefits of high school graduation relative to high school dropout status. We use a method that allows us to compare the intervention costs directly with the public benefits. We use the same discount rate (3.5 percent) and express all money figures from the perspective of a 20-year-old in 2005. We assume that some of the new high school graduates will proceed to college at the modest rates reported in chapter 1. We summarize the public benefits in terms of additional tax revenues and savings in government expenditures on health, crime, and welfare.[31] These benefits are summarized in table 9-5.

We report estimates by race and gender, taking account of the significant disparities in dropout rates across groups. Importantly, we are not proposing that policy be based crudely on net present values across subgroups of the population. We present benefit results by subgroup to show that the conclusions are not driven by one group and that population-wide interventions are easily justified. A broader perspective must be adopted in order to decide where the most urgent investments should be made, and it is necessary to understand the causes of any differences. These causes might include the potency of education's effects based on the quality of available schools, the progression rates to college, the extent of involvement in the labor market, and the receipt of pub-

31. Our calculations are summarized on the basis of a full analysis conducted by Henry Levin, Clive Belfield, Peter Muennig, and Cecilia E. Rouse in 2007, available at www.cbcse.org.

Table 9-5. *Lifetime Public Savings per New Expected High School Graduate*[a]
2004 dollars[b]

	Extra tax payments	*Public health savings*[c]	*Criminal justice system savings*[d]	*Welfare savings*[e]	*Total*
Male					
White	202,700	27,900	30,200	1,200	262,000
Black	157,600	52,100	55,500	3,300	268,500
Hispanic	119,000	37,800	38,300	1,200	196,300
Other	168,600	39,000	30,200	1,200	239,000
Female					
White	109,100	39,600	8,300	5,000	162,000
Black	94,300	62,700	8,600	9,000	174,600
Hispanic	85,000	46,500	8,300	3,100	142,900
Other	96,700	49,200	8,300	3,100	157,300
Average	139,100	40,500	26,600	3,000	209,200

a. An expected high school graduate is one who probabilistically either terminates education after graduation, completes some college, or completes a B.A. degree. See chapter 1 for progression rates. Discount rate is 3.5 percent. The benefits are gross and do not take into account the investment costs of additional educational attainment.

b. Figures are rounded to hundreds.

c. Includes Medicaid and Medicare.

d. Annual criminal activity is assumed to decay to zero by age 65. The decay rate is based on the actual incidence of crime for each age group (Federal Bureau of Investigation [2004, table 1]).

e. Lifetime welfare savings are adjusted for the decline in these forms of welfare receipt with age. Welfare programs are TANF, housing assistance, food stamps, and state-level programs on a proportionate basis.

lic services. Other important considerations are the extent of labor market discrimination within and across education groups and the value society places on work outside the labor market.[32] Investigation of all these factors is beyond our scope, and so we emphasize that the gross public benefits from graduation are very large for all cases.

Benefits in Labor Market Income and Tax Revenues

One of the best documented relationships in economics is the link between education and income: more highly educated people have higher incomes. Failure to graduate from high school has both private and public consequences: income is lower, which means lower tax contributions to finance public services.

32. Altonji and Blank (1999).

As Cecilia Rouse showed in chapter 5, dropouts are less likely to be employed and earn much less than high school graduates. Their lower levels of employment are due to both lower participation in the labor force and higher unemployment rates among those within the labor force. The lower earnings reflect both the inferior wages of dropouts and their depressed employment levels, and these effects hold for all subgroups. The lower incomes of high school dropouts translate into reduced tax revenues relative to those derived from high school graduates.

We calculate earnings and tax payments across a person's working life, expressed in present values at age 20. To account for additional payments in property taxes and sales taxes, we add 5 percent to total income tax payments. The extra lifetime earnings from graduation are substantial. Male high school graduates earn $117,000 to $322,000 more than dropouts. Those with some college earn significantly more, and the difference in lifetime earnings between a high school dropout and a college graduate is $950,000 to $1,387,000. Similarly, female high school graduates earn $120,000 to $244,000 more than dropouts. Female college graduates also do well, earning roughly $800,000 more than high school dropouts. This translates into considerably higher tax payments. Male dropouts pay approximately $200,000 in taxes over their lifetime. Male high school graduates pay an additional $76,000 to $153,000, and those who graduate from college pay an extra $503,000 to $674,000. Female dropouts pay less than $100,000 in taxes. Female high school graduates pay $66,000 to $84,000 extra, and female college graduates contribute $348,000 to $407,000 extra.

The additional tax revenue per expected high school graduate is given in table 9-5. The average lifetime benefit in terms of additional taxes is substantial, at $139,100. The amounts vary by race and gender, but for each subgroup they are significant.

Education and Health

High school graduates have improved health status and lower rates of mortality than high school dropouts. Those with higher educational attainment are less likely to use public programs such as Medicaid, and they typically have higher quality jobs that provide health insurance. As Peter Muennig described in chapter 6, increasing educational attainment will likely produce the following effects. First, given the causal link between educational attainment and income, the public sector will save money by reducing enrollment in Medicaid and other means-tested programs. Second, if there is a causal link between educational attainment and disability, then the public sector will save money by reducing enrollment in Medicare among persons under the age of 65.

National data show that Medicaid and Medicare coverage rates decrease with greater educational attainment. High school graduates enroll at half the rate of dropouts, and those with college degrees enroll at very low rates. These differences in coverage rates—reflecting genuine differences in health—translate into differences in annual per capita costs and so into lifetime costs. The costs vary by gender and race, but the educational effects are significant. Among white females, for example, a dropout will receive $60,800 in Medicaid and Medicare payments or services over her lifetime up to age 65 when measured in present value at age 20. A high school graduate will receive $23,200, and a college graduate, $3,600.

The second column of table 9-5 shows the lifetime public health savings per new high school graduate. Over a lifetime, the average saving to the public health system per expected high school graduate is $40,500 in present value terms at age 20. The savings are greater for females but are also substantial for males.

Effects of Education on Crime Behavior

Broadly, crime researchers find that higher educational attainment reduces crime by both juveniles and adults. As Enrico Moretti showed in chapter 7, the economic cost of crime attributable to inadequate education is high. From the public perspective, there are four main costs: criminal justice system costs for policing and for trials and sentencing, incarceration costs (including parole and probation), state-funded victim costs (medical care and lost tax revenues), and expenditures by government crime prevention agencies.[33]

We use a five-stage procedure to calculate the public costs of crime. First, we derive the annual incidence of arrests and crimes per dropout. We focus on high-cost crimes: murder, rape and sexual assault, violent crime, property crime, and drugs offenses. Then we use the analyses of Lochner and Moretti to caculate the reduction in crime if the dropout were to become a high school graduate.[34] Overall, crime rates are reduced by 10 to 20 percent, and this reduction is assumed to have a corresponding effect on incarceration rates. Next we apply Bureau of Justice Statistics data and survey information to calculate the public cost per crime and per arrest for each of the five types of

33. Victims bear most of the costs of crime, but these are not directly counted in the public's balance sheet.

34. Lochner and Moretti (2004).

crimes. Each crime imposes costs in terms of policing, government programs to combat crime, and state-funded victim costs. Each arrest also imposes costs in terms of trials, sentencing, and incarceration.[35] Then we multiply the reduction in the incidence of crime by the unit cost to get an annual cost. Finally, we extrapolate these annual costs over a lifetime, on the basis of the observed rate of criminal activity by age.

The resulting lifetime cost savings to the criminal justice system are reported in table 9-5. The average saving per new high school graduate calculated in present value at age 20 is $26,600. Savings are significantly higher for males than for females, reflecting the big difference between the genders in criminal activity. Most of the savings are from lower incarceration costs, although substantial savings are also gained from lower criminal justice system costs.

Effects on Welfare Expenditures

Greater educational attainment is associated with lower receipt of public assistance payments or subsidies. As shown by Jane Waldfogel, Irwin Garfinkel, and Brendan Kelly in chapter 8, the relationship may be caused directly by lower rates of single motherhood or teenage pregnancy associated with high school graduation. More education produces higher incomes, which reduce eligibility for means-tested welfare programs. However, persons with more education are better able to navigate the welfare system and claim benefits to which they are entitled, offsetting somewhat the gains from reducing welfare entitlements.

The effect of education on welfare payments may be significant. Annually, the federal government spends $168 billion and state governments spend $25 billion on cash aid, food benefits, housing aid, training, and energy aid as needs-tested benefit programs.[36] Receipt of Temporary Assistance to Needy Families (TANF) varies by level of education. Almost half of all recipients are high school dropouts, a proportion much higher than the representation of dropouts in the population, and people with any college education are highly unlikely to receive welfare.[37] Similarly, of the 1.6 million persons annually receiving housing assistance, a disproportionate number consists of dropouts. The most extensive program is food stamps, in which 9.6 million non-elderly

35. Costs per crime and arrest vary according to type of crime, mainly because of differences in prison sentences.

36. Congressional Research Service (2004).

37. Barrett and Poikolainen (2006); U.S. Department of Health and Human Services (2005); Rank and Hirschl (2005).

adults participated in 2004. Again, receipt rates for dropouts are almost double those for high school graduates. Over a lifetime, 64 percent of adult dropouts will have used food stamps, in comparison with 38 percent of high school graduates.[38]

Data from the Current Population Survey show that being a high school graduate is associated with a lower probability of receipt of TANF by 40 percent, of housing assistance by 1 percent, and of food stamps by 19 percent. For those with some college or above, welfare receipt is even more sharply reduced: by 62 percent for TANF, by 35 percent for housing assistance, and by 54 percent for food stamps. Overall, there are likely to be significant cost savings from reducing welfare caseloads across all three programs by raising high school graduation rates. For TANF, the average monthly benefit is approximately $355, and for food stamps it is $85.[39] We add administrative costs to these figures to assess the full fiscal burden. For housing assistance, we calculate spending of $3,100 per person annually, on the basis of reported total expenditures in 2002.[40] Total costs per year are calculated as the number of recipients times the unit cost. Annual figures can be extrapolated to calculate lifetime effects of increasing educational attainment.

Lifetime cost savings per new expected high school graduate are reported in column 4 of table 9-5. The average saving per expected new graduate is $3,000 over the lifetime, expressed as a present value at age 20.[41] The average figure is low relative to those for the other domains, because welfare is time limited, because children and the elderly receive large proportions of welfare funds, and because males receive little welfare but constitute a large proportion of all dropouts. Also, we have omitted benefits for other welfare programs, mostly at the federal level, for which we have insufficient evidence. Nevertheless, the cost savings are significant, particularly for female dropouts.

Total Savings per New Expected High School Graduate

The total public savings or public benefits per new high school graduate, in terms of extra tax payments and savings in health, crime, and welfare costs, are substantial (table 9-5). The savings vary by sex and race but are all large in absolute terms. The differences are caused by many factors, including the

38. Rank and Hirschl (2005, p. 142).

39. U.S. Department of Health and Human Services (2005); Barrett and Poikolainen (2006).

40. Congressional Research Service (2004).

41. The largest proportion of the saving comes from reductions in TANF payments, although there are nontrivial savings in housing assistance and food stamps as well. Further details are available in a technical appendix available from the authors.

strengths of educational effects, the progression rates to college, and the involvement of the different populations in the labor market. The average lifetime saving from an additional high school graduate is $209,200, a present value figure from the perspective of a 20-year-old in 2005. This is a gross figure; it accounts neither for the additional public costs of educating a person through high school nor for the public costs of college for those who progress. Nevertheless, it is a substantial amount.

The Public Costs and Benefits of High School Graduation

We now compare the cost of an intervention to raise the rate of high school graduation with the cost saving or benefit that would result. We adopt the public perspective and apply a discount rate of 3.5 percent, expressing all figures in present values at age 20.

The comparison is summarized in table 9-6. The intervention costs vary according to the cost effectiveness of the intervention, ranging from $59,100 to $143,600. (To repeat, these are the amounts necessary to ensure one extra graduate when the intervention is delivered to a group of students some of whom would already be likely to graduate and some of whom would not.) Each new graduate will, on average, generate economic benefits to the public sector of $209,100. The benefit-to-cost ratios for all interventions are strongly positive, showing that these are highly profitable public investments. For even the median intervention—teacher salary increase—the benefits are 2.55 times greater than the costs.

The aggregate consequences of raising the high school graduation rate for each age cohort are economically significant. Each cohort of 20-year-olds includes more than 700,000 high school dropouts (assuming the GED is not considered as high school graduation). The fiscal consequence is $148 billion in lost tax revenues and additional public expenditures over the cohort's lifetime. If the number of dropouts were reduced by half through successful implementation of the median educational intervention, and if the costs of that investment are taken into account, then the net present-value economic benefit would be $45 billion. This figure is an annual one because each cohort includes about the same number of dropouts. And it does not count the private benefits of improved economic well-being that accrue directly to the new graduates themselves. If the interventions reduced the number of dropouts by only one-fifth, the net economic benefit would be $18 billion.

The net economic benefits of investments to raise high school graduation rates appear to be very large. This conclusion is unlikely to change if alterna-

Table 9-6. *Net Investment Returns from High School Graduation per Additional High School Graduate*[a]
2004 dollars except as indicated

Variable	*First Things First*	*Chicago Parent-Child Centers*	*Teacher salary increase*	*Perry Preschool Program*	*Class size reduction*
Costs (C)	59,100	67,700	82,000	90,700	143,600
Benefits (B)	209,100	209,100	209,100	209,100	209,100
Benefit:cost ratio (B:C)	3.54	3.09	2.55	2.31	1.46
Net present value (B–C)	150,000	141,400	127,100	118,400	65,500

a. Numbers are rounded to nearest $100. Costs include delivering the intervention and any subsequent public subsidies for high school and college. Discount rate is 3.5 percent.

tive assumptions are applied. In our economic analysis, based on the best available evidence, we have used conservative assumptions. Clearly, if we can identify more effective interventions or if the interventions we have discussed prove less effective when scaled up, then net benefits will be affected. These influences are not easily measured. Our main alternative assumptions and the ways in which they would affect the results are listed in box 9-1.

Net benefits would increase significantly if educational interventions could be targeted more accurately toward at-risk individuals. (The results given previously assume that interventions must be given to all students, regardless of whether or not they would drop out.) Net benefits would also go up if we counted other effects of education, such as lower juvenile crime and teenage pregnancy, and the deadweight loss in collecting taxes. Increased education will also improve civic engagement.[42] Because sample surveys undercount people in poverty, benefits would likely increase if more accurate data were available. In contrast, factors that would reduce the return include a fall in market wages as more graduates enter the labor market; an increase in the cost of delivering each intervention; no progression to college by new high school completers; and a higher discount rate. We tested the two most conservative assumptions—no college progression and a discount rate of 5 percent—and found that the net economic benefits were still strongly positive.

The returns on educational investments in high school graduation are substantial, but they could be higher if benefits were increased and costs reduced. Clearly, the most direct way of raising benefits is to establish more powerful methods of improving high school graduation rates. More recent approaches

42. National Conference on Citizenship (2006).

Box 9-1. *Key Assumptions and Their Consequences*

Assumption	*Effect on net economic benefits*[a]
Educational interventions can be more accurately targeted toward at-risk groups	+++
Juvenile benefits (reduced crime, teenage pregnancy) are added	++
Higher taxes, which impose economic distortion on taxpayers through lost economic efficiency (deadweight loss), are added	++
Intergenerational, family, and civic benefits from graduation are added	++
Persons in poverty are more accurately counted	+
Wages fall with more graduates in the labor market	–
The costs of delivering each intervention are higher	– –
High school graduates do not progress to college	– –
Discount rate is higher	– –

a. Number of plus or minus signs indicates the approximate strength of the effect.

may have even more potent effects in improving educational results. If so, schools can raise benefits by shifting to interventions that are shown to be most productive according to evaluation methods based on high standards of validity.

In addition, one strategy that could cut costs considerably is to target the intervention at the students most likely to drop out or most likely to benefit from it. When the intervention is targeted toward an entire school, including students who would have graduated anyway, it requires more resources than if it were targeted toward a particular group of vulnerable students. Targeting the intervention or portions of it, if possible, represents a way of reducing the cost for each additional student who graduates. This is not always possible, because it tends to stigmatize those most at risk.

In summary, it seems unlikely that sensitivity tests using alternative assumptions would overturn the fundamental conclusion of this analysis—that the net present value of public investments to ensure high school graduation is significantly positive across all subgroups of the population.

Educational Interventions for Future Generations

The monetary value of the public benefits of reducing the high school dropout rate exceeds considerably the public costs of getting results through demonstrably successful educational interventions. We selected only interventions for which rigorous and credible evaluations were available and which showed positive effects in reducing the number of high school dropouts. Although dependence only on interventions that have demonstrated their effectiveness is supported by mainstream authorities in evaluation,[43] only five interventions met these criteria.[44] Promise is also shown by a large number of potential approaches, even if such support falls short of what is needed for a rigorous cost-benefit analysis. At the high school level, for example, there are interventions such as career academies, Talent Search, the Institute for Student Achievement model, and Twelve Together. Our conclusions need not be narrowly tied to the smaller set of interventions we included in our calculations. Indeed, it is highly unlikely that "one best intervention" exists. Given the total number of dropouts and the variations in their circumstances and educational needs, a variety of interventions, possibly in combination, should be implemented. Rigorous evaluations should be conducted for all reforms that show promise, so that they can be included in future cost-benefit studies.

The next two chapters examine the potential of large-scale reforms—within the education system and across society—to improve the rate of high school graduation and educational attainment more broadly.

References

Altonji, Joseph G., and Rebecca M. Blank. 1999. "Race and Gender in the Labor Market." In *The Handbook of Labor Economics*, vol. 3, edited by Orley Ashenfelter and David Card, pp. 3143–259. Amsterdam: Elsevier Science.

Barrett, Allison, and Anni Poikolainen. 2006. *Food Stamp Program Participation Rates, 2004*. Department of Agriculture.

Belfield, Clive R., and others. 2006. "Cost-Benefit Analysis of the High/Scope Perry Preschool Program using Age 40 Follow-Up Data." *Journal of Human Resources* 41, no. 1: 162–90.

Brewer, Dominic J., and others. 1999. "Estimating the Costs of National Class Size Reductions under Different Policy Alternatives." *Educational Evaluation and Policy Analysis* 21, no. 2: 179–92.

Congressional Research Service. 2004. "Cash and Non-Cash Benefits for Persons with Limited Income: Eligibility Rule, Recipient, and Expenditure Data, FY 2000–2002." Report RL32233. Washington, D.C.

Federal Bureau of Investigation. 2004. *Uniform Crime Report: Crime in the United States*. Department of Justice.

43. Mervis (2004).

44. New and promising interventions, however, should be considered. We did not include these interventions in our calculations because of a lack of reliable information about their effectiveness. It is our hope that over time we will obtain excellent evaluations of their effects and that they will show even more powerful results.

Finn, Jeremy D., and Charles M. Achilles. 1999. "Tennessee's Class Size Study: Findings, Implications, Misconceptions." *Educational Evaluation and Policy Analysis* 21, no. 2: 97–109.

Finn, Jeremy D., Susan B. Gerber, and Jayne Boyd-Zaharias. 2005. "Small Classes in the Early Grades, Academic Achievement, and Graduating from High School." *Journal of Educational Psychology* 97, no. 2: 214–23.

Harris, Douglas, and David Plank. 2000. "Making Policy Choices: Is Class Size Reduction the Best Alternative?" Working paper. Michigan State University.

Krueger, Alan B. 1999. "Experimental Estimates of Education Production Function." *Quarterly Journal of Economics* 114, no. 2: 497–532.

Levin, Henry M., and Clive R. Belfield. 2002. "Families as Contractual Partners in Education." *UCLA Law Review* 49, part 6: 1799–1824.

Levin, Henry M., and Patrick J. McEwan. 2001. *Cost-Effectiveness Analysis: Methods and Applications.* Thousand Oaks, Calif.: Sage.

Lochner, Lance, and Enrico Moretti. 2004. "The Effect of Education on Crime: Evidence from Prison Inmates, Arrests, and Self-Reports." *American Economic Review* 94, no. 1: 155–89.

Loeb, Susanna, and Marianne E. Page. 2000. "Examining the Link between Teacher Wages and Student Outcomes: The Importance of Alternative Labor Market Opportunities and Non-pecuniary Variation." *Review of Economics and Statistics* 82, no. 3: 393–408.

Mervis, Jeffrey. 2004. "Educational Research: Meager Evaluations Make It Hard to Find Out What Works." *Science* 304 (June 11): 1583.

Molnar, Alex, and others. 1999. "Evaluating the SAGE Program: A Pilot Program in Targeted Pupil-Teacher Reduction in Wisconsin." *Educational Evaluation and Policy Analysis* 21: 165–77.

Moore, Mark A., and others. 2004. "Just Give Me a Number! Practical Values for the Social Discount Rate." *Journal of Policy Analysis and Management* 23 (Fall): 789–812.

Mosteller, Frederick. 1995. "The Tennessee Study of Class Size in the Early School Grades." *Future of Children* 52: 113–27.

National Center for Education Statistics. 2002. *Short-term Enrollment in Postsecondary Education: Student Background and Institutional Differences in Reasons for Early Departure, 1996–98.* NCES 2003-153. Department of Education.

———. 2003. *Public High School Dropouts and Completers from the Common Core of Data: School Year, 2000–01.* NCES 2004-310. Department of Education.

National Conference on Citizenship. 2006. *Broken Engagement: America's Civic Health Index* (www.ncoc.net/conferences/2006civichealth.pdf).

Ogawa, Rodney T., Deborah Huston, and Deborah E. Stine. 1999. "California's Class Size Reduction Initiative: Differences in Teacher Experience and Qualifications across Schools." *Educational Policy* 13: 659–73.

Quint, Janet. 2006. *Meeting Five Critical Challenges of High School Reform.* New York: Manpower Development Research Corporation.

Quint, Janet, and others. 2005. *The Challenge of Scaling Up Educational Reform: Findings and Lessons from First Things First.* New York: Manpower Development Research Corporation.

Rank, Mark R., and Thomas A. Hirschl. 2005. "Likelihood of Using Food Stamps during the Adulthood Years." *Journal of Nutrition Education and Behavior* 37, no. 3: 137–46.

Reynolds, Arthur J., and others. 2001. "Long-term Effects of an Early Childhood Intervention on Educational Achievement and Juvenile Arrest: A Fifteen-Year Follow-up of Low-

Income Children in Public Schools." *Journal of the American Medical Association* 285, no. 18: 2339–46.

Rothstein, Richard. 2004. *Class and Schools: Using Social, Economic, and Educational Reform to Close the Black-White Achievement Gap.* Washington, D.C.: Teachers College Press and Economic Policy Institute.

Shadish, Wil, Thomas D. Cook, and Donald T. Campbell. 2002. *Experimental and Quasi-Experimental Designs for Generalized Causal Inference.* New York: Houghton Mifflin.

Temple, Judy, and Arthur Reynolds. 2007. "Benefits and Costs of Investments in Preschool Education: Evidence from the Child-Parent Centers and Related Programs." *Economics of Education Review* 26, no. 1: 126–44.

U.S. Department of Health and Human Services. 2005. *TANF Sixth Annual Report to Congress.* Government Printing Office.

10 CLIVE R. BELFIELD

The Promise of Early Childhood Education Interventions

To WHAT EXTENT can pre-kindergarten education (pre-K) reduce social and economic inequalities?[1] For pre-K advocates, the answer is straightforward. Substantial gaps exist between children as they enter school, and these gaps persist and are reinforced throughout childhood. Judging from its effectiveness as demonstrated by high quality research investigations, an expansion of preschooling would significantly close these initial gaps and improve children's economic well-being over the longer term. And because the state incurs much of the burden of economic and social inequalities, there is no efficiency-versus-equity trade-off from investing public funds in preschooling. Investing in preschool serves both goals.

The story is simple—but does it hold true? To answer this question, I begin by documenting initial gaps among children as they enter school and juxtaposing these gaps with differences in access to preschooling. Next I discuss how initial gaps are reinforced and give rise to larger disparities in later childhood and adulthood. I then document how preschool programs may reduce educational and economic inequalities and thereby yield a high social return. Finally, I consider policy issues relating to the expansion of early childhood education. I ask, What would such interventions cost? What proportion of children would be eligible? How well do actual programs correspond to model

1. Here pre-K, preschool, and early childhood education are not distinguished. Throughout, pre-K refers to an educational program for children in the one to two years immediately before kindergarten.

programs? The answers shed light on whether increases in equity can in fact be realized.

Educational Status in Early Childhood

Table 10-1 shows initial gaps between white and black and Hispanic children upon entry to school.[2] The academic gaps, as measured by test scores, are substantial. Behavioral gaps are smaller and even negative in some cases, suggesting that in some ways black and Hispanic children are better prepared for school. However, these numbers are based on subjective teacher ratings that may be socially conditioned, and the most academic of the measures—"approaches to learning"—shows an advantage for white children over blacks and Hispanics. Moreover, white children typically have advantages in other critical areas, such as health status and home environment, that provide the foundation for many of the skills needed to progress in school.[3]

However, the trajectories for achievement in the early years differ according to the child's characteristics. Table 10-2 gives results from longitudinal survey data from the Early Childhood Longitudinal Study–Kindergarten (ECLS-K) on 11,210 children in kindergarten in 1998.[4] The effect of socioeconomic status on reading and math achievement is broadly consistent regardless of how old the children are (with an effect size of 0.2–0.3). Once in school, children from families with lower socioeconomic status do not fall much farther behind each year, because a large component of the gap is evident upon entry to school. The achievement gap does widen, leading to striking disparities in a much broader set of measures of well-being after twelve years of schooling, but the initial disparity is substantial.

The pattern by race is more complex. For blacks and Hispanics, most of the initial (kindergarten) achievement difference is eliminated when a few controls are included (for example, for socioeconomic status and birth weight). But over the next few years, the early gap widens for blacks and narrows for Hispanics (table 10-2).[5] Black children fall behind by about 0.1 standard deviation for the first four years. Hispanic children improve their relative standing

2. The table identifies the effect of each characteristic in isolation, so these numbers understate the real disparities between, for example, high-income white children and low-income black children.

3. In a full analysis, Rothstein and Wilder (this volume) catalog differences between whites and blacks in terms of parental commitments of books, time, and activities for their young children. In terms of health, they report that the average black child is in the 37th percentile in terms of neonatal outcomes.

4. Fryer and Levitt (2004b).

5. Fryer and Levitt (2004b).

Table 10-1. *Academic and Behavioral Gaps between Whites and Minorities upon Entry to School*
Standard deviation

	White-Black		*White-Hispanic*	
	Raw	*Adjusted*[a]	*Raw*	*Adjusted*[a]
Academic measures				
Math test	0.64	0.09	0.72	0.20
Reading test	0.40	0.12	0.43	0.06
Vocabulary	1.41	0.81	. . .	. . .
IQ	1.25	0.32	. . .	. . .
Behavioral measures				
Approaches to learning	0.36	. . .	0.21	. . .
Self-control	0.38	. . .	0.13	. . .
Externalizing behavior	–0.31	–0.21	0.01	. . .
Internalizing behavior	–0.06	–0.16	–0.05	. . .

Source: Rock and Stenner (2005, tables 1 and 2).
a. Adjusted gaps account for family background characteristics and home behaviors.

by 0.025 standard deviation each year. These gains, however, do little to compensate for the early disadvantages Hispanic children face, especially because many of them also come from low-income families. These large, unadjusted gaps in achievement at school entry are the sources of inferior economic outcomes in adulthood for both Hispanics and blacks.

Table 10-2. *Children's Reading and Mathematics Gaps*[a]
Standard deviation

Comparison categories	*Fall kindergarten*	*Spring grade 1*	*Spring grade 3*
Socioeconomic status			
Reading	0.300	0.277	0.294
Math	0.306	0.256	0.288
Black-white			
Reading	0.130	–0.078	–0.282
Math	–0.099	–0.279	–0.382
Hispanic-white			
Reading	–0.071	–0.014	–0.050
Math	–0.197	–0.122	–0.078

Source: Fryer and Levitt (2004b, tables 2 and 3).
a. Effect sizes control for age, birth weight, female, number of books, mother age, WIC benefits, teenage parent. $N = 11{,}201$.

Table 10-3. *Preschool Enrollments for Children Ages 3–5*
Percent

Group	*Enrollment*[a]
White	59
Black	64
Hispanic	40
Family income below poverty	47
Family income at or above poverty	59
Ages under 6	
White	26
Black	33
Hispanic	19
Family income below 100 percent poverty	23
Family income 100–200 percent poverty	20
Family income above 200 percent poverty	28
Head Start[b]	
White	27
Black	31
Hispanic	32

Sources: For children under 6, Magnuson and Waldfogel (2005, table 1); for Head Start, 2005 data from Head Start Bureau, U.S. Department of Health and Human Services (www.acf.hhs.gov/programs/ ohsb/).

a. Figures are for enrollment in center-based early childhood care and education programs in the United States.

b. Percentage of total enrollment of 905,000 children.

One possible explanation for such large gaps upon entry to school is that access to preschooling is less available to blacks, Hispanics, and children from families with fewer resources.[6] Yet as a result of changes since 1995, participation in preschooling has grown considerably. In 2005 just over half of 3-year-olds and two-thirds of 4-year-olds in the United States attended school.[7]

Table 10-3 shows the percentages of children ages 3 and 4 who are in early education programs across the United States. It shows that the simple story—that of limited access for disadvantaged groups—immediately needs qualification, at least for 4-year-olds. The evidence of current disparities cannot be

6. Fryer and Levitt (2004b) found weak evidence that school quality explained the gap, and no evidence for testing differences or influences across types of parental inputs. In comparing coefficients from their comprehensive analysis of kindergarten and first grade scores (Fryer and Levitt [2004a]), center-based care also appears to be relatively powerful.

7. Barnett and Belfield (2006).

attributable to an absence of preschooling. Indeed, black children are enrolled in Head Start at five times the rates of white children; for Hispanics, the rate is almost four to one.

Moreover, the effect of family income is complex. Although preschool enrollments rise with income, families with the lowest income levels are eligible for publicly funded preschooling. Hence the lowest rates of pre-K are found for children in families just above the poverty line. Income is therefore not a good indicator of participation.[8] Analysis of data from the National Household Expenditure Survey shows that mother's education is a much stronger indicator of preschool participation. Mothers who are high school dropouts enroll their children at considerably lower rates.

The relationship between income and preschool access is further muddied by the imperfect allocation of places. Although Head Start targets children in poverty, self-report data on program participation indicate that by the second half of the school year about half the children are not poor but "near poor." Some children have fallen out of eligibility, been granted exemptions, or been enrolled despite not meeting the criteria. Across the United States, there is tremendous variation by state. Children in the West, for example, are considerably less likely to receive pre-K schooling, independent of need.[9]

Of course access to preschooling does not mean that all children receive the same quality of provision. There is great variability among providers of programs and what they provide, not only in duration but also in educational content, regulations, and resources. The quality of programs may be lower for minority and disadvantaged children, or insufficiently high to offset the disadvantages of family background. These disparities are not easy to estimate.[10]

Broadly, existing public preschool programs go some way toward closing gaps.[11] For 4-year-olds, access could be widened, but many children are enrolled; for 3-year-olds, there is more scope simply to expand access to disadvantaged children. More important, to achieve equality in total investments during early childhood, it would be necessary to substantially upgrade the pre-K programs in which some children are already enrolled.

8. Fuller, Livas, and Bridges (2005) reported further complexity when race and income effects interacted in California.

9. Barnett and Belfield (2006).

10. State programs vary considerably (National Institute for Early Education Research [2005]). For data on children enrolled in myriad private programs, it is necessary to use the U.S. Census, but it does not disaggregate provision by either program type or quality.

11. Magnuson and Waldfogel (2005, p. 180) estimated that if Head Start were unavailable, blacks would be 9 percentage points less likely to enroll in pre-K, and Hispanics would be 31 percentage points less likely.

How Might Early Education Programs Improve Outcomes?

There are four pathways through which preschool education can affect later development.[12] The first is that preschooling generates a cognitive advantage for the child. This pathway is the most plausible and has been subjected to the most intensive testing. However, cognitive advantages typically fade out,[13] and the most disadvantaged need many other skills to advance through school successfully.

The second pathway is that preschooling enhances family support for the child. Preschool programs with home visits or parental participation are expected to change parenting practices and influence family functioning; they may even affect parental investments and expectations.[14] Health status may be included here. Dental caries, ear infections, and allergies are common, chronic childhood ailments, and preschool programs may include health and nutritional support to ameliorate them and help families cope.

The third pathway is that preschooling is the educational foundation for success in school. Preschooling may allow children to enter school better prepared, not so much giving them an academic advantage as making them more comfortable in educational settings and ensuring that they are in the optimal instructional setting.[15] The effect may be an artifact of the way children are screened or tracked. Children who are behind in kindergarten may be classified as having "specific learning disabilities" or "developmental delay" and may then be tracked into alternative educational paths for a number of years. They may also be more likely to face sanctions such as retention, suspension, and expulsion that can impede future educational progress.[16]

The fourth pathway is that preschooling provides early socialization into behaviors that are effective in later life. Preschooling may affect children's motivations and attitudes toward learning. This may encourage them to regard schooling as an opportunity for advancement.

Each of these pathways has been found to have some empirical support.[17] In practice the four are likely to be mutually reinforcing, so that collectively they add up to a significant and persistent developmental advantage.[18]

12. Ramey and Ramey (2004); Reynolds and others (2001).

13. See Currie (2001); Lee and Loeb (1995).

14. On ethnic differences in parenting efficacy, see Brooks-Gunn and Markham (2005).

15. For example, survey data from more than 2,500 public school teachers indicate that 62 percent (strongly) agree that "pre-kindergarten is an important pre-condition for success in kindergarten" (Belfield [2005a]).

16. Annually, 13 percent of black students are suspended from school for disciplinary reasons (Wald and Losen [2003]).

17. Reynolds and others (2002).

18. Economists might argue that adults respond to immediate incentives. The tendency to engage in juvenile crime, for example, depends on the immediate costs and benefits of the act. But the costs are

Does Early Education Close the Initial Gap?

There is strong evidence that pre-K programs could close the gap upon entry to school if allocated to at-risk children who are either not served or are in low quality programs. Such programs are effective in comparison with alternative environments for children.[19]

Barnett and Belfield have summarized the results from the large number of studies and literature reviews on the short-term benefits of pre-K.[20] The average initial effect on cognitive abilities is 0.5 standard deviation above the mean score; for behavioral outcomes, the effects are smaller but still positive. When one adjusts for the quality of the study, the effects are somewhat smaller. Family support programs yield a gain of 0.1 standard deviation for cognitive and social development. "Two-generation" programs for mothers and children also yield small gains,[21] although nurse home visitations appear to be more effective.[22] Thus, influencing child development indirectly through parents appears to be relatively ineffective, in part because the programs are not intensive.

Child care studies find that in comparison with home and other types of care, center-based care generates a gain of 0.10 to 0.33 standard deviation above the mean for cognitive abilities.[23] State-wide programs also yield achievement advantages.[24] Participants in Oklahoma's universal program showed strong academic gains (of 16 percent) in overall language and cognitive skills tests.For Tulsa school children, Gormley and Gayer reported that preschooling increased cognitive and knowledge scores by approximately 0.24 standard deviation, motor skills by the same figure, and language scores by 0.38 standard deviation.[25] Similarly positive—but less powerful—academic effects are found in evaluations of the universal pre-K program in Georgia.[26]

---

based on a series of cumulative events that have shaped the child's options to that point. An alternative economic explanation for expecting beneficial effects could assume borrowing constraints for low-income families such that they do not invest optimally in preschool.

19. See Campbell and Ramey (1994, 1995); Currie and Thomas (1995); Johnson and Walker (1991); Karoly and others (1998); McCarton and others (1997); Montes and others (2003); Ramey and Ramey (2004); Reynolds, Ou, and Topitzes (2004); Reynolds and Robertson (2003); Reynolds, Temple, and Ou (2003); Reynolds and others (2001, 2002).

20. Barnett and Belfield (2006).

21. St. Pierre and Layzer (1999).

22. Olds and others (1999).

23. Barnett and Belfield (2006).

24. Gilliam and Zigler (2004) cataloged the developmental competence measures used in state-level evaluations. However, many state-level evaluations are inadequate to identify causal effects.

25. Gormley and Gayer (2005).

26. Universal pre-K programs might generate peer effects on achievement. However, the evidence is mixed. Henry and Rickman (2007) found strong peer effects on value-added achievement for the universal pre-K program in Georgia.

Achievement gains are also evident in analyses using the ECLS-K data set. On initial reading and math tests in kindergarten, children in center-based care earned the highest scores in comparisons with children who received preschooling care from parents, relatives, or nonrelatives or in mixed settings. In their broad specification, Fryer and Levitt found the effects of center-based preschooling to be extremely large, even exceeding those of a one standard deviation increase in socioeconomic status.[27] Magnuson and others found that pre-K attendance raised math and reading scores by 0.1 standard deviation at school entry; for children from low-income families these academic gains persisted into first grade.[28] Puzzlingly, they also found that pre-K education had adverse effects on self-control and externalizing behavior.[29] But these behaviors do not correlate strongly with later academic performance.

A wide range of effects measures exist for Head Start. The best were provided by a recent national randomized trial. The magnitude of estimates for immediate effects of one year of Head Start was quite small, at 0.10–0.24 standard deviation for standardized measures of language and cognitive abilities.[30] This echoes findings from the Early Head Start randomized trial, in which cognitive and language effects were 0.1 standard deviation or smaller.[31] Both Head Start and Early Head Start randomized trials have yielded small decreases in antisocial behavior, about 0.1 standard deviation in magnitude, and there is no evidence at all in Head Start studies of negative effects on social and emotional development.[32]

Evidence for the effects of more intensive interventions up to the age of school entry comes from the two randomized trials that have been carried out with disadvantaged populations, the Perry Preschool Program and the Abecedarian Early Childhood Intervention. In these studies, the estimated effects of the programs on cognitive and language abilities ranged from 0.75 to 1.50 standard deviation—at least twice as large as the effects of the better state preschool programs and eight times larger than the effects of Early Head Start and Head Start.[33]

27. Fryer and Levitt (2004a, table A2).

28. Magnuson and others (2004).

29. See Magnuson, Ruhm, and Waldfogel (2007).

30. Garces, Thomas, and Currie (2002); NICHD and Duncan (2003).

31. Love and others (2001).

32. The Head Start study did not estimate the effect of Head Start relative to no program but relative to whatever experiences children received otherwise. The percentage remaining at home was remarkably high, perhaps because of the way the sample was selected (in situations of excess demand for Head Start). However, effect estimates that were adjusted for participation in other programs did not differ appreciably from simple estimates.

33. In the older studies the estimates might be somewhat larger, because the control group had little access to alternative services. Even in the Abecedarian study, however, the control group had considerable access to center-based child care, so that change in control group experience is unlikely to have much influence on comparisons with more recent studies.

The Perry Preschool study also found that program participation had a positive effect on social behavior in the first year of school. In contrast, the Abecedarian study, which looked at intensive education through full-day child care over five years, found negative effects on social behavior at school entry, although these were transitory. Across all studies of early education interventions, intensive research programs, and large-scale public programs including Head Start, the estimated short-term effects average 0.25 to 0.40 standard deviation across domains such as self-esteem and problem behavior. It is difficult to assess the extent to which these measurements reflect a real difference in outcomes between these programs and typical child care or are simply artifacts of research design. However, the Abecedarian study results are suggestive that the effects are related to program differences.

Some evidence shows fade-out of achievement gains.[34] In rebuttal, pre-K may set children on a different trajectory as "skills beget skills."[35] More emphatically, as I show later, research does not show behavioral fade-out. This discrepancy could reflect measurement error in tests or more rapid progression of high-achieving students. The most plausible resolution is that pre-K benefits are not restricted to gains in test scores.

To address inequities, it is critical to establish either that high quality programs produce strong returns—on the assumption that such programs could be targeted at the most disadvantaged—or that programs are differentially effective, such that children from disadvantaged backgrounds benefit from them most.

Clearly, the differences in outcomes between well-funded model programs and generic state programs suggest that higher quality programs are more effective. (The attributes of high quality programs include better prepared and higher paid teachers, smaller class sizes, teacher-parent interactions, and teachers' aides.) Other studies have found that higher program quality, measured in various ways, may lead to small improvements (0.04–0.08 standard deviation) in cognitive and language ability and in behavior.[36] Similarly, looking at Head Start, Currie and Neidell found evidence that increased spending generated enhanced outcomes, although they were unable to identify the categories of increased spending that most raised effectiveness.[37]

As for differential effects, Barnett and Belfield concluded that pre-K programs appeared to be most effective for those who were most disadvantaged, although there was little evidence about the effects of intensive educational

34. Currie and Thomas (1995); Lee and Loeb (1995).
35. Carneiro and Heckman (2003).
36. NICHD and Duncan (2003).
37. Currie and Neidell (2007).

interventions on children from middle-income or even highly advantaged families.[38] Perhaps most promising have been results showing differential effectiveness in the Oklahoma pre-K program. The effects for black and Hispanic children were two and four times as large, respectively, as those for whites, with effects evident only for those in receipt of free or reduced-price lunches.[39]

Finally, Loeb and others examined the effects of duration (years) and intensity (hours per year) of pre-K schooling.[40] Their results offered mixed support for either returns on quality or differential effectiveness. Longer durations produced a greater advantage in reading and math (the greatest benefit was for children starting at ages 2 and 3), but the results did not vary across income groups or races. However, for black and Hispanic children, some intensity (15–30 hours per week) raised student achievement to the same extent as full intensity (30+ hours per week). In contrast, for low-income children and white children, the rate of learning increased with the number of hours of instruction.

Does Early Education Reduce Disparities during Childhood?

Even if the achievement advantage from preschooling appears to fade out after a few years, a set of more general advantages is maintained. These advantages have been identified using high quality randomized field trials, sibling comparisons, and matched-pair analyses and with longitudinal data.[41]

The durable effects of preschooling on educational performance are reported in table 10-4. Model pre-K programs show extremely powerful effects over the long term.[42] There are significant reductions in special educational placement and grade retention. Pre-K participation reduces high school dropout rates dramatically. High school completion rates are higher for Head Start children, as is college progression, although these effects hold only for white children in Head Start.

Table 10-5 shows the differences in adolescent and adult behavior between children who went to preschool and an appropriate comparison group. Former preschoolers exhibit lower rates of teenage parenting, health problems, abortions, child abuse or neglect, and criminal activity. These behaviors all have durable effects on economic well-being. In addition, table 10-6 shows the effects of preschooling on earnings (present values). These are strong for the model programs but undetectable for Head Start.

38. Barnett and Belfield (2006).
39. Gormley and Gayer (2005).
40. Loeb and others (2007).
41. For discussion, see Barnett (2005).
42. For details on these programs, see Barnett (2004).

Table 10-4. *Effects of Early Childhood Interventions on Educational Performance*
Percent

Variable and program	*Change resulting from participation in program*
Special education placement	
Abecedarian Early Childhood Intervention (ABC)	–8
Perry Preschool Program (PPP)	–43
Chicago Child-Parent Centers (CPC)	–32
Head Start	–28
Retained in grade	
ABC	–47
PPP	–13
CPC	–33
Early Childhood Longitudinal Study—Kindergarten (ECLS-K)	Negative effect
High school dropout likelihood	
ABC	–32
PPP	–25
CPC	–24
High school completion	
Head Start: white children	+20
Head Start: African American children	No clear effect
College progression	
Enrollment in four-year college (ABC)	3 times as likely
PPP	No clear effect
Head Start: white children	+28
Head Start: African American children	No clear effect

Sources: Belfield and others (2006); Centers for Disease Control and Prevention (2002); Currie (2001); Garces, Thomas, and Currie (2002); Masse and Barnett (2002); Reynolds and others (2002); Temple, Reynolds, and Miedel (2000).

Is Early Childhood Education a Good Investment for the State?

Preschooling clearly delivers significant private benefits, as shown by the studies I have cited. But the public effect of pre-K may be just as important. For example, preschooling may have an important effect on state budgets by reducing crime or reliance on welfare. Such public benefits play a central role in any effort to measure the rate of return on investments in pre-K programs.

Table 10-5. *Effects of Early Childhood Interventions on Adolescent and Adult Behaviors*
Percent

Behavior	*Control or comparison group*	*Group receiving early childhood program*
Teenage parenting		
Abecedarian Early Childhood Intervention (ABC)	45	26
Perry Preschool Program (PPP)	37	26
Chicago Child-Parent Centers (CPC)	27	20
Well-being		
Health problem (PPP)	29	20
Drug use (ABC)	39	18
Needed treatment for addiction (PPP)	34	22
Abortion (PPP)	38	16
Abuse or neglect by age 17 (CPC)	9	6
Criminal activity		
Felony violent assault (PPP)	0.37	0.17
Juvenile court petition (CPC)	25	16
Booked or charged with a crime (Head Start)	. . .	–12

Sources: Belfield and others (2006); Garces, Thomas, and Currie (2002); Masse and Barnett (2002); Reynolds and others (2002).

I use a balance sheet approach to evaluate whether pre-K is a worthwhile investment for the state. On one side is the cost of the program, with details about its ingredients (for example, teacher quality, class size, curricula). On the other side are the benefits, which may be classified according to agency (local, state, or federal government, society, or private individual) and the time frame of the program (short, medium, or long term). For example, where preschool reduces rates of special education, it generates savings for both state governments and the federal government, because each contributes funding for special education programs. Economic studies compare the costs with the discounted benefits to estimate whether pre-K is a good investment when gains only to the general public (and not to the private individual) are counted.

For the general public, there are gains in terms of expenditure savings as schools become more efficient (fewer grade repeaters and special education students; table 10-4); cost savings through reduced need for criminal justice system expenditures (table 10-5); income tax revenues from parents' released time; and income tax revenues as participants earn more (table 10-6).

Table 10-6. *Effects of Early Childhood Interventions on Present-Value Earnings*
Dollars

Program	*Net earnings gain for participant in early childhood program*
Abecedarian Early Childhood Intervention	35,531
Perry Preschool Program	38,892
Chicago Child-Parent Centers	30,638
Head Start	No effect

Sources: Belfield and others (2006); Centers for Disease Control and Prevention (2002); Currie (2001); Garces, Thomas and Currie (2002); Masse and Barnett (2002); Reynolds and others (2002).

Table 10-7 summarizes the results from the available cost-benefit studies of small-scale, high quality pre-K programs. For the three complete cases—the Abecedarian Early Childhood Intervention, the Perry Preschool Program, and the Chicago Child-Parent Centers—the general fiscal benefits are more than sufficient to pay for the costs of provision. The benefits are spread across the various domains.[43] They are also estimated conservatively; as shown in table 10-5, pre-K affects general behavior and the prevalence of risk factors associated with problem conditions.[44] For example, health gains are associated with improved access to screening, immunization, and nutrition through preschool. The Centers for Disease Control and Prevention reported that the effect size for social risks after preschooling was –0.41; the gain in health screening rates was 44 percent.[45] These effects in turn reduce a child's reliance on health support services and welfare programs. Such savings, however, are not typically included in cost-benefit analyses.[46]

Several studies have extrapolated from the micro-evidence to estimate the economic consequences of large-scale preschool programs.[47] These studies calibrate the effects of model programs and apply those effects to large proportions of a given age cohort. State-level data are applied to calculate the costs

43. The benefits are not just a consequence of the lower crime rates of participants. Crime savings do represent 65 percent of total savings for the Perry Preschool Program, but 28 percent for the Chicago Child-Parent Centers (CPC) and 0 percent for the Abecedarian Early Childhood Intervention (ABC). Earnings savings range from 23 percent for ABC to 58 percent for CPC.

44. Johnson and Walker (1991); McCarton and others (1997).

45. Centers for Disease Control and Prevention (2002); see Smokowski and others (2004).

46. Other benefits, such as intergenerational benefits, are difficult to identify causally, even as they apply to the domains of crime, earnings, and welfare, as well as to education and general family life (Belfield [2004b]). Lower adult welfare expenditures are also itemized as a benefit from pre-K. Economically, this is unimportant: welfare differences are not substantial across pre-K children and control groups, and discounted welfare payments are not large sums.

47. Belfield (2005a, 2005c); Karoly and Bigelow (2005); Lynch (2004).

Table 10-7. Cost-Benefit Analyses of Preschool Programs

Program	*Cost-benefit results for state or society*
Abecedarian Early Childhood Intervention	Every $1 investment returns $2–$3.66
Perry Preschool Program	Every $1 investment returns $5.67
Chicago Child-Parent Centers	Every $1 investment returns $7.14
Head Start	Short- and medium-term benefits offset 40–60 percent of total costs

Sources: Belfield and others (2006); Currie (2001); Masse and Barnett (2002); Reynolds and others (2001).

and resulting benefits of investment in preschooling.[48] Each model finds that large-scale programs should generate positive net present values at a 5 percent discount rate. Although the reductions in crime associated with pre-K must be emphasized if universal pre-K programs are to yield high returns, the benefits of pre-K appear to be widespread across domains.[49] Taxpayer savings and societal gains appear to be substantial.

What is more, investment in preschooling can promote important goals that are difficult to capture in dollar-equivalent terms. For example, investing in preschool may increase intergenerational socioeconomic mobility by causing more children from poorer families to go to college. In a four-period model of parent-child investments, Restuccia and Urrutia measured intergenerational mobility contingent on public expenditures on elementary-secondary and higher education.[50] Using their model results, and assuming an increase in public spending on early education of $90 billion (sufficient funding for preschooling for all children in the United States for approximately two years), intergenerational earnings correlations should fall from 0.40 to 0.36, and intergenerational education correlations should fall from 0.35 to 0.28, indicating an increase in mobility.[51] These results, however, are driven

48. Karoly and Bigelow (2005) calibrated benefits using CPC data. Belfield (2005c) assumed that only high school dropouts would generate the majority of social benefits.

49. Importantly, recent evidence shows that the potential returns on additional education may be increasing, because the rate of placement in special education is growing, public school costs are rising in real terms, and the costs of incarceration are also rising.

50. Restuccia and Urrutia (2004).

51. Relative to the effects of other educational investments, these effects appear substantial. Restuccia and Urrutia (2004) showed that spending on higher education would have zero or even a negative effect on intergenerational earnings correlations (the effect on intergenerational education was mixed). College subsidies cannot influence students' ability to graduate from college, and credit constraints on educational investments occur at a much younger age (Cameron and Heckman [1999]).

mainly by the equalization of college enrollment rates for the three middle-income quintiles; increasing spending on preschool does little to raise educational attainment for the lowest quintile.

In rebuttal to these arguments, the obvious counter to investing in preschooling is that there may be better investment alternatives. If most of the benefits of pre-K are mediated through lower rates of high school dropout, then why not address dropout directly with programs for youths that will take effect within two to three years? If most of the state benefits are mediated through crime, then why not improve policing systems so that acts of crime are less likely? On the basis of current evidence, a plausible answer to both questions is that there is no proven alternative program that has such beneficial effects.[52]

An equally important concern is that bureaucratic politics or procedures may make it difficult to capture some of the benefits associated with preschooling or to match those against the necessary investments. The returns on pre-K depend in large part on cost savings from reduced pressure on other programs, such as special education. In order for these gains to be realized, budget allocations for special education must fall along with the need for services. This may not happen: government funds are allocated in part using historical formulas, and government agencies may be reluctant to accept reduced budgets regardless of need. Such inertia applies to many investments, but it is particularly salient for an investment that is reliant on cost savings.

A related concern is that pre-K yields benefits to many separate levels of government (federal versus state and local) and agencies (Department of Education versus criminal justice system versus child welfare). As each level and agency benefits, it should contribute to the financing of pre-K in proportion to the size of the benefits. Yet this coordination may be inoperable. The danger, then, is that even if pre-K is a strong investment, it is insufficiently worthwhile for a Department of Education to allocate enough funds to it.

The Effects of Preschooling on Equity

There appears to be a strong efficiency justification for investing in preschooling. But will this investment reduce educational and social inequalities? The answer depends critically on how the provision of preschooling is organized,

52. On dropouts, see Rumberger (2004). A series of cost-benefit analyses for many government programs in the state of Washington was reported by Aos and others (2004). Although pre-K ranked highly, other programs had higher returns. However, the quality of the evidence for pre-K was much better than that for many other proposed policies. First, pre-K programs had high quality costs data; for many of the comparators, Aos and others (2004) used program prices (not costs). Second, pre-K programs generated

and particularly on whether public provision is targeted to certain children or provided universally.

In theory, programs targeted to those who are most disadvantaged would satisfy equity goals most directly. A targeted program would obviously generate benefits for those who enrolled. However, many of those who would newly enroll would either be white, meaning that simple racial differences would largely be preserved (table 10-3), or in the lower-middle quartile of income distribution, meaning that the genuinely worst off would not benefit from program expansions. Moreover, identifying these new enrollees and exhorting them to participate might not be easy.[53] Screening, regulating, and monitoring eligibility would also be costly. Unit costs are therefore likely to increase, and as I discuss later, a financing constraint will bind. Instead, because many low-income and minority children are already in Head Start pre-K programs, redressing inequities would require the upgrading of existing provision. It is also important to recognize the positive returns to the taxpayer from investments in pre-K, which mean that even if a targeted program is funded by high-income families, those families should not experience an increase in their net taxes.

Magnuson and Waldfogel simulated the effects on achievement of the expansion of pre-K programs.[54] Expanding the enrollment of black and Hispanic children to 80 percent (that is, one-third higher than the rate for white children) would close the initial gap by 4 to 20 percent for black children and 12 to 52 percent for Hispanic children. However, race-specific policies are likely to be difficult to implement. Expanding enrollment to cover all children below the poverty line would reduce the black-white gap by at most 12 percent and the Hispanic-white gap by at most 16 percent. If the cutoff is twice the poverty line, the reductions are 12 percent and 38 percent, respectively.

The alternative is to offer a universal pre-K program for all children. Inequalities might still be reduced, because program effects for low-income and

---

an array of benefits that other programs did not appear to generate. Of course the justification for investing in pre-K is that it yields a high return relative to other educational options that might be implemented. It is not essential to establish that pre-K is the best investment, but only that it yields a positive net present value.

53. Families will have to invest resources even if provision is publicly provided. Even with zero fees, some families do not enroll, so presumably the costs and inconvenience of enrollment must outweigh the benefits. It is possible that an informational problem exists: families do not appreciate the benefits of preschooling. The more likely explanation is that pre-K is inconvenient for many families or that even relatively small direct expenses (such as for transportation) are too much. (Scrivner and Wolfe [2003, p. 10] estimated average parental payments in 1996 at $3,726; families were investing in pre-K for their children.)

54. Magnuson and Waldfogel (2005).

minority children are larger than those for advantaged children. The forgoing evidence suggests that pre-K programs are differentially effective across race and socioeconomic status; at issue is the strength of the differential. Magnuson and Waldfogel found pre-K to be equity enhancing for Hispanic children but not for black children.[55] Moreover, public funding would generate an income effect for advantaged families; any reduction in inequalities caused by differential program effects would be offset, if not cancelled out, by additional private gains to higher income families.

The dilemma here is that there may be an efficiency-equity trade-off. A targeted program would have a greater effect on inequities, but it would not generate as high a return. Steven Barnett compared the returns on universal and targeted programs and found that the former were likely to yield the highest returns.[56] A program that is perfectly targeted at the lowest family income quintile would generate enough fiscal surplus to fund a universal program, even if the other four quintiles generated no savings. And if a program targeted at the lowest quintile was only 50 percent accurate (that is, half the participants were not actually from the lowest quintile), then it would generate smaller returns than a universal program. In addition, universal programs are much more likely to garner political support and generate spillover benefits.[57]

Assuming that in general pre-K programs reduce inequities, it remains to be determined whether these programs can be afforded and which specific ingredients should be included in them. The question "What does pre-K cost?" is difficult to answer. Pre-K is an investment, and potentially any amount could be invested, the appropriate amount depending on the size of the benefits. It might be expected that tailored programs with specific sets of ingredients would average costs that could be set down. But these costs will vary across states, across localities (urban, rural), according to local wage rates, and according to the availability of facilities (public, private). Factors such as class size and economies of scale will also affect costs. Where pre-K program ingredients are not exactly prescribed, costs will vary according to the way the program is delivered. Hence, costs may not be easily estimated.[58] And limited information exists

55. Magnuson and Waldfogel (2005, table 2).

56. Barnett (2005, table 4).

57. Belfield (2005c).

58. Many pre-K programs exist in different settings, and these require either expansion or upgrading. Little information exists on how unit costs might change. Marshall and others (2002) estimated upgraded provision costs at 27 percent more for Massachusetts. For California the figure was 51 percent (Muenchow and others [2004]), and for Head Start, 11 percent. Settings matter even for model programs: the ABC, or Abecedarian, program is one-sixth more expensive in a public school center than in a child care development center (Masse and Barnett [2002]). Also, cost accounting information is poor.

about marginal costs as participation rates rise. The relationship between expenditures and enrollment numbers is not helpful, because quality is not constant.[59] Building new capacity for pre-K may require high fixed costs.[60]

These difficulties notwithstanding, a number of researchers have investigated the costs of pre-K, others have reported expenditures from state pre-K programs, and the unit costs of tailored programs are available. The typical annual investment per child can therefore be estimated, as summarized in table 10-8. Expenditures across state pre-K programs averaged $3,470 per child in 2004, considerably less than the figures for Head Start and first grade in public schools.[61] For the three field-trial programs considered here, annual costs per child ranged from $4,900 to $13,900 in 2002 dollars.

Economic models of pre-K typically assume that a year of pre-K costs between $4,500 and $6,500 per child. For California, Muenchow and others estimated the cost of universal, full-day pre-K at $4,671 to $5,375.[62] In a separate study for California, Karoly and Bigelow applied unit costs of $5,700 per child.[63] If the program includes a child care component, however, unit costs rise to $12,205.

Clearly, in comparison with specific programs, Head Start, and public schooling, investment as part of state pre-K programs is relatively small. For budgeting purposes it might be appropriate to assume that one year of part-day pre-K can be funded for $6,000 per child, or at least that this is a maximum amount taxpayers would be willing to pay. This is probably a suboptimal investment in terms of potential returns, but even this amount is far more than most states appear willing to invest in preschool programs, judging from current spending levels.[64]

Budget documents use very general terms such as "direct services to children" (Governor's Task Force [2002]). A costing template that prescribes the specific ingredients for different pre-K programs, states, and cities is available but is rarely used (Barnett and Kelley [2002]).

59. No large enterprise has taken over the market (see Helburn and Bergmann [2002]; on inelastic supply in California, see PACE [2002]). Therefore, extra supply will require significantly more funding.

60. Gill, Dembosky, and Caulkins (2002) reported very high fixed costs in Pennsylvania.

61. See Magnuson, Ruhm, and Waldfogel (2006); National Child Care Information Center (2004); National Institute for Early Education Research (2005).

62. Muenchow and others (2004); see also Golin, Mitchell, and Gault (2003); Marshall and others (2002).

63. Karoly and Bigelow (2005).

64. A range of financing options is possible. Ryan and Heise (2002) argued for a voucher system. Scrivner and Wolfe (2003) itemized the types of funding that might be considered for pre-K, distinguishing between foundation programs (state allocations based on an amount of per student funding to districts from state and local contributions) and categorical programs (with funding for a specific service). Together with funding mechanisms, studies of equity must take into account the burden of financing in relation to tax systems. Such discussions are beyond the scope of this chapter.

Table 10-8. *Estimated Expenditures and Unit Costs of Pre-K Programs*
Dollars

Source	*Annual expenditure or unit cost per enrolled child*
Pre-K expenditures	
All states with pre-K	3,470
Two states with universal pre-K (Georgia, Oklahoma)	3,096
Ten highest-funded states with pre-K	5,476
Comparable expenditures	
Head Start	7,100
First grade in public schools	8,600
Program costs per year	
Abecedarian Early Childhood Intervention	13,900
Perry Pre-School Program	9,800
Chicago Child-Parent Centers	4,900
Economic models (range)[a]	4,500–12,205

a. Belfield (2004a, 2005a, 2005b); Karoly and Bigelow (2005); Muenchow and others (2004).

The second significant concern relates to program ingredients: What should the pre-K program include? It is unclear which particular types of pre-K offer the best investment. Existing programs vary considerably in timing, duration, content, resources, and management. Gilliam and Zigler rightly concluded that "evaluations almost never attempt to address fundamental questions regarding what types of pre-kindergarten services work best and under what conditions of implementation."[65] Even when researchers identify successful programs, it remains unclear whether they could be implemented to the same effect in different settings.

In principle, it should at least be possible to adjudicate between full-day and half-day programs, between Head Start and center-based programs, between well-resourced and poorly resourced programs, and between one-year and multiyear programs. Evidence on these issues remains fragmentary, however, and the effects that are found often require qualification. As a start, current child care options might be improved. As Ramey and Ramey noted, many programs do not include preservice training for teachers, are not very intensive, are reme-

65. Gilliam and Zigler (2004, p. 38).

dial rather than preventive, and are aimed at supporting families as much as children.[66] Some have argued that the content of these programs should include more general provision (for example, nurse home visitation).[67] Others maintain that only intensive, long-lasting programs that engage both children and families will ameliorate the most adverse outcomes (for example, child abuse).[68] Or, if pre-K programs are not full-year or full-day, their usefulness will be limited for Head Start–eligible families who need workday child care.[69]

Philip DeCicca found that full-day kindergarten generated academic advantages over half-day programs in the first few years, but these advantages faded out after a few years. In their simulations, Magnuson and Waldfogel found that upgrading all types of existing preschooling had no effect on gaps across ethnic groups.[70] Improving the quality of Head Start reduced racial gaps by at most 10 percent for black children and 8 percent for Hispanic children. And although Currie and Neidell found evidence that increased spending did generate enhanced outcomes, an additional $1,600 per children (or 35 percent more funding) would be necessary to eliminate reading and vocabulary gaps across children.[71] The cost consequences for more intensive pre-K programs, as described by Loeb and others, have not been calculated.[72] But these costing exercises leave unknown the extent to which successful programs could be implemented to the same effect in different settings and whether it is feasible to operate a licensing or accreditation system that maintains quality control over time to ensure that standards are maintained.

In short, it remains to be established that model programs exist whose implementation would meet goals of efficiency and equity and that political willingness to allocate funds for such programs exists.

Conclusion

The simple pre-K story faces challenges. Important elements of the story hold true: preschooling programs do have long-lasting effects on behaviors, especially for the most disadvantaged, and these effects are strongly predictive of

66. Ramey and Ramey (2004).
67. See Olds and others (1999).
68. Reynolds and others (2002).
69. As found by Chang and others (2007).
70. DeCicca (forthcoming).
71. Currie and Neidell (2007).
72. Loeb and others (2007).

adult well-being. (Even here, though, the effects are weakest for Head Start, the program catering to the most disadvantaged.) In consequence, pre-K programs yield clear net positive returns on public investments. By raising economic well-being and reducing public expenditures, they represent an attractive investment to reduce the economic burden of inadequate education.

But delivering on the promise of pre-K is far from simple. Existing programs already play a sizable—although far from complete—role in redressing differences in access to early childhood education. To reduce inequalities would therefore require reorganizing current programs as much as expanding enrollments to underserved populations. Yet the evidence to guide such reorganizations is far from complete, and the funding to implement them adequately may not be forthcoming.

References

Aos, Steve, and others. 2004. *Benefits and Costs of Prevention and Early Intervention Programs for Youth*. Policy Brief 04-07-3901. Olympia: Washington State Institute for Public Policy (www.wsipp.wa.gov/rptfiles/04-07-3901.pdf).

Barnett, W. Steven. 2004. "An Overview of the Returns on Investments in Quality Preschool Programs." Rutgers University, National Institute for Early Education Research (nieer.org/resources/files/PreschoolInvestmentReturns.pdf).

———. 2005. "Maximizing Returns from Prekindergarten Education." Federal Reserve Bank of Cleveland.

Barnett, W. Steven, and Clive R. Belfield. 2006. "Early Childhood Development and Social Mobility." *Future of Children* 16, no. 2: 73–98.

Barnett, W. Steven, and Pamela J. Kelley. 2002. *Measuring Preschool Costs and Revenues: Issues and Answers. A Summary Report of the 2002 Early Education Cost Symposium.* Rutgers University, National Institute for Early Education Research.

Belfield, Clive R. 2004a. "Early Childhood Education: How Important Are the Cost-Savings to the School System?" Working paper. Albany: Winning Beginning New York.

———. 2004b. "Intergenerational Benefits from Investments in pre-K." Working paper. Washington, D.C.: Committee for Economic Development.

———. 2005a. "Should Ohio Invest in Universal Preschooling?" Federal Reserve Bank of Cleveland.

———. 2005b. "Investments in 4K in Wisconsin." Working paper. Washington, D.C.: Pre-K Now.

———. 2005c. "The Fiscal Impacts of Universal pre-K: Case Study Evidence from Four States." Working paper. Washington, D.C.: Invest in Kids Working Group.

Belfield, Clive R., and others. 2006. "Cost-Benefit Analysis of the High/Scope Perry Preschool Program Using Age Forty Follow-up Data." *Journal of Human Resources* 41, no. 1: 162–90.

Brooks-Gunn, Jeanne, and Lisa B. Markham. 2005. "The Contribution of Parenting to Ethnic and Racial Gaps in School Readiness." *Future of Children* 15, no. 1: 139–68.

Cameron, Stephen, and James Heckman. 1999. "Can Tuition Policy Combat Rising Wage Inequality?" In *Financing College Tuition: Government Policies and Educational Priorities,* edited by Marvin Kosters, pp. 76–124. Washington, D.C.: AEI Press.

Campbell, Frances A., and Craig T. Ramey. 1994. "Effects of Early Intervention on Intellectual and Academic Ability: A Follow-up Study of Children from Low-Income Families." *Child Development* 65, no. 2: 684–98.

———. 1995. "Cognitive and School Outcomes for High-Risk African American Students at Middle Adolescence: Positive Effects at Early Intervention." *American Educational Research Journal* 32, no. 4: 743–72.

Carneiro, Pedro, and James J. Heckman. 2003. "Human Capital Policy." In *Inequality in America: What Role for Human Capital Policies?* edited by James J. Heckman and Alan B. Krueger, pp. 77–239. MIT Press.

Centers for Disease Control and Prevention. 2002. "Community Interventions to Promote Healthy Social Environments: Early Childhood Development and Family Housing." *Morbidity and Mortality Weekly Report* 51, no. RR01 (February 1): 1–8.

Chang, Young Eun, and others. 2007. "The Effects of Welfare and Employment Programs on Children's Participation in Head Start." *Economics of Education Review* 26, no. 1: 17–32.

Currie, Janet. 2001. "Early Childhood Programs." *Journal of Economic Perspectives* 15, no. 2: 213–38.

Currie, Janet, and Matthew Neidell. 2007. "Getting Inside the 'Black Box' of Head Start Quality: What Matters and What Doesn't." *Economics of Education Review* 26, no. 1: 83–99.

Currie, Janet, and Duncan Thomas. 1995. "Does Head Start Make a Difference?" *American Economic Review* 85, no. 3: 341–64.

DeCicca, Philip. 2007. "Does Full-Day Kindergarten Matter? Evidence from the First Two Years of Schooling." *Economics of Education Review* 26, no. 1: 66–82.

Fryer, Roland G., and Steven D. Levitt. 2004a. "Understanding the Black-White Test Score Gap in the First Two Years of School." *Review of Economics and Statistics* 86, no. 2: 447–64.

———. 2004b. "The Black-White Test Score Gap through Third Grade." Harvard University.

Fuller, Bruce, Alexandra Livas, and Margaret Bridges. 2005. "How to Expand and Improve Preschool in California: Ideals, Evidence, and Policy Options." Working Paper 05-01. PACE (Policy Analysis for California Education), University of California, Berkeley.

Garces, Eliana, Duncan Thomas, and Janet Currie. 2002. "Longer-term Effects of Head Start." *American Economic Review* 92, no. 4: 999–1012.

Gill, Brian P., Jacob W. Dembosky, and Jonathan P. Caulkins. 2002. *A "Noble Bet" in Early Care and Education: Lessons from One Community's Experience.* Santa Monica, Calif.: RAND.

Gilliam, Walter S., and Edward F. Zigler. 2004. "State Efforts to Evaluate the Effects of Prekindergarten: 1977–2003." Working paper. Yale University Child Study Center.

Golin, Stacie Carolyn, Anne W. Mitchell, and Barbara Gault. 2003. *The Price of School Readiness: A Tool for Estimating the Cost of Universal Preschool in the States.* Working paper. Washington, D.C.: Institute for Women's Policy Research (www.iwpr.org/pdf/G713.pdf).

Gormley, William T., and Ted Gayer. 2005. "Promoting School Readiness in Oklahoma: An Evaluation of Tulsa's pre-K program." *Journal of Human Resources* 40, no. 3: 533–58.

Governor's Task Force on Universal Access to Preschools. 2002. *Ready, Set, Grow: Illinois Preschool—A Framework for Universal Access to Quality Preschool in Illinois.* Springfield, Ill.: Office of the Governor.

Helburn, Suzanne, and Barbara Bergmann. 2002. *America's Child Care Problem.* New York: Palgrave.

Henry, Gary T., and Dana K. Rickman. 2007. "Do Peers Influence Children's Skill Development in Preschool?" *Economics of Education Review* 26 (1): 100–12.

Johnson, Dale L., and Todd Walker. 1991. "A Follow-up Evaluation of the Houston Parent Child Development Center: School Performance." *Journal of Early Intervention* 15, no. 3: 226–36.

Karoly, Lynn A., and James H. Bigelow. 2005. *The Economics of Investing in Universal Preschool Education in California.* Pittsburgh, Pa.: RAND.

Karoly, Lynn A., and others. 1998. *Investing in Our Children: What We Know and Don't Know about the Costs and Benefits of Early Childhood Interventions.* Santa Monica, Calif.: RAND.

Lee, Valerie, and Susanna Loeb. 1995. "Where Do Head Start Attendees End Up? One Reason Why Preschool Effects Fade Out." *Educational Evaluation and Policy Analysis* 17 (1): 62–82.

Loeb, Susanna, and others. 2007. "How Much Is Too Much? The Influence of Preschool Centers on Children's Social and Cognitive Development." *Economics of Education Review* 26 (1): 52–66.

Love, John M., and others. 2001. "Early Head Start Research: Building Their Futures: How Early Head Start Programs Are Enhancing the Lives of Infants and Toddlers in Low-Income Families." Princeton, N.J.: Mathematica Policy Research.

Lynch, Robert G. 2004. *Exceptional Returns: Economic, Fiscal, and Social Benefits of Investment in Early Childhood Development.* Washington, D.C.: Economic Policy Institute.

Magnuson, Katherine A., Christopher J. Ruhm, and Jane Waldfogel. 2006. "Does Prekindergarten Improve School Preparation and Performance?" *Economics of Education Review* 26, no. 1: 33–51.

Magnuson, Katherine A., and Jane Waldfogel. 2005. "Early Childhood Care and Education: Effects on Ethnic and Racial Gaps in School Readiness." *Future of Children* 15, no. 1: 169–88.

Magnuson, Katherine A., and others. 2004. "Inequality in Preschool Education and School Readiness." *American Educational Research Journal* 41, no. 1: 115–57.

Marshall, Nancy L., and others. 2002. "Early Care and Education in Massachusetts Public School Preschool Classrooms." Working paper. Wellesley, Mass.: Wellesley Centers for Women (www.wcwonline.org/earlycare/earlycareII.pdf).

Masse, Leonard N., and W. Steven Barnett. 2002. "A Benefit-Cost Analysis of the Abecedarian Early Childhood Intervention." In *Cost-Effectiveness and Educational Policy,* edited by Henry M. Levin and Patrick J. McEwan, pp. 157–76. Larchmont, N.J.: Eye on Education.

McCarton, Cecilia M., and others. 1997. "Results at Age Eight Years of Early Intervention for Low-Birth-Weight Premature Infants." *Journal of the American Medical Association* 277, no. 2: 126–32.

Montes, Guillermo, and others. 2003. *Rochester Early Childhood Assessment Partnership, 2002–2003 Annual Report.* Rochester, N.Y.: Children's Institute.

Muenchow, Susan, and others. 2004. "Estimating the Cost of Preschool for All." Washington, D.C.: American Institutes for Research.

National Child Care Information Center. 2004. *Early Care and Education Funding.* Washington, D.C.

National Institute for Early Education Research. 2005. *The State of Preschool Yearbook.* Rutgers University, National Institute for Early Education Research (nieer.org/yearbook/pdf/yearbook.pdf).

NICHD (National Institute of Child Health and Human Development) Early Child Care Research Network and Greg Duncan. 2003. "Modeling the Impacts of Child Care Quality on Children's Preschool Cognitive Development." *Child Development* 74, no. 5: 1454–75.

Olds, David L., and others. 1999. "Prenatal and Infancy Home Visitation by Nurses: Recent Findings." *Future of Children* 9, no. 1: 44–65.

PACE (Policy Analysis for California Education). 2002. "A Stark Plateau: California Families See Little Growth in Child Care Centers." Policy Brief 02-2. University of California-Berkeley, PACE (pace.berkeley.edu/policy_brief_02-2.pdf).

Ramey, Craig T., and Sharon L. Ramey. 2004. "Early Learning and School Readiness: Can Early Intervention Make a Difference?" *Merrill-Palmer Quarterly* 50, no. 4: 471–91.

Restuccia, Diego, and Carlos Urrutia. 2004. "Intergenerational Persistence of Earnings: The Role of Early and College Education." *American Economic Review* 94, no. 5: 1354–78.

Reynolds, Arthur J., Suh-Ruu Ou, and James W. Topitzes. 2004. "Paths of Effects of Early Childhood Intervention on Educational Attainment and Delinquency: A Confirmatory Analysis of the Chicago Child-Parent Centers." *Child Development* 75, no. 5: 1299–1328.

Reynolds, Arthur J., and Dylan L. Robertson. 2003. "School-Based Early Intervention and Later Child Maltreatment in the Chicago Longitudinal Study." *Child Development* 74, no. 1: 3–26.

Reynolds, Arthur J., Judy A. Temple, and Suh-Ruu Ou. 2003. "School-Based Early Intervention and Child Well-Being in the Chicago Longitudinal Study." *Child Welfare* 82, no. 5: 633–56.

Reynolds, Arthur J., and others. 2001. "Long-term Effects of an Early Childhood Intervention on Educational Achievement and Juvenile Arrest: A Fifteen-Year Follow-up of Low-Income Children in Public Schools." *Journal of the American Medical Association* 285, no. 18: 2339–46.

Reynolds Arthur J., and others. 2002. "Age Twenty-One Cost-Benefit Analysis of the Title I Chicago Child-Parent Centers." *Educational Evaluation and Policy Analysis* 24, no. 4: 267–303.

Rock, Donald A., and A. Jackson Stenner. 2005. "Assessment Issues in the Testing of Children at School Entry." *Future of Children* 15, no. 1: 15–34.

Rumberger, Russell. 2004. "Why Students Drop Out of School." In *Dropouts in America,* edited by Gary Orfield, pp. 131–56. Cambridge, Mass.: Harvard Education Press.

Ryan, James E., and Michael Heise. 2002. "The Political Economy of School Choice." *Yale Law Review* 111, no. 8: 2043–2136.

Scrivner, Scott, and Barbara Wolfe. 2003. "Universal Preschool: Much to Gain, But Who Will Pay?" Discussion Paper 1271-03. Institute for Research on Poverty, University of Wisconsin, Madison.

Smokowski, Paul R., and others. 2004. "Childhood Risk and Protective Factors and Late Adolescent Adjustment in Inner-City Minority Youth." *Children and Youth Services Review* 26: 63–91.

St. Pierre, Robert G., and Jean I. Layzer. 1999. "Using Home Visits for Multiple Purposes: The Comprehensive Child Development Program." *Future of Children* 9, no. 1: 134–51.

Temple, Judy A., Arthur J. Reynolds, and Wendy T. Miedel. 2000. "Can Early Intervention Prevent High School Drop-out? Evidence from the Chicago Child-Parent Centers." *Urban Education* 35, no. 1: 31–56.

Wald, Johanna, and David Losen. 2003. "Defining and Redirecting a School to Prison Pipeline." *New Directions in Youth Development* 99: 9–15.

11

RONALD F. FERGUSON

Toward Excellence with Equity: The Role of Parenting and Transformative School Reform

Closing the achievement gap between children of different racial and ethnic backgrounds is a long-term challenge with long-term implications for the United States. There are reasons to be hopeful. Progress has been made in narrowing racial test-score gaps since the early 1970s, when the National Assessment of Educational Progress (NAEP) began tracking test scores at the national level by racial group.[1] For example, the black-white reading score gap for 17-year-olds narrowed by more than 60 percent between 1971 and 1988 (although it then widened slightly), and evidence exists that the black-white IQ gap is narrowing.[2] Further, recent national data show virtually no racial differences in measured ability among children approaching their first birthday.[3] The nation's long-term experience establishes clearly that progress is possible. Now, progress needs to continue and even accelerate. A social movement is developing to meet this challenge.

1. U.S. Department of Education (2005).

2. See Ferguson (2005) for a discussion of possible reasons progress in narrowing the reading score gap stopped at the end of the 1980s. Also see Neal (2005). Dickens and Flynn (2005) found evidence that the black-white IQ gap had narrowed since 1972. See also note 20.

3. U.S. Department of Education, National Center for Education Statistics, Early Childhood Longitudinal Study, Birth Cohort (ECLS-B), Restricted-Use File (NCES 2004–093), previously unpublished tabulation (January 2005), viewed at agi.harvard.edu/Topics/coe_table_35_3.xls?tableID=303, February 19, 2007. Also see Fryer and Levitt (2006).

I believe that skillful parenting and deeply transformative, community-level school reforms are two important and feasible goals to pursue within the broader national movement for "excellence with equity"—a movement aimed relentlessly at high standards of achievement among children from all racial, ethnic, and social class backgrounds. In this chapter I first look briefly at the "movement" idea and introduce some basic principles. Next I review evidence on socioeconomic inequalities, disparities in parenting practices (some of which help predict achievement gaps), and the effectiveness of parenting interventions. Some aspects of this discussion are unflattering to blacks and Latinos, and as a black American I am aware that bigots may cite these findings for racist purposes. However, I believe scholars must not allow bigots to intimidate them into silence on issues that need to be addressed. The point is to look forward with hope at opportunities and responsibilities for progress, not to look backward in order to craft excuses or assign blame. Parenting should be a serious focus of strategies for raising achievement and closing gaps, even for college-educated households, among which gaps are also large.

Finally, I discuss ways of improving schools by transforming whole school systems from within. Whole-school reform models and other types of programs that originate outside school systems have their roles to play. Experimental evaluations show they often have positive effects. But if achievement gaps are to close dramatically across the nation, school systems will need their own internal capacities and supportive political constituencies for long-term excellence.

Why a Movement?

A movement is a diffuse collection of people mobilized by a common sense of purpose to change the world in a particular way. In the United States, female suffrage and civil rights were the pivotal movements of the twentieth century. Now, early in the twenty-first century, there is an emergent movement to raise academic achievement and close skill gaps between children from different racial, ethnic, and social class backgrounds. Universities, governments, and civic organizations around the country are changing policies, launching institutes, developing projects, and conceiving campaigns. In every instance, raising achievement and closing gaps are the goals.

The focus on achievement gaps is inspired by concern for the nation's future. By 2050 racial, ethnic, and socioeconomic groups that are overrepresented among low achievers and underrepresented among high achievers will make up the majority of the population and the workforce. Even more than today, technology and trade will pit workers head-to-head in competition with others around the world. The elderly will be more numerous. When young parents lack reading, math, and job skills to avoid poverty, they will compete with the elderly poor for public supports. Tax burdens on working-age adults are likely to be high. Meanwhile, internationally, the most elevated standards of living will obtain in nations where workers are most skilled and politics most stable. Where the United States will rank in this mix is uncertain. It depends on us. More than we might like to acknowledge, the social stability and vitality of the nation we leave our children depends fundamentally upon how relentlessly and effectively we pursue excellence with equity now and over the next several decades.

Social movements depend upon people who frame and debate ideas and endeavor to mobilize others to embrace particular images of the cause. The movement to raise achievement and narrow gaps is no different. Framing and mobilization are key. In crafting the strategies, policies, programs, and projects that such a movement entails, movement leaders should target adults in all the many roles in which they influence child learning and development. In effect, we need to mobilize across the entire socioecological system that supports child and youth development.

At base this system includes people in their roles as parents, teachers, and leaders in homes, in classrooms, on playgrounds, and even in doctors' and nurses' offices—places where face-to-face experiences most directly produce learning and development.[4] Beyond individual settings, adults affect the ways in which multiple settings connect, in order to achieve consistency and synergy for the children who move back and forth between them.[5] Adults make decisions in workplaces, in central administration offices, and on committees of various kinds, venues in which children typically do not participate but where adults shape many of the rules, resources, and routines that apply in the settings where children do participate.[6] Finally, adults craft and maintain the nation's shared "cultural blueprint," which comprises the laws, languages, religions, property relations, and norms by which Americans live. Important norms include the ways in which race, ethnicity, and social class affect access to power and privilege.[7] Adults in all their many roles affect the way our schools operate and the way our children grow and develop. Leaders in the movement for excellence with equity should seek ways to enlist them all.

4. Bronfenbrenner's (1979) micro-ecologies.

5. Bronfenbrenner's (1979) meso-ecologies.

6. Bronfenbrenner's (1979) exo-ecologies.

7. Bronfenbrenner's (1979) macro-ecology.

Some Basic Principles

A movement for excellence with equity should aspire to high quality learning opportunities for children and adults alike. Fortunately, substantial agreement exists on the types of experiences children and adults need in order to learn and thrive and on the conditions most likely to produce those experiences. The National Research Council (NRC) Committee on Community-Level Programs for Youth reviewed a wide range of youth development studies—quantitative, qualitative, and theoretical—and found broad commonality in frameworks and findings.[8] Semantics varied, but the ideas were consistent. The following eight "features of positive developmental settings" synthesize a great deal of research. Although the committee was focused on youths, the list is universal, and a movement for excellence with equity would do well to promote these features for every home, classroom, and workplace in which people learn and develop.

1. *Physical and psychological safety* (to prevent feelings of fear and anxiety that might interfere with concentration or motivate withdrawal from participation)
2. *Appropriate structure* (for example, rules that make clear which forms of individual initiative are to be rewarded or penalized and that provide boundaries within and around which individuals can set and pursue goals)
3. *Supportive relationships* (to foster positive emotional states and willingness to take risks that might require social support)[9]
4. *Opportunities to belong* (with an emphasis on accommodating individual skills and interests)
5. *Positive social norms* (to induce healthy behaviors and aspirations, avoiding incentives to be self-destructive or do harm to others)
6. *Support for efficacy and mattering* (to inspire and enable initiative and persistence toward individual and group goals and provide opportunities to make contributions that others value)

8. Eccles and Gootman (2002).

9. In discussing the attributes of supportive relationships, the NRC report emphasized the importance of responsiveness and fit: "On the surface these appear to be objective qualities, but research suggests that these qualities reside less in the adult than in the adolescent's perception of the adult and in the adolescent's experience of interactions with the adult. . . . Inasmuch as there is an underlying essential element here, it consists of attentiveness and responsiveness to adolescents' subjective worlds" (Eccles and Gootman, 2002, pp. 94–95). The same can be said of interactions of adults in training to be better parents or teachers, wherein parent or teacher receptivity to trainers or supervisors depends importantly upon subjective experiences of feeling valued and respected. It depends as well on perceptions of whether or not the trainer or supervisor is well meaning, competent, and reliable.

7. *Opportunities for skill building* (to support development of physical, intellectual, social, psychological, and emotional skills)

8. *Integration of family, school, and community efforts* (to reduce inconsistencies and promote supportive synergies across settings)[10]

The more consistently children and adults encounter these conditions across multiple settings, the more they will develop the skills and proclivities that prepare them for success. Beware, however, against thinking that the list is a blanket endorsement of peace and harmony under all conditions. As every parent knows, conflict and stress are sometimes necessary. Moreover, conflict and stress are to be expected during periods of dramatic change, when vested interests or attachments to old ways pose resistance in homes, schools, and communities. Indeed, some substantial share of people's work in the movement for equity and excellence will entail challenging social and structural conditions in the society that bias the allocation of public resources and access to opportunity.[11]

Nonetheless, my focus in this chapter is on the two institutions that interface most directly with children and young people as they develop—families and schools. Even before major changes take place in broader social and structural conditions, participants in the excellence with equity movement can take advantage of unexploited opportunities to improve parenting and schooling in ways that raise achievement. We can exploit these opportunities more effectively if we make doing so a priority.

Parenting

Especially when children are young, home is an important place and parents are extremely important people. Parents have profound influence over the way homes rate on the features just listed, some of which ratings turn out to be correlated with race and socioeconomic status (SES). Within racial groups, research is clear that higher SES parents provide more opportunities at home for academic skill building (item 7) and tend to have greater resources for integrating family, school, and community efforts (item 8).

10. Eccles and Gootman (2002, pp. 90–91). The chapter in which these appear elaborates on each condition, with examples.

11. Key concerns include racial discrimination in hiring, promotion, and lending, which affects the family incomes and wealth that provide resources for rearing children. Further, it seems unfair that some segments of society benefit from exclusive social networks that carry valuable information or protect control over decisionmaking in key institutions. There is much about society that may stand in the way of reaching full potential in the domains addressed in this book.

Similar differences obtain between racial groups, for whom home literacy practices are among the factors contributing to higher achievement by whites and Asians relative to blacks and Hispanics. In this section I report on racial and SES patterns in parenting practices, review key findings on the relationship of parenting to achievement, and summarize evidence on the effectiveness of parenting interventions.

Resources

Resource disparities are important to the story of why parenting practices and opportunities for effective parenting differ across groups. In comparison with typical white parents, poor whites and nonwhites on average have lower incomes. They have fewer years of schooling and fewer academic skills for any given length of schooling.[12] They work fewer weeks per year, earn lower average wages, and have accumulated less wealth.[13] They are more stigmatized by assumptions of inferiority and have fewer social network ties to people and institutions that control information or have the capacity to provide other forms of assistance.[14]

Resource disparities do predict achievement gaps. Further, policies and programs that raise income for very poor households have been found to boost achievement among young children. On the basis of a variety of studies, Duncan and Magnuson concluded that socioeconomic resource disparities predicted about 0.5 standard deviation of the test score gap between whites, on the one hand, and blacks and Hispanics, on the other.[15] This magnitude is robust across a number of studies covering different age groups. One-half standard deviation is typically between one-half and two-thirds (occasionally more) of the total racial achievement gap in any given study.

Although causation can never be completely proved, many mechanisms have been suggested to explain why income and other socioeconomic resources are such strong predictors of student achievement. For example, parents with greater resources have access to safer neighborhoods with better schools and more studious peers.[16] Teachers are more likely to welcome input from high-SES parents and treat them respectfully.[17] High-SES parents can afford more learning tools and materials in the home, may be less stressed by survival pres-

12. Phillips and others (1998).
13. Neal (2005).
14. Dickens (1999); Loury (2002).
15. See discussion and references in Duncan and Magnuson (2005).
16. See, for example Hanushek, Kain, and Rivkin (2002); Orfield (2005).
17. Lareau and Horvat (1999).

sures and therefore have more patience in helping their children, and may have better and more reliable health services.[18] The list goes on.

To help redress these inequities, policymakers and administrators of programmatic interventions over the years have endeavored to improve school quality in poor areas, increase access to better neighborhoods, improve parent-teacher communication, supplement home learning resources, help parents with stress management, provide access to health care services, and more. All these things are expected to complement or substitute for parental resources. Experience has produced both successes and failures, with no magic bullets but many helpful lessons to build on.[19]

Learning-at-Home Disparities

In an authoritative review of the literature on the contribution of preschool parenting to racial and ethnic gaps in school readiness, Brooks-Gunn and Markman identified racial and ethnic differences on five dimensions of preschool parenting.[20] All involved learning at home, and research has established that all five are contributors to school readiness.[21] The dimensions were nurturance (expressions of love, affection, and care); discipline (responses to

18. Brooks-Gunn and Markman (2005); Conger, Conger, and Elder (1997); McLoyd (1998).

19. Standard assessments of the degree to which socioeconomic resources affect achievement may be underestimates if important resource variables such as social network resources are poorly measured or absent from the analysis. Conversely, estimates may be too high if genetic differences correlate positively with SES. Specifically, if genetics contribute to parental income and education and also to offspring's achievement levels, then contributions to achievement that are typically attributed to parental income and achievement may be at least partly due to genetics. Researchers tend to agree that genetics account for some within-race achievement disparities, but the importance of genetics for between-race disparities remains a matter of considerable dispute. Some researchers have concluded that genetics account for much of the correlation between family resources and student achievement—even between racial groups. Most prominently, Rushton and Jenson (2005) concluded that fixed, immutable genetic differences, not resources, discrimination, or environmental forces, accounted for half or more of racial IQ and achievement gaps. Supporting environmental (as opposed to genetic) explanations, Dickens and Flynn (2005) found that the black-white IQ gap narrowed between one-fifth and one-third (three to six points) between 1972 and 2002. They attributed this narrowing to environmental forces, although their work to identify such forces was only beginning. Research leaves little doubt that environmental forces are critically important determinants of achievement levels as well as achievement disparities. And among environmental forces, parenting constitutes the most important cluster in children's lives (Shonkoff and Phillips [2000]).

20. Brooks-Gunn and Markman (2005).

21. Epstein (1995) characterized six types of parental involvement: parenting, communicating, volunteering, learning at home, decisionmaking, and collaborating with community. Of the six, she argued that learning at home was the most reliably associated with gains in achievement. Typologies by other researchers (Bamber, Berla and Henderson [1993]; Eccles and Harold [1993]); Shartrand and others [1997]) fit well with Epstein's.

behaviors that parents regarded as inappropriate); teaching (strategies for transmitting information or skills to the child); language (amount and characteristics of verbal communication with the child); and materials (books, recordings, and other materials to support learning). These variables resemble the eight features of positive developmental settings summarized from the NRC report. There is more evidence on which to base black-white than Hispanic-white comparisons, but when the average for blacks or Hispanics differs from that for whites in any given study, whites almost always rate higher on the measured practices. Generally, the best studies find racial differences in preschool parenting ranging from one-fifth to three-fifths of a standard deviation, depending on the particular parenting practices.[22] Programming that reduces these differences can shrink achievement gaps at kindergarten entry.

But should middle-class whites be the models? Many people question the validity of using standards from one group to draw conclusions or prescriptions for another. Brooks-Gunn and Markman recounted the way their black graduate students resisted using the two-way contrast between *authoritative* parenting (warm but with firm control) and *authoritarian* parenting (negative, lacking warmth, harsh control) that had become the standard for differentiating parental styles. The students suggested that some very effective black parents might be misclassified under this scheme, and they were correct. Brooks-Gunn and Markman explained:

> We did an exploratory analysis using a sample of about 700 black and white mothers of toddlers, attempting to identify clusters of mothers based on our videotaped ratings on both domains [authoritative and authoritarian]. We identified not two but four groups of mothers—those who were high in warm, firm control and low in negative, harsh control (the classic authoritative behavior); those who were high in negative, harsh control and low in warm, firm control (the classic authoritarian behavior); those who were relatively high in both (what we termed "tough love"); and those who were low in both (what we termed "detached").[23]

Teenage mothers of both racial groups dominated the standard authoritarian group, and many were high school dropouts. In contrast, the "tough love" group was mostly older black mothers with at least a high school education. The standard formulation would have cast them as authoritarian—a less effec-

22. Brooks-Gunn and Markman (2005).
23. Brooks-Gunn and Markman (2005, p. 148).

tive form of parenting. But the children of these "tough love" mothers had higher IQ scores and larger vocabularies than the children of detached or authoritarian mothers.[24]

"Tough love" is an example of a practice that differs in prevalence and effectiveness across racial groups. Nonetheless, the general finding in the literature is that there are more similarities than differences regarding which practices predict positive child outcomes. Closing racial and SES gaps in the prevalence of practices that are positively associated with learning can help close achievement gaps.

Whereas much of the literature focuses on low-income and poorly educated parents, learning-at-home gaps appear at all levels of parental education and for students at all grade levels. In the nationally representative Early Childhood Longitudinal Survey–Kindergarten (ECLS-K), numbers of children's books in the home for kindergarten children reported by college-graduate African American mothers were more similar to numbers reported by high-school-educated whites than by college-educated whites (table 11-1). Findings were similar for records, audiotapes, and compact discs.

The survey also found black-white differences in the frequency with which parents read to children, discussed nature and science, sang, and played games. Whites reported more reading and conversations about nature; blacks reported more singing, playing games, and doing puzzles (table 11-2).[25] Fryer and Levitt used the ECLS-K to explore how SES, books in the home, and other measures predicted scores as children entered kindergarten. After controlling for an index of standard SES measures, they found that adding the number of children's books to the equation reduced the residual black-white gaps in arithmetic and reading readiness scores by an additional 0.13 standard deviation—equal to one-fifth of the black-white arithmetic gap and one-third of the black-white reading gap.[26] Obviously, this does not mean that buying more books should in itself be a prescription for any group to raise achievement. Surely, the associated literacy practices are what matter—including the ways books are read *and discussed.*[27]

Fryer and Levitt noted that when patterns were examined separately by racial group, the payoff to higher SES in the form of higher school readiness scores

24. McLoyd and Smith (2002) found that spanking had less deleterious effects in black than in white households. The differential meaning of "tough love" in black families may help to explain why.

25. "Playing games and doing puzzles" is a single category in the ECLS-K; puzzles are not distinguished from other forms of playing.

26. See Fryer and Levitt (2004, table 2).

27. For example, the number of books may matter because new books provide new opportunities for parent-child discussions requiring higher-order thinking.

Table 11-1. *Numbers of Children's Books and Records, Audiotapes, or CDs in the Home*

Number, with (standard deviation; sample size) in parentheses

	African Americans		*European Americans*	
Mother's years of schooling	*Median*	*Mean*	*Median*	*Mean*
Books[a]				
12 or fewer	20	30 (33; 1,304)	50	76 (55; 3,099)
13–15 years	30	46 (40; 826)	100	97 (59; 3,042)
16 or more	50	65 (51; 258)	100	114 (59; 2,777)
Records, audiotapes, or CDs[b]				
12 or fewer	4	8 (13; 1,306)	10	15 (18; 3,114)
13–15	8	13 (16; 827)	12	18 (18; 3,072)
16 or more	10	16 (16; 260)	20	22 (19; 2,814)

Source: Author's tabulations using ECLS-K Base Year Public Use File. This table also appears in Ferguson (2005).

a. Responses to the question, "About how many children's books does your child have in your home now, including library books?"

b. Responses to the question, "About how many children's records, audiotapes, or CDs do you have at home, including any from the library?"

was somewhat lower for blacks than for whites, but the basic patterns in the findings remained.[28] Similarly, Selcuk Sirin used seventy-four independent samples in which the relationship of SES to achievement had been estimated and published in journal articles between 1990 and 2000. The meta-analysis he conducted found, as expected, that nonwhites had fewer resources than whites, and this predicted lower achievement among their children. Like Fryer and Levitt, however, he found that parental SES tended to be a stronger predictor of achievement for white students than for minorities. Why? Sirin suggested that "neighborhood and school SES, not family SES, may exert a more powerful effect on academic achievement in minority communities, particularly in African American communities."[29] This is one possibility, but not the only one.

For example, differences in the payoff to higher SES can exist among students of different racial groups living in the same community and attending

28. Fryer and Levitt (2004).

29. Sirin (2005, p. 441).

Table 11-2. *Selected Family and Child Learning Practices, by Mother's Years of Schooling, Fall 1998*
Percent

Mother's years of schooling	*Never*	*Once or twice a week*	*Three to six times a week*	*Daily*	*Sample size*
A. Family Members Read Books to the Child					
African American					
12 or fewer	2.0	38.0	29.1	30.9	1,313
13–15	0.6	25.5	36.6	37.4	828
16 or more	1.2	14.2	37.3	47.3	260
European American					
12 fewer	1.0	19.4	38.1	41.6	3,118
13–15	0.3	11.5	41.4	46.8	3,074
16 or more	0.1	5.7	34.1	60.1	2,815
B. Adults Discuss Nature or Do Science Projects with the Child					
African American					
12 or fewer	37.0	40.1	13.1	9.8	1,311
13–15	24.8	47.6	17.8	9.9	828
16 or more	16.5	53.9	20.0	9.6	260
European American					
12 or fewer	22.2	48.4	20.2	9.2	3,116
13–15	14.6	51.2	23.7	10.6	3,071
16 or more	8.5	49.5	31.0	11.0	2,814

(continued)

the same school. Studies would tend to find this result if, for instance, there were differences in course placements, peer culture, or learning-at-home environments among students from different racial groups who had the same measured SES.

I have estimated the relationship of SES to achievement for almost 40,000 middle and high school students from the fifteen suburban districts (across six states) of the Minority Student Achievement Network (MSAN).[30] On average, white and Asian students in these communities arrive at school with greater socioeconomic background advantages relative to blacks and Hispanics. But they also attend the same schools and live in similar neighborhoods. These are

30. MSAN formed around 1998 so that these districts could share ideas and activities aimed at narrowing their racial achievement gaps. See Ferguson (2002); www.msanetwork.org.

Table 11-2. *Selected Family and Child Learning Practices, by Mother's Years of Schooling, Fall 1998* (Continued)
Percent

Mother's years of schooling	*Never*	*Once or twice a week*	*Three to six times a week*	*Daily*	*Sample size*
C. Family Members Sing Songs with the Child					
African American					
12 fewer	5.5	21.5	19.2	53.9	1,313
13–15	3.1	18.0	24.4	54.5	829
16 or more	2.3	18.9	24.6	54.2	260
European American					
12 fewer	5.5	25.3	25.8	43.4	3,118
13–15	3.6	21.9	30.7	43.8	3,075
16 or more	2.6	21.5	33.3	42.7	2,815
D. Family Members Play Games or Do Puzzles with the Child					
African American					
12 or fewer	6.5	36.3	27.0	30.2	1,313
13–15	3.9	33.3	36.3	26.5	829
16 or more	4.6	29.3	38.5	27.7	260
European American					
12 or fewer	3.6	36.7	39.8	20.2	3,118
13–15	2.4	34.2	44.0	19.4	3,076
16 or more	1.7	30.4	48.6	19.3	2,815

Source: Author's tabulations using ECLS-K Base Year Public Use File.

not bad neighborhoods. Nonetheless, the MSAN data, like Sirin's meta-analysis, show a stronger relationship of SES to achievement for whites and Asians than for non-Asian students of color. SES measures here include parents' years of schooling, household structure (two parents, step-parents, and so forth), number of siblings, and numbers of books and computers in the home.

Table 11-3 shows the distribution of households by SES category in the MSAN data.[31] Most whites and Asians are in the upper-middle and highest SES

31. I simulated achievement for each of the four standardized SES profiles. To form the SES categories, I began by using all the SES measures in the data, but not race, to predict grade point average (GPA). This multiple regression produced regression coefficients to use as weights in composite SES measures. The equation used an indicator variable for each value of each SES variable, in order to allow for nonlinearity in estimated effects. The equation also included school-grade-level fixed effects and gender.

Table 11-3. *Distribution of Racial and Ethnic Groups by Socioeconomic (SES) Category*[a]
Percent

SES	*Black*	*White*	*Hispanic*	*Asian*	*Mixed*	*Total*
Lowest	24	3	19	7	12	10
Lower middle	55	25	59	39	44	40
Upper middle	19	57	19	41	37	40
Highest	2	16	3	12	8	10

a. Data are for secondary schools in fifteen Minority Student Achievement Network (MSAN) districts.

categories, whereas most blacks, Hispanics, and mixed-race students are in the lower-middle and lowest categories.[32] These disparities alone would predict differences in achievement. But in addition, table 11-4 shows that achievement disparities in MSAN communities are greatest at the highest SES levels. Other data sets, too, have shown greater racial disparities at higher SES levels.[33] So, equalizing SES, at least by standard measures, would go only part of the way toward equalizing school achievement among racial groups if racial differences exist in parenting practices or peer dynamics even within SES categories.

In 2005 I surveyed elementary school students in twenty-nine public schools across a dozen school districts. Most were suburban districts similar to the MSAN districts already mentioned, but some were inner city. Survey items included several pertaining to learning conditions at home. Table 11-5 shows the percentages of Asian, black, Hispanic, and white students who responded "yes," instead of "maybe" or "no," to selected items. All were first through sixth graders in May 2005. The table shows responses for both "advantaged" and "disadvantaged" students. The "advantaged" were defined as those who reported at least one computer and two adults in the home; the "disadvantaged" lived in single-parent homes, lacked a computer in the home, or both.

Missing values for explanatory variables were handled using dummy variables. The adjusted R-square for the equation was 0.23. Using the results, some students' SES characteristics (ignoring race or ethnicity) put them in the bottom 10 percent of predicted GPA. I labeled this group the "lowest SES" group. Others' characteristics predicted that they would be in the 40 percent of the distribution from the 10th to the 50th percentile (labeled "lower middle SES") or the 50th to the 90th percentile (labeled "upper middle SES"). Finally, some would be in the top 10 percent, and this group was labeled "highest SES."

32. Shaker Heights, Ohio, is one of these districts. Ogbu (2003) was incorrect when he suggested that blacks and whites in Shaker Heights had essentially equal SES.

33. See U.S. Department of Education (1995). Here, there is greater racial disparity in NAEP reading scores among 17-year-olds who say their parents are college graduates than among those who say their parents are high school graduates or dropouts.

Table 11-4. *Simulations by SES Category and Race or Ethnicity for Three Achievement Measures*[a]
Units as indicated

SES	*Black*	*White*	*Hispanic*	*Asian*	*Mixed*
Mean grade point average (4-point scale)					
Lowest	2.38	2.52	2.61	2.66	2.30
Lower middle	2.65	2.91	2.88	3.07	2.73
Upper middle	2.88	3.36	3.13	3.36	3.17
Highest	3.18	3.68	3.34	3.67	3.49
Degree to which student reports "completely" understanding teachers' lessons (standard deviation, mean = 0)					
Lowest	–0.38	–0.54	–0.44	–0.58	–0.59
Lower middle	–0.23	–0.22	–0.21	–0.26	–0.26
Upper middle	0.00	0.20	0.01	0.06	0.22
Highest	0.04	0.35	0.11	0.35	0.31
Degree to which student reports understanding material read for school "very well" (standard deviation, mean = 0)					
Lowest	–0.56	–0.59	–0.65	–0.64	–0.57
Lower middle	–0.36	–0.15	–0.39	–0.29	–0.31
Upper middle	–0.07	0.25	–0.06	0.17	0.17
Highest	0.06	0.44	0.17	0.41	0.36

a. Simulations are for fixed SES profiles, where achievement predictions use regression coefficients estimated separately by race or ethnicity.

Table 11-5 shows interesting differences in learning-at-home environments.[34] Blacks, Hispanics, and whites appear to have more supportive home conditions than Asians (items 1–4). In comparison with Asians, larger percentages of blacks, Hispanics, and whites reported that help with homework was always available if needed, that parents expressed curiosity about what they were learning at school, and that parents tried to make learning fun. These are all conditions one assumes would support learning.

However, upon inspecting items 5–11, one suspects that Asians (and whites) nonetheless have the net advantage. These items seem more related to the amount of time children spend on academic learning activities at home. Asians agreed most that "I read almost every day at home." Advantaged Asians were the only students more likely to have a computer than a television in

34. Future work may link the data in this table to achievement disparities. Currently, however, the data have not been combined with grades or test scores.

Table 11-5. Responses of First through Sixth Graders to Selected Statements about Home Life

	Percent responding "yes" (advantaged, disadvantaged)[a]			
Survey item	*Asian*	*Black*	*Hispanic*	*White*
1. At home, someone is always there to help me with my homework if I need it.	52, 34	78, 76	80, 73	80, 74
2. My parents want me to tell them what I learned in school.	46, 45	65, 62	61, 61	62, 61
3. Someone reads with me almost every night before I go to sleep.	9, 18	17, 20	19, 32	22, 23
4. At home, we try to make learning fun.	50, 44	60, 59	56, 59	50, 56
5. I read almost every day at home.	66, 56	45, 42	50, 54	59, 52
6. I have a computer in my bedroom.	45, 29	30, 18	33, 15	23, 20
7. I have a television in my bedroom.	36, 46	81, 83	70, 69	39, 53
8. At home, I watch television more than I do anything else.	13, 22	30, 36	14, 27	13, 22
9. At home, I watch rap videos on television.	11, 19	55, 61	35, 50	15, 24
10. On many days, I get very sleepy at school.	11, 19	35, 35	18, 30	25, 32
11. Sometimes my teacher says I don't pay attention as I should.	24, 27	41, 45	28, 45	25, 37

Source: Author's tabulations using Tripod Project student surveys from spring 2005.

a. Advantaged: Asian, $N = 458$; Black, $N = 659$; Hispanic, $N = 152$; White, $N = 1{,}364$. Disadvantaged: Asian, $N = 63$; Black, $N = 409$; Hispanic, $N = 71$; White, $N = 187$.

their bedrooms. Both advantaged and disadvantaged Asians indicated less television watching than blacks and Hispanics (and far less watching of rap videos). Moreover, a smaller percentage of Asians than of other groups reported becoming sleepy at school. This might partly explain why a smaller percentage of Asians than of other groups agreed that "Sometimes my teacher says I don't pay attention as I should." Whites responded similarly to blacks and Hispanics on items 1–5 and similarly to Asians on items 5–11.

This constellation of findings should cause those of us who are parents of school-age children to take notice. We might respond in any of several ways. One is simply to await more evidence. Another is to campaign against presenting such data in public because they might stigmatize and contribute to stereotypes. A more constructive response is to consider whether there are things we should be changing in our own homes and then act on what we decide while joining with others to more fully explore the potential of parenting.

Preschool Parenting and School Readiness Interventions

According to Brooks-Gunn and Markman, "when researchers measuring school readiness gaps control for parenting differences, the racial and ethnic gaps narrow by 25 to 50 percent. And it is possible to alter parenting behavior to improve readiness."[35] Brooks-Gunn and Markman reported that center-based preschool programs that had parenting components tended to improve both parenting and school readiness among poor children. They reported that family literacy programs could improve school readiness as well. Home-based parenting programs without a center-based child-care component tended to benefit the mother but not the child, at least over the time span covered by most studies.

These encouraging findings for preschool programs with parenting components came mainly from high quality experimental studies. The authors of an NRC review in 2001, titled *Eager to Learn: Educating Our Preschoolers,* concluded, as Brooks-Gunn and Markman did, that *high quality* preschool programs with parenting components could have positive and lasting effects. They added, however, that the parenting components of most current programs needed to be improved in order to be comparable to those shown by evaluations to be most effective. They wrote: "The extent to which program effects on children could be enhanced by improved parent involvement is unclear. Although the theoretical basis for efficacy is clear, many current efforts to work with parents do not appear to be effective. Given this apparent discrepancy, rigorous research aimed at identifying highly effective parent involvement strategies would be extremely valuable."[36]

Interventions with Parents of School-Age Children

Policies and programs to involve parents in support of their school-age children's learning have proliferated since the 1960s, encouraged by findings from research.[37] In the early 1990s a publication of the U.S. Department of Education proclaimed: "Three decades of research have shown that parental participation improves students' learning. This is true whether the child is in preschool or the upper grades, whether the family is rich or poor, whether the parents finished high school [or not]."[38] In the often-cited report *A New Gen-*

35. Brooks-Gunn and Markman (2005, p. 139).

36. National Research Council (2001, p. 149).

37. Carey, Lewis, and Farris (1998); Christenson, Rounds, and Franklin (1992); Epstein (1996); Fruchter, Galletta, and White (1993); Moles (1993).

38. Ballen and Moles (1994, p. 2).

eration of Evidence: The Family Is Critical to Student Achievement, Henderson and Berla went so far as to claim that "the evidence is now beyond dispute. When schools work together with families to support learning, children tend to succeed not just in school but throughout life."[39]

While optimistic that parent involvement can help raise student achievement, some researchers are more cautious.[40] Baker and Soden critically analyzed hundreds of studies and found that a "lack of scientific rigor in the research informing practice and policy" had contributed greatly to the confusion faced by those attempting to understand the field of parent involvement.[41] One reason research on parental involvement is often "messy" is that programs cover a broad range of activities and most have multiple components. Complexity is compounded when programs are embedded in comprehensive school reform initiatives such as the Accelerated Schools Project, Success for All, and the School Development Program. Isolating the effects of parent involvement in complex interventions is extremely difficult and seldom attempted.[42]

A well-known saying by the late evaluation expert Donald Campbell exhorts one to "evaluate no program before it is proud." Appropriately, the vast majority of books and articles on parent involvement are focused not on the evaluation of parental involvement programs but on what it takes to make them work—to help them become "proud." Challenges to becoming proud include limited skills and knowledge on which to build collaboration; lack of resources (of all types); misperceptions between parents and teachers about each other's motives and beliefs; low expectations and negative attitudes; cultural differences between families and schools; lack of interest; lack of trust; lack of systemic support; and problems in parent-professional interactions, such as negative communication around poor student performance. Implementation can be profoundly challenging, especially for schools serving middle and high school students in low-income neighborhoods.[43]

39. Henderson and Berla (1994, p. 1).

40. Ascher (1988); Baker and Soden (1998); Christenson, Rounds, and Franklin (1992); Rutherford, Billig, and Kettering (1993).

41. Baker and Soden (1998, p. 1). Joyce Epstein, a leader in this field, writes, "Research about school, family, and community connections needs to improve in many ways. Early research was often based on limited samples, too global or too narrow measures of involvement, and limited data on student outcomes. As research proceeds with clearer questions and better data, measurement models should be more fully specified, analyses more elegant, and results more useful for policy and practice" (Epstein [1996, p. 218]).

42. See, for example, Cook and others (1998); Davies (1993); Haynes and Comer (1993); Madden, Slavin, and Karweit (1993); Wong (1995).

43. See Chavkin (1993); Christenson, Rounds, and Franklin (1992), Dauber and Epstein (1989); Eccles and Harold (1993); Garlington (1992); Leitch and Tangri (1988); Moles (1993); Reglin (1993); Shartrand and others (1997); Swap (1993); Swick (1991); Wolfendale (1983).

William Jeynes reported on findings from a meta-analysis of fifty-three studies of parental involvement. All of them measured effects on secondary school students' academic achievement. The researchers used a variety of methodologies, so the analyses are most accurately understood as showing a pattern of associations—the estimated effects might or might not be causal. The expected positive correlation between parental involvement and student achievement was confirmed for most aspects of parental involvement covered by the studies, although relationships were statistically significant more often for grades than for standardized test scores. Jeynes reported that effect sizes for "overall educational outcomes, grades, and academic achievement" averaged on the order of 0.5 standard deviation. The magnitude was similar for whites and racial minorities.[44]

Jeynes concluded: "Parental involvement programs . . . influenced educational outcomes, although to a lesser degree than preexisting expressions of parental support."[45] He found that activities such as communication about school and participation in school functions had smaller estimated relationships to achievement than did measures of parental style (for example, authoritativeness and warmth) and expectations (for example, for grades and years of schooling).

Turner, Nye, and Schwartz reported on a meta-analysis of parental involvement and academic achievement for students in grades K–5.[46] To be included in their analysis, an intervention had to meet the following criteria: the treatment had to involve parental activities outside of formal schooling aimed at enhancing student achievement; academic achievement had to be measured as an outcome; and treatment and control groups had to be selected using random assignment. By the end of an exhaustive search they had identified nineteen such studies among hundreds of books and articles. Results were mixed, but the overall effect-size estimate was statistically significant and quantitatively meaningful, at 0.43 standard deviation. The average duration of programs in these studies was less than half a year of schooling. Because the studies were all randomized field trials, this effect size can be interpreted as causal.

My research assistant spent much of 1999 searching for studies that used random assignment or good quasi-experimental designs to test whether it was possible to change parenting in ways that enhanced achievement. She found only five studies that used these methodologies. They showed the following:

—In comparison with a control group that received extra help neither at school nor at home, students' first- and second-grade reading achievement

44. Jeynes (2004).

45. Jeynes (2004, p. 6).

46. Turner, Nye, and Schwartz (2004).

increased when parents listened to their children read school books at home two to four times each week. In comparison with an alternative treatment group given extra reading help at school, however, no improvement was found.[47]

—An intervention including parental involvement for at-risk, urban fourth and fifth graders improved scholastic and behavioral self-concept ratings but not academic achievement.[48]

—A homework intervention for sixth graders entailed three alternative treatments: (1) neither the student nor the family received guidance on involving family members in mathematics assignments; (2) the student received guidance on how to involve a family member; (3) both the student and the family received guidance on how to involve family in math assignments. The study found that such guidance did not increase student achievement.[49]

—Low-achieving, inner-city seventh graders assigned for ten weeks to a reading group that included parents showed the largest gains in fundamental reading skills six months later, in comparison with a control group that received no treatment, a reading class without parent involvement, and a school-based tutoring group.[50]

—Inner-city elementary school students whose parents participated in a program designed to teach tutoring skills in reading and mathematics demonstrated positive effects, with experiment students showing a significant increase in achievement over students in the control group.[51]

The strongest support for the value of parental involvement came from the three studies that focused on parents' involvement in reading.[52] Balli, Demo, and Wedman found that efforts to involve parents did not significantly affect mathematics achievement (estimated effects were positive but not statistically significant).[53] Evidence from a correlational study by Joyce Epstein lends support to the differential effect of parental involvement on reading versus mathematics achievement. Specifically, on the basis of a survey of teachers and principals and using achievement test scores of 293 third and fifth graders, Epstein found a positive correlation between teachers' efforts to achieve parent involvement and students' reading achievement, but no such correlation for mathematics.[54]

Because experimental studies randomly assign people to be treated or not, there is no systematic difference at baseline between the treated and the

47. Tizard, Schofield, and Hewison (1982).
48. Fantuzzo, Davis, and Ginsberg (1995).
49. Balli, Demo, and Wedman (1998).
50. Rodick and Henggeler (1980).
51. McKinney (1976).
52. McKinney (1976); Rodick and Henggeler (1980); Tizard, Schofield, and Hewison (1982).
53. Balli, Demo, and Wedman (1998).
54. Epstein (1991).

untreated. This makes it very likely that any post-treatment differences are due to the treatment and not to something else. People trained in evaluation research tend to dismiss non-experimental studies as unreliable. I usually count myself among them, but some non-experimental studies are worth taking seriously. Operation Higher Achievement, for example, was aimed at helping the parents of 826 African American children in one inner-city elementary school to create conditions in the home to promote academic learning. Results showed that students intensively exposed to the program gained a 0.5 to 0.6 grade equivalent more during the year than those who were less intensively exposed.[55]

In the end, evaluation studies find that some parenting interventions produce achievement gains and some do not. No one program model produces the same effects in every application. Nonetheless, enough interventions have produced gains with at least moderately large effect sizes, even in rigorously conducted experimental trials, that further consideration of parenting programs as achievement-gap interventions is warranted.

A great deal of activity focused on helping parents to be effective is already in motion around the United States. It is worth learning more about this activity and making it more central to both research and intervention efforts aimed at helping children achieve at higher levels. Strategies should differ depending upon the populations involved and their capacity to help themselves. Future work with middle-class households, especially among blacks and Latinos, might best be pursued by asking organizations that blacks and Latinos control to take lead roles in designing, implementing, and monitoring new efforts.

Transformative School Reform

Over the past few decades, educators have designed and implemented a huge number of programs to help teachers become more effective. Few of them have been widely replicated. Among those that have, a small number have been evaluated rigorously for effect, and among these some have proved effective enough to justify broader replication. Although no program is guaranteed to work under all conditions, and findings are almost always mixed, evaluation results have been encouraging for Success for All, Direct Instruction, Comer's School Development Program, First Things First, Talent Development, Job Corps, and several others. Those with more finely specified components, better training for teachers, and professionally managed implementation tend to show the most consistent results. Generally, implementation tends to be

55. Walberg, Bole, and Waxman (1980).

stronger when the program developer and his or her organization are directly involved. I believe, however, that state and local leaders in the movement for excellence with equity should depend on such programs only as a means toward the longer-term goal of institutionalizing excellence in the people and social networks embedded in the everyday lives of their districts.

There is plenty of evidence that interventions can have positive effects on achievement in schools and communities.[56] Whether or not they actually do in any particular case depends on a number of factors. For example, in a survey of teachers that I conducted in the spring of 2005, I listed seventeen reasons that a program might have little, if any, effect on teaching or learning. The survey instruction read: "Recall the last professional development program at your school that had little or no effect on teaching or learning in your class. With that program in mind, please check all the following responses that apply."[57] The four items teachers checked most often were:

—It was just too much on top of everything else the school was trying to do (37 percent)

—There was too little support and training (30 percent)

—Teachers were not held accountable for doing it (25 percent)

—The way it was introduced didn't inspire me to try (25 percent)

Altogether, 67 percent of elementary school respondents and 88 percent of secondary school respondents checked at least one of these four responses. In contrast, only 7 percent checked "I really tried to make it work, but it just didn't help my students." Only 8 percent responded that "I never thought it could work with my students." Instead, the pattern of responses suggests that the main reasons the programs did not work was that the teachers did not implement them. This highlights the importance of capacity and leadership in the selection, introduction, scheduling, provision of support and training, and overall management of professional development programs.

If school systems could keep talented leaders in curriculum and instruction jobs for as long as a decade, with stable political support for long-term strategic planning and implementation, including frequent reviews and midcourse corrections, might the result be the wholesale transformation of teaching and instruction? Might labor relations function more smoothly? Might teachers be better trained and instruction better differentiated to meet the needs of all

56. For example, see the compendium of evaluation findings issued by the American Youth Policy Forum (James, Jurich, and Estes [2002]). Also see reviews in Molnar (2002).

57. Responses were voluntary; 82 elementary teachers from 21 schools and 233 secondary teachers from 20 schools responded. None was a deeply troubled school, but all were schools in cities, towns, and suburbs that had racial and ethnic achievement gaps that school officials were addressing with various types of professional development.

students? Might people hold one another more accountable for giving their best effort? Would achievement rise? Would gaps become narrow? Could districts become highly effective design and implementation organizations for achieving excellence with equity? We should try to find out. Some large cities are making a start.

Large Cities

The Council of Great City Schools is the membership organization for most large city school districts in the United States.[58] In 2001 the council convened an advisory committee of school superintendents and education researchers to help design a study. The committee would identify cities making the most impressive progress in narrowing racial gaps while raising overall average scores and would try to understand the reasons for their successes. The research and evaluation firm MDRC would help design the study, conduct the site visits, and write the main report.

The advisory committee scanned the data looking for districts that met the following three criteria: improvement in both reading and math in all or nearly all grades from the beginning of their state's testing program through the spring of 2001; faster rates of improvement than their respective states had achieved for at least three years; and simultaneous narrowing of racial-ethnic achievement gaps. The districts selected for case studies were Charlotte-Mecklenburg, North Carolina; Houston, Texas; and Sacramento, California. For these three districts, positive trends in elementary school scores were evident and better than the respective state averages. Progress was greatest for the lowest scoring groups, so gaps had narrowed. Middle schools had achieved some progress as well, although less than elementary schools, and high schools had made no progress at all.

The study was admittedly exploratory—it would not be definitive. Some members of the advisory committee (including me) thought there would be no valid basis for judgments about which district actions or policies might be contributing to achievement. Still, the committee selected two anonymous comparison districts that had experienced little improvement and proceeded. The MDRC researchers would look for political and managerial differences between the case study districts and the comparison districts and would offer judgments concerning whether some of those differences might help explain why the case study districts had done better.

58. This section is based on Casserly and Snipes (2005); Casserly and others (2002); and Snipes, Doolittle, and Herlihy (2002).

What the MDRC researchers found was more coherent than anyone had a right to expect. All three case study districts had begun from very low levels. Each had a chaotic political history before the reforms that led to improvement. There had been political factionalism on the school boards, infighting among school departments, and bad relations between schools and central administration. District-level operations were sometimes managed by people who had been promoted into their positions because of seniority instead of qualifications. There was no coherent focus on teaching and learning. Teacher recruitment and retention were difficult. The curriculum was undemanding, instruction was unaligned with state standards, and professional development was in disarray.

By the time MDRC arrived in the case study districts, conditions had changed. In a summary of the report, Casserly and Snipes distinguished what they called "preconditions for reform" and "district strategies for reform." They wrote that they found in place the following preconditions for reform:

—A new role for the school board, whereby a new board majority (or other governing unit) focused on policy-level decisions that supported improved student achievement rather than day-to-day operations of the district

—A vision shared by the chief executive or superintendent of the school district and the school board regarding the goals and strategies of reform

—An ability to sell the leadership's vision for reform to city and district stakeholders

—A focus on revamping district operations to serve and support the schools, including a capacity to diagnose instructional problems

—Resources to support reform and improvement

Grounded in the forgoing preconditions, the case study districts were pursuing the following district strategies for reform:

—Specific goals for student achievement had been set at the school and district levels, and these were associated with fixed schedules and consequences for failure; accountability systems held district and building-level staff personally responsible

—District-level curricula and instructional approaches were developed and adopted, aligned with state standards

—Districtwide professional development supported the reforms, striving for consistent, districtwide implementation of the curriculum and instructional approaches

—A commitment had been made to data-driven decisionmaking about instruction, and the district was investing in the capacity to follow through on that commitment

—Lower-performing schools received special attention, including extra resources and an infusion of qualified teachers[59]

The emphasis in the early stages of reform was on elementary schools, which may help explain why progress at the high school level had not occurred.

Officials in the two comparison districts said they were implementing many of the same reforms seen in the case study districts. But as Casserly and Snipes described it:

—They lacked consensus among key stakeholders about district priorities or an overall strategy for reform

—They lacked specific, clear standards, achievement goals, time lines, and consequences

—The districts' central offices took little or no responsibility for improving instruction or creating a cohesive instructional strategy throughout the district

—The policies and practices of the central office were not strongly connected to intended changes in teaching and learning in the classrooms

—The districts gave schools multiple and conflicting curriculum and instructional expectations, which they were left to decipher on their own.[60]

Progress in the case study districts was not achieved easily. There was resistance. Principals and teachers complained as jobs became more demanding and stressful. Parents and students complained as more time on reading and math meant less time for music, art, and field trips. Experienced teachers complained that the new approaches to instruction were inferior to what they already were doing, although test scores provided no justification for continuing old practices. Advocates for the gifted and talented complained that devoting so much attention to low achievers was causing the highest achievers to be neglected. District officials responded to such complaints in a number of ways, some more effective than others. Some complaints had merit. But with strong preconditions for reform in place, the superintendent and other leaders had the incentives and clout to push ahead with the district strategies for reform that were beginning to make a difference in student achievement.

School-Level Transformation without the District

The preceding focus was on districts because transformative, district-level reform may be the only way to make progress at the scale the nation needs. Currently, most districts, whether city, suburban, or rural, are only steps from the starting line—and some seem to stand behind it. In the meantime, many

59. Casserly and Snipes (2005, pp. 162–63).

60. Casserly and Snipes (2005, pp.164–65).

schools have not waited for their districts but have pushed ahead, guided by the same strategic practices and principles that the Council of Great City Schools examples have in common.

For example, David Jacobson and I selected several schools from the Ohio State Department of Education's "Ohio Schools of Promise" list.[61] These were schools that ranked high on Ohio's state standardized exams. From the longer list we chose schools with relatively large concentrations of racial minority and free-lunch-eligible students. What we saw in site visits to these high-performing, high-poverty schools was the same basic pattern for achieving improvement that other researchers have reported in recent years. Specifically:

—Teachers and administrators analyze student work to identify particular weaknesses

—On the basis of these analyses they select a limited number of skills or topics as priorities for improvement

—They shop around to find (or eventually craft) instructional resources and practices to address their chosen priorities (for some schools, these resources and practices come from whole-school-reform vendors)

—They work in groups to learn the new teaching materials and procedures, sometimes with professional development support from outside the school

—They plan the logistics, especially scheduling, necessary to follow through with implementation

—They monitor implementation, make midcourse corrections, assist teachers who need help, and put pressure on teachers who seem not to be trying

—They monitor student progress and repeat the cycle.

Whether or not a school can initiate and follow through on this type of process depends on the professional climate in the school and the available resources. It also depends on leadership. Recall the top four reasons from my survey for the failure of professional development to be effective: "It was just too much," "There was too little support and training," "Teachers were not held accountable," and "The way it was introduced didn't inspire me to try." Considering each in turn, one would not be surprised to discover that effective school leaders manage professional development in ways that make time in the schedule for new work, provide adequate support and training, monitor teacher participation for accountability, and from the outset introduce and develop ideas in ways geared to attract and sustain participation.

61. The study with Jacobson applies our framework from the Tripod Project for School Improvement (www.tripodproject.org) to classify the ways leaders in higher and lower performing schools introduce ideas to teachers; balance administrative control with teacher autonomy; get teachers to define and adopt school and personal goals; manage resistance, especially following setbacks; and celebrate success.

It would be ideal if every school principal were able and inclined to achieve excellence for students from all backgrounds and with minimal district interference. There would be no need for districtwide reforms that restrict school-level autonomy. After all, autonomy restrictions on schools that are already highly effective could do more harm than good. But if many schools need help and districts lack the capacity to support multiple school-level approaches to professional development, then district-level approaches make a great deal of sense.[62] It follows that efforts to build a political movement to mobilize and sustain the will to develop and protect such district-level reforms and associated leadership make a great deal of sense as well.

Conclusion

The United States is at the cutting edge of a dramatic shift in national identity. There will be no racial majority group in the country by the middle of the present century. The economic vitality and social stability of the nation that future generations will inherit will depend upon how effectively Americans now alive help all their children, beginning now, to reach their academic potential. Great progress is possible. Earlier I recounted how more than 60 percent of the reading score gap between blacks and whites disappeared between 1971 and 1988. For fourth graders in the NAEP series, recent evidence indicates that gaps are narrowing even as scores for all groups are rising. Working through all the many roles in which they operate, adults today have a duty to help these fourth graders and their contemporaries continue making progress as they pass through high school and college and eventually into the workplace.

Success will require more than changes in policy. Individuals, families, communities, school systems, and nations have *lifestyles*—routine ways of allocating time, effort, attention, and resources to activities. Progress in a national movement for excellence with equity will require lifestyle changes in the ways in which the nation does schooling. Similarly, for most parents, of any racial or social class background, it is not difficult to imagine lifestyle changes likely to raise their children's achievement. Examples are required daily leisure reading, discussions in which children explain their homework answers to parents, and appropriate bedtimes, routinely enforced.

62. Especially in large districts, the right answer may be to grant exceptions on the basis of high levels of student performance. But equity concerns would remain even with this idea if schools work with different student populations, some more difficult than others.

No such changes will happen consistently without adults who take steps to commence and sustain them, often against initial resistance. Sometimes adults can be induced by public policies that provide incentives or persuaded by the information gleaned from special programs or public information campaigns. Multiple means of influencing adults should be tried and studied for their effectiveness. In the end, developing and sustaining the collective will, skill, and discipline of adults to effectively prioritize learning by children, *including other people's children*, is the central challenge we face in a long-term, nationwide movement for building excellence with equity.

References

Ascher, C. 1988. "Improving the School-Home Connection for Poor and Minority Urban Students." *Urban Review* 20, no. 2: 109–23.

Baker, A., and L. M. Soden. 1998. *The Challenges of Parent Involvement Research*. ERIC/CUE Digest 134. ED419030. New York: ERIC Clearinghouse on Urban Education.

Ballen, J., and O. Moles. 1994. *Strong Families, Strong Schools: Building Community Partnerships For Learning*. Department of Education (eric-web.tc.columbia.edu/families/strong/key_research.html).

Balli, S. J., D. H. Demo, and J. F. Wedman. 1998. "Family Involvement with Children's Homework: An Intervention in the Middle Grades." *Family Relations* 47: 149–57.

Bamber, C., N. Berla, and A. T. Henderson. 1996. *Learning from Others: Good Programs and Successful Campaigns*. Washington, D.C.: Center for Law and Education.

Bronfenbrenner, U. 1979. *The Ecology of Human Development*. Harvard University Press.

Brooks-Gunn, Jeanne, and Lisa Markman. 2005. "The Contribution of Parenting to Racial and Ethnic Gaps in School Readiness." *Future of Children* 15, no. 1: 139–68.

Carey, N., L. Lewis, and E. Farris. 1998. *Parent Involvement In Children's Education: Efforts by Public Elementary Schools*. Statistical Analysis Report, ED416027. National Center for Education Statistics.

Casserly, M., and J. C. Snipes. 2005. "Foundations for Success in the Great City Schools." In *Scaling Up Success: Lessons Learned from Technology-Based Educational Improvement*, edited by C. Dede, J. Honan, and L. Peters, pp. 153–75. New York: Jossey-Bass.

Casserly, M., and others. 2002. "Beating the Odds II: A City-by-City Analysis of Student Performance and Achievement Gaps on State Assessments." Washington, D.C.: Council of Great City Schools.

Chavkin, N. F., ed. 1993. *Families and Schools in a Pluralistic Society*. State University of New York Press.

Christenson, S., T. Rounds, and M. J. Franklin. 1992. "Home-School Collaboration: Effects, Issues, and Opportunities." In *Home-School Collaboration: Enhancing Children's Academic and Social Competence*, edited by S. Christenson and J. C. Conoley. ED353492. Silver Spring, Md.: National Association of School Psychologists.

Conger, Rand, Katherine Conger, and Glen Elder. 1997. "Family Economic Hardships and Adolescent Adjustment: Mediating and Moderating Processes." In *Consequences of Growing Up Poor*, edited by Greg Duncan and Jeanne Brooks-Gunn. New York: Russell Sage Foundation.

Cook, Thomas D., and others. 1998. "Comer's School Development Program: A Theory-Based Evaluation." Evaluation report. Northwestern University.

Dauber, S. L., and Joyce L. Epstein. 1989. "Parent Attitudes and Practices of Involvement in Inner-City Elementary and Middle Schools." Paper presented at the annual meeting of the American Educational Research Association, San Francisco.

Davies, D. 1993. "The League of Schools Reaching Out." *School Community Journal* 3, no. 1: 37–46.

Dickens, William T. 1999. "Rebuilding Urban Labor Markets: What Community Development Can Accomplish." In *Urban Problems and Community Development,* edited by R. Ferguson and W. Dickens. Brookings Institution Press.

Dickens, William T., and James R. Flynn. 2005. "Black Americans Reduce the Racial IQ Gap: Evidence from Standardization Samples." Brookings Institution.

Duncan, Greg J., and Katherine A. Magnuson. 2005. "Can Family Socioeconomic Resources Account for Racial and Ethnic Test Score Gaps?" *Future of Children* 15, no. 1: 35–54.

Eccles, Jacquelynne, and Jennifer Appleton Gootman, eds. 2002. *Community Programs to Promote Youth Development.* Washington, D.C.: National Academies Press.

Eccles, J. S., and R. D. Harold, 1993. "Parent-School Involvement during the Early Adolescent Years." *Teachers College Record* 94, no. 3: 568–87.

Epstein, J. L. 1991. "Effects on Student Achievement of Teachers' Practices of Parent Involvement." In *Advances in Reading/Language Research,* vol. 5: *Literacy through Family, Community, and School Interaction,* edited by S. Silvern, pp. 261–76. Greenwich, Conn.: JAI Press.

———. 1995. "School/Family/Community Partnerships: Caring for the Children We Share." *Phi Delta Kappan* 76, no. 9: 701–13.

———. 1996. "Perspectives and Previews on Research and Policy for School, Family, and Community Partnerships." In *Family-School Links: How Do They Affect Educational Outcomes?* edited by A. Booth and J. F. Dunn, pp. 209–46. Mahwah, N.J.: Lawrence Erlbaum.

Fantuzzo, J. W., G. Y. Davis, and M. D. Ginsberg. 1995. "Effects of Parent Involvement in Isolation or in Combination with Peer Tutoring on Student Self-Concept and Mathematics Achievement." *Journal of Educational Psychology* 87, no. 2: 272–81.

Ferguson, Ronald. 2002. "What Doesn't Meet the Eye: Understanding and Addressing Racial Disparities in High-Achieving Suburban Schools." Oak Brook, Ill.: North Central Regional Educational Laboratory (www.ncrel.org/gap/ferg).

———. 2005. "Why America's Black-White School Achievement Gap Persists." In *Ethnicity, Social Mobility and Public Policy: Comparing the U.S. and Great Britain*, edited by G. Loury, T. Modood, and S. Teles, pp. 309–41. Cambridge University Press.

Fruchter, N., A. Galletta, and J. L. White. 1993. "New Directions in Parent Involvement." *Equity and Choice* 9, no. 3: 33–43.

Fryer, Roland, and Steven Levitt. 2004. "Understanding the Black-White Test Score Gap in the First Two Years of School." *Review of Economics and Statistics* 86, no. 2: 447–64.

———. 2006. "Testing for Racial Differences in the Mental Ability of Young Children." Working Paper 12066. Cambridge, Mass.: National Bureau of Economic Research.

Garlington, J. A. 1992. *Helping Dreams Survive: The Story of a Project Involving African-American Families in the Education of Their Children.* Washington, D.C.: National Committee for Citizens in Education.

Hanushek, Eric A., John F. Kain, and Steven G. Rivkin. 2002. "New Evidence about *Brown* v. *Board of Education:* The Complex Effects of School Racial Composition on

Achievement." Working Paper 8741. Cambridge, Mass.: National Bureau of Economic Research.

Haynes, Norris M., and James P. Comer. 1993. "The Yale School Development Program: Process, Outcomes, and Policy Implications." *Urban Education* 28, no. 2: 166–99.

Henderson, A. T., and N. Berla, eds. 1994. *A New Generation of Evidence: The Family Is Critical to Student Achievement.* Washington, D.C.: National Committee for Citizens in Education.

James, D. W., S. Juri ch, and S. Estes. 2002. *Raising Minority Academic Achievement: A Compendium of Education Programs and Practices.* Washington, D.C.: American Youth Policy Forum.

Jeynes, William H. 2004. "Parental Involvement and Secondary School Student Educational Outcomes: A Meta-Analysis." *Harvard Family Research Project: The Evaluation Exchange* 10, no. 4.

Lareau, Annette, and Erin McNamara Horvat. 1999. "Moments of Social Exclusion and Inclusion: Race, Class, and Cultural Capital in Family-School Relationships." *Sociology of Education* 72, no. 1: 37–53.

Leitch, L. M., and S. S. Tangri. 1988. "Barriers to Home-School Collaboration." *Educational Horizons* 66: 70–74.

Loury, Glenn C. 2002. *The Anatomy of Racial Inequality (The W. E. B. Du Bois Lectures).* Harvard University Press.

Madden, N. A., R. E. Slavin, and N. L. Karweit. 1993. "Success for All: Longitudinal Effects of a Restructuring Program for Inner-City Elementary Schools." *American Educational Research Journal* 30: 123–48.

McKinney, J. A. 1976. "The Development and Implementation of a Tutorial Program for Parents to Improve the Reading and Mathematics Achievement of Their Children." Ed.D. practicum, Nova University. ERIC Document Reproduction Service, ED113703.

McLoyd, Vonnie. 1998. "Socioeconomic Disadvantage and Child Development." *American Psychologist* 53, no. 2: 185–204.

McLoyd, Vonnie, and Julia Smith. 2002. "Physical Discipline and Behavior Problems in African-American, European American, and Hispanic Children: Emotional Support as a Moderator." *Journal of Marriage and Family* 64, no. 1: 40–53.

Moles, O. C. 1993. "Collaboration between Schools and Disadvantaged Parents: Obstacles and Openings." In *Families and Schools in a Pluralistic Society*, edited by N. F. Chavkin, pp. 21–52. State University of New York Press.

Molnar, Alex, ed. 2002. *School Reform Proposal: The Research Evidence*. Greenwich, Conn.: Information Age Publishing.

National Research Council. 2001. *Eager to Learn: Educating Our Preschoolers.* Washington, D.C.: National Academy of Sciences.

Neal, Derek. 2005. "Why Has Black-White Skill Convergence Stopped?" Working Paper 11090. Cambridge, Mass.: National Bureau of Economic Research.

Ogbu, John. 2003. *Black American Students in an Affluent Suburb: A Study in Academic Disengagement.* Mahwah, N.J.: Lawrence Erlbaum.

Orfield, Gary. 2005. "Why Segregation Is Inherently Unequal: The Abandonment of *Brown* and the Continuing Failure of *Plessy*." *New York Law School Law Review* 49, no. 4: 1041–52.

Phillips, Meredith, and others. 1998. "Family Background, Parenting Practices, and the Black-White Test Score Gap." In *The Black-White Test Score Gap,* edited by Christopher Jencks and Meredith Phillips. Brookings Institution Press.

Reglin, G. L. 1993. *At-Risk "Parent and Family" School Involvement: Strategies for Low-Income Families and African-American Families of Unmotivated and Underachieving Students.* Springfield, Ill.: Charles C. Thomas.

Rodick, J. D., and S. W. Henggeler. 1980. "The Short-Term and Long-Term Amelioration of Academic and Motivational Deficiencies among Low-Achieving Inner-City Adolescents." *Child Development* 51: 1126–32.

Rushton, J. Philippe, and Arthur R. Jenson. 2005. "Thirty Years of Research on Race Differences in Cognitive Ability." *Psychology, Public Policy, and Law* 11, no. 2: 235–94.

Rutherford, B., S. Billig, and J. F. Kettering. 1993. *Parent and Community Involvement in the Middle Grades: Evaluating Education Reform.* Denver, Colo.: RMC Research.

Shartrand, A. M., and others. 1997. *New Skills for New Schools: Preparing Teachers in Family Involvement.* Harvard Family Research Project, Harvard Graduate School of Education.

Shonkoff, Jack P., and Deborah A. Phillips, eds. 2000. *From Neurons to Neighborhoods: The Science of Early Childhood Development.* Washington, D.C.: National Academies Press.

Sirin, Selcuk R. 2005. "Socioeconomic Status and Academic Achievement: A Meta-Analytic Review of Research." *Review of Educational Research* 75, no. 3: 417–53.

Snipes, Jason, Fred Doolittle, and Corinne Herlihy. 2002. *Foundations for Success: Case Studies of How Urban School Systems Improve Student Achievement.* Washington, D.C.: Council of Great City Schools.

Swap, S. M. 1993. *Developing Home-School Partnerships: From Concepts to Practice.* Teachers College Press.

Swick, K. J. 1991. *Teacher-Parent Partnerships to Enhance School Success in Early Childhood Education.* Washington, D.C.: National Education Association of the United States.

Tizard, J., W. N. Schofield, and J. Hewison. 1982. "Collaboration between Teachers and Parents in Assisting Children's Reading." *British Journal of Educational Psychology* 52: 1–15.

Turner, Herbert, Chad Nye, and Jamie Schwartz. 2004. "Assessing the Effects of Parent Involvement Interventions on Elementary School Student Achievement." *Harvard Family Research Project: The Evaluation Exchange* 10, no. 4.

U.S. Department of Education. 1995. *Nation's Report Card: Reading 1994 for the Nation.* National Assessment of Educational Progress (nces.ed.gov/nationsreportcard/).

———. 2005. *The Nation's Report Card: NAEP 2004 Trends in Academic Progress. Three Decades of Student Performance in Reading and Mathematics* (nces.ed.gov/nationsreport card).

Walberg, H. J., R. E. Bole, and H. C. Waxman. 1980. "School-Based Family Socialization and Reading Achievement in the Inner City." *Psychology in the Schools* 17: 509–14.

Wolfendale, S. 1983. *Parental Participation in Children's Development and Education.* New York: Gordon and Breach.

Wong, P. L. 1995. "Accomplishments of Accelerated Schools." Accelerated Schools Project, Stanford University.

12

MICHAEL A. REBELL

The Need for Comprehensive Educational Equity

The inadequate and inequitable opportunities offered to most low-income and African American and Latino youths today are the greatest challenge facing America's schools and social institutions, and they pose a major threat to our country. Lack of opportunity is a social threat because inadequately educated people are more likely to be arrested and incarcerated, become pregnant, use drugs, experience violence, and require public assistance. It is an economic threat because it diminishes the competitiveness of America's current and future workforce. And it is a civic threat because a person's ability to function productively as a civic participant, to be a capable voter, juror, and involved citizen who feels a personal stake in society, clearly mirrors his or her educational level. Finally, the lack of adequate and equitable educational opportunities for so many children constitutes a moral threat. In an age when the best jobs require higher levels of skills and knowledge than ever before in history, the fact that many students do not get the education to compete for them, simply because of their parents' skin color or income, is a blight on the moral standing of the United States.

The research findings reported in this volume paint the most detailed and accurate portrait to date of the increased costs in crime, compromised health, poor preparation for competitive employment, and lost income and tax revenue that the United States incurs because of its inadequate and inequitable educational institutions. They also characterize damage to the social and civic fabric of the nation—an equally heavy toll that accumulates annually with each cohort of high school dropouts. And they provide a glimpse of a future, only several decades hence, when, if present trends continue, the "minority" groups with the lowest overall levels of education will account for more than 50 percent of the U.S. student population.

Fortunately, state and national educational policies today recognize the seriousness of this challenge. The stated purpose of the federal No Child Left Behind Act (NCLB) is to meet the educational needs of low-achieving children in the nation's highest-poverty schools by ensuring "that all children have a fair, equal and significant opportunity to obtain a high-quality education and reach, at a minimum, proficiency on challenging State academic achievement standards and state academic assessments . . . by the end of the 2013–2014 school year."[1] Similarly, the standards-based reforms that have been adopted by virtually all the states are based on the premise that "all children can learn; and we can change our system of public elementary, middle and secondary education to ensure that all children do learn at world class levels."[2]

Unfortunately, the federal and state policies that have been in place since the late 1990s seem not to have brought about dramatic improvements. Although some gains have been made, and achievement gaps have narrowed slightly, the 2005 scores on the National Assessment of Educational Progress (NAEP) indicate that over the preceding two years—the period of major implementation of NCLB—reading scores at the fourth grade level were essentially flat, and at the eighth grade level they actually declined. In math the NAEP scores showed a modest gain at the fourth grade level and a 1 percent increase at eighth grade level. Extrapolating the significance of these trends, the Northwest Evaluation Association projected that on the basis of these eighth grade reading score results, it would take 200 years to close the achievement gap between black and white students.[3]

Other indicators also portend difficulty in reaching the nation's goals. For example, high school graduation rates seem to be declining rather than im-

1. P.L 107-110, §§ 1001, 1111.

2. New York State Board of Regents (1993).

3. See Sam Dillon, "Bush Education Law Shows Mixed Results in First Test," *New York Times*, October 20, 2005. The gaps narrowed steadily from the 1970s through the late 1980s but then leveled out through 1999, before narrowing slightly again. See also Sam Dillon, "Schools Slow in Closing Gaps between Races," *New York Times*, November 20, 2006. The gains in terms of NAEP scores are not actually as bleak as they seem, because of a phenomenon known as "Simpson's paradox." This occurs when, because of a changing sample population, an overall average remains stable while every demographic group in the sample is making significant gains. Since 1970, for example, eighth graders have improved by only 7 points on the NAEP reading assessment, but this increase hides a 10 point increase for white students, a 14 point increase for Hispanic students, and a 21 point increase for black students. The overall average is lower than

proving. Whereas in 2000, 16.1 percent of the U.S. population lacked a high school diploma, in 2020, if current trends continue, 18.5 percent of the population will not have attained this minimal educational credential (Bailey, this volume). The dropout problem relates primarily to racial and ethnic minorities and students from low-income backgrounds. For example, 10 percent of blacks and 41 percent of Latinos have less than a high school education, versus 10 percent of whites.[4]

The United States' efforts to rectify the blatant inadequacies and inequities that plague its educational system seem not to be succeeding at an acceptable pace. The reason is that reform efforts to date simply have not matched the magnitude of the problem as revealed by the data and analyses presented in this volume. Our comprehensive assessment of the costs of inadequate education reflects the breadth and depth of the causes and effects of educational inequity. And it points to the need for comprehensive solutions. To meet the global challenges of an increasingly flat world, to prepare students to be capable civic participants in a democratic society, and to ensure that children's racial or ethnic, socioeconomic, or family background no longer strongly predicts their access to educational opportunity or their ultimate level of achievement, school reform must address the full array of factors that affect students' educational performance.[5]

Poverty and the conditions it creates are the core causes of educational underachievement. The United States has the highest rate of childhood poverty by far among the affluent nations in the world and few methods in place to help families out of poverty or mitigate its effects on children. The rate of childhood poverty in America is 21.9 percent, in comparison with less than 3 percent in Denmark and Finland, the countries with the lowest rates among the rich countries in the world. The United States also leads the industrialized world in the percentage of its population that is permanently poor (14.5 percent), an indication that "unlike other wealthy nations, we have few mechanisms to get people out of poverty once they fall into poverty."[6]

---

any of the subgroup increases because of the rapid expansion in the proportion of the lower-scoring groups (see Bracey [2004].) For present purposes, the significance of the pattern of NAEP score gains of recent decades is twofold. It shows that additional expenditures and reform efforts do yield positive results. The greatest gains came during the initial period of Title I funding and the initial round of fiscal equity litigations; modest gains in recent years followed the implementation of standards-based reforms and the growing success of the adequacy cases. At the same time, it illustrates the magnitude of the challenge of educating all the students in the United States' rapidly diversifying culture to high educational levels.

4. Jane Junn, "The Political Costs of Unequal Education" (www.tc.columbia.edu/centers/EquitySymposium/symposium/resourceDetails.asp?PresId=9).

5. Friedman (2005); National Center on Education and the Economy (2007).

6. Berliner (2006, pp. 956–61).

As Richard Rothstein and Tamara Wilder documented in chapter 2, the effect of poverty on children's readiness to learn is profound. Children from low-income households are more likely to have exposure to lead dust and lead poisoning, vision and hearing problems, untreated cavities, and asthma, all of which directly relate to capacity for learning. Lead exposure, for example, is connected with lowered IQ scores.[7] Undetected hearing and vision impairments impede classroom attentiveness and effectiveness. Asthma keeps children up at night, so if they make it to school the next day, they are likely to be drowsy and less attentive and to exhibit behavioral problems that depress achievement. Hunger, lack of adequate housing, and residential mobility also clearly affect poor children's performance in school.[8]

Children spend, on average, 1,000 hours a year in school but 5,000 hours in the neighborhood and with their families.[9] This means that if we seek to deal effectively with the impediments to learning that surround children from poverty backgrounds, then we must provide them a broad range of "supplementary educational interventions" during their nonschool hours.[10] Such services would include early childhood education programs, after-school and summer programs, family and community support, health care, and good nutrition. Unless we attend to these broad needs, we will never overcome the significant achievement gaps between low-income and minority students and their more advantaged peers.

Because out-of-school factors directly impede academic achievement, they can no longer be relegated to the sidelines of the education policy dialogue; they must be tackled head on. The potential benefits of providing such comprehensive supports and services have actually been long recognized.[11] In the nineteenth century, the settlement houses were an early model for providing a variety of services to children and their families. The War on Poverty of the 1960s expanded programs for children, although it left them largely uncoordinated. Spurred by research in the social sciences in the 1970s and 1980s, a widespread understanding emerged of the benefits of the coordinated delivery of a wide range of health, mental health, family, and educational services to children.

Since the 1990s, in the United States and elsewhere, there has in fact been a burgeoning of initiatives, programs, projects, and activities that seek to integrate education and supports. The delivery models employed include com-

7. Brooks-Gunn and Duncan (1997).
8. Rothstein (2004, pp. 37–42).
9. Berliner (2006).
10. Gordon, Bridglall, and Meroe (2004).
11. Soler and Shauffer (1990).

munity, full-service, and extended schools; comprehensive early childhood programs; school-linked services projects; school-community partnerships; private interagency commissions; family support and education programs; integrated-services initiatives; comprehensive community initiatives; and state programs and broad national legislation.[12]

Although the importance of taking a comprehensive approach to the well-being of children has been widely recognized, these past efforts have not been well coordinated or evaluated for their effectiveness in ensuring educational opportunity. Nor have successful models of coordinated, comprehensive services been publicized, replicated, funded, or advanced as the critical core of the effort to provide meaningful educational opportunity to all children. Therefore we must both learn from past efforts and vastly expand our understanding and advocacy of effective mechanisms for providing comprehensive educational equity if we are to meet the nation's stated goals for educational opportunity and educational achievement. In short, a serious and realistic approach to educational policy and practice must encompass the complex relationship between education, class, and poverty. While not attempting to eliminate poverty entirely or to right all social and political wrongs, we must not ignore their profound effects on children's ability to learn.

A comprehensive approach to educational opportunity should be focused on children's needs in at least the following dozen critical in-school and out-of-school areas:

1. High quality early childhood education programs
2. Rigorous and challenging curricula and assessments
3. High quality teaching
5. Effective, sustained educational leadership
5. Appropriate class sizes
6. Mental and physical health care services
7. Appropriate academic support for English language learners
8. Appropriate academic support for special education students
9. Appropriate academic support for children in areas of highly concentrated poverty
10. Effective after-school, community, and summer programs

12. The United Kingdom recently initiated national reforms to move the country toward comprehensive educational equity. See www.everychildmatters.gov.uk. With the goal of improving children's outcomes defined comprehensively, the government passed a new Children's Act 2004. The act expands services for children and legislates broad changes in the way children's services work together. Under the new legislation, beginning in 2006, localities must develop "children's trust" arrangements, working with schools to "integrate front-line services, backed up by integrated processes, planning and interagency governance" U.K. Department for Education and Skills (2004, p. 2).

11. Effective parental involvement and family support

12. Policies that foster racially and economically diverse schools[13]

Some people who oppose efforts to ensure adequate funding for all public school students invert the reality of the need for comprehensive services by arguing that investments in educational opportunities for low-income and minority students are ill advised. They claim that most of these children will not become academically proficient, because poverty and other elements of family background put them at too great a disadvantage. Although it is true that many poor children enter school with severe learning deficiencies, this is a reason to provide them greater resources, both in school and to supplement what can be provided by the schools. Certainly it is not a reason to provide them with less. As the justices of the Supreme Court of New Jersey eloquently put it: "If the claim is that these [disadvantaged] students simply cannot make it, the constitutional answer is, give them a chance. The Constitution does not tell them that since more money will not help, we will give them less; that because their needs cannot be fully met, they will not be met at all. It does not tell them they will get the minimum, because that is all they can benefit from."[14]

Ironically, despite the enormity of the deprivations suffered by children from poverty backgrounds and the magnitude of their learning needs, in the United States today the children with the greatest needs by and large have the fewest resources provided to them. The Education Trust has estimated that on average throughout the United States, spending on children in high poverty districts is $907 less per student than spending on students in low poverty districts. The situation is even worse in certain states. New York, for example, stands at the apex of national inequities, reporting a funding gap of $2,280 between students in rich and low-income districts.[15] Although legal challenges to this pattern of inequity triggered a vigorous debate over the past few decades about whether "money matters" in education, the overwhelming consensus of the research on this question has established that "a broad range of school inputs are positively related to student outcomes, and . . . the magnitude of the

13. This list covers programs and services that schools can provide on their own or in collaboration with other governmental and community agencies. Certain other critical conditions of poverty that affect readiness to learn, such as insufficient family income support and inadequate housing, are beyond the realm of intervention by schools but need to be ameliorated by other societal entities. In addition, providing a meaningful opportunity for a quality education for all students requires the following implementation essentials: (1) adequate funding; (2) effective methods for building and sustaining capacity at the school, community, district, and state levels; (3) appropriate governance structures; (4) meaningful public engagement processes; and (5) effective accountability mechanisms.

14. *Abbott* v. *Burke II*, 1990.

15. Education Trust (2005, pp. 2–3).

effects are sufficiently large to suggest that moderate increases in spending may be associated with significant increases in achievement.[16]

Of course funding for public education is not and cannot be unlimited. Money that is appropriated for school-based services and for critical supplementary services must be spent in ways that are both strategic and accountable. There is broad agreement today that money certainly matters—but only when it is spent well.[17] Research and careful analysis must determine which health, family support, or social service deficits in each area of comprehensive educational equity most directly affect children's readiness to learn and which should be targeted for a focused infusion of resources. As Levin and Belfield demonstrated in chapter 9, the benefits of some interventions, such as the Perry Preschool Program, the Chicago Child-Parent Centers program, and the First Things First comprehensive school reform approach, easily exceed the costs of delivering them. Strategic investments in certain supplementary interventions, such as asthma prevention, are also likely to yield high academic dividends. Each year 21 million school days are lost because of this disease, and blacks are 80 percent more likely than whites to miss seven days of school and to suffer severe learning consequences because of lack of treatment.[18]

The provision of services in each of the comprehensive educational opportunity areas needs to be approached through careful cost-benefit analyses of likely gains and with continuing oversight of the effectiveness of methods of delivering the services.[19] The critical concerns should be how to get better results for present investments and which new investments are most likely to yield the greatest long-range educational gains. The type of cost-benefit study undertaken by Levin and Belfield needs to be replicated and expanded. Future cost studies for determining legislative appropriations for in-school and out-of-school educational services need to be correlated with analyses of best practices and most promising practices in particular areas of education.[20]

Some may ask, Why take this comprehensive approach when a number of studies point to high-poverty, high-minority schools that are "beating the odds" and distinguishing themselves with good outcomes thanks to quality teaching and great leadership? Our goal must go beyond helping some schools to beat the odds against success; we must aim to lower those odds for all schools. We need to study the broad range of factors that have contributed to

16. Greenwald, Hedges, and Laine (1996, p. 362).

17. Hanushek (2006); Rebell (2007b).

18. Berliner (2006); Rothstein (2004).

19. Allgood (2006); Schuck and Zeckhauser (2006).

20. Levin and Belfield (this volume); Rebell (2007a).

success in particular initiatives and determine the extent to which these practices are replicable and can be implemented on a larger scale and for sustained time periods.

Even with careful cost-benefit analyses and effective accountability mechanisms, additional revenues will need to be raised to provide the range of comprehensive services that children who are poor need in order to reach national educational goals. But three critical facts must be kept in mind in considering this reality. First, although currently the United States makes the highest per capita expenditures in the world for postsecondary education, it is only third highest in spending for elementary education, fourth highest for secondary education, and at the bottom of the heap in preschool spending.[21] Second, recent studies and recent education policy reform initiatives have demonstrated that major increases in educational appropriations can be accomplished through innovative and equitable taxing policy without major increases in income, sales, or property taxes.[22] Finally, state and national polls have revealed a consistent willingness on the part of overwhelming majorities of the American public (59–75 percent) to pay higher taxes for education—especially if there is a reasonable expectation that the money will be spent well.[23] As the earlier chapters in this volume clearly established, if the additional funding is invested well, the overall dividends to society will be enormous.

An immediate action agenda must bridge the current divide between education research and policy focused on school-based improvements and research and policy focused on family, health, and social services. Research and demonstration projects must examine how best to ensure poor children the resources, services, and supports determined most critical for school success—not only the most important educational resources, such as high quality teaching, but also the most important resources in areas such as physical and mental health, early education, and family support. Cost-benefit analyses targeting the areas and programs that are the best bets for productive investment of existing and enhanced resources need to be undertaken. The piecemeal nature of many

21. Centre for Educational Research and Innovation (2004).

22. Hunter (2002); Institute on Taxation and Economic Policy (2005).

23. A report on a National Public Radio poll in 1999 was headlined "Three out of four Americans say they would be willing to have their taxes raised by at least $200 a year to pay for specific measures to improve community public schools" (www.npr.org/programs/specials/poll/education/education.front.html). A report on a PEN/Education Week poll in 2004 was titled "A majority of voters (59 percent) say they are willing to pay higher taxes to improve public education" (209.85.165.104/search?q=cache:pXSi6GqIo_AJ:www.publiceducation.org/doc/2004_Poll_Press_Release.doc). And a *Phi Delta Kappan*/Gallup poll in 2006 found that 66 percent of Americans responded affirmatively to the question "Would you be willing to pay more taxes for funding preschool programs for children from low-income or poverty-level households?" (www.pdkintl.org/kappan/k0609pol.htm).

past and existing endeavors to combine the forces of these fields must be set aside, and a new commitment to comprehensive educational equity for all children must be broadly accepted and implemented at both the federal and state levels.

Consistent with its heritage as a revolutionary, egalitarian society, the United States has adopted as its national policy a serious commitment to overcoming historic achievement gaps between low-income and minority students and their more advantaged peers and achieving equity in the foreseeable future. These are not abstract goals; they are legal mandates, as judges in school-funding lawsuits around the nation have recognized in establishing students' constitutional right to the opportunity for a quality education and ordering states to ensure adequate funding to provide this.[24] Though difficult to accomplish, these ambitious but vital national commitments can be realized. If there is sufficient will, comprehensive educational equity can provide the way.

References

Allgood, Whitney C. 2006. "The Need for Adequate Resources for At-Risk Children." Working paper. Washington, D.C.: Economic Policy Institute.

Berliner, David. 2006. "Our Impoverished View of Educational Research." *Teachers College Record* 108, no. 6: 949–95.

Bracey, Gerald W. 2004. "Simpson's Paradox and Other Statistical Mysteries." *American School Board Journal* 191, no. 2: 32–34.

Brooks-Gunn, Jeanne, and Greg J. Duncan. 1997. "The Effects of Poverty on Children." *Future of Children* 7, no. 2: 55–71.

Centre for Educational Research and Innovation. 2004. "Education at a Glance: OECD Indicators 2004." *OECD Transition Economies* 2004, no. 20: 1–461.

Education Trust. 2005. "The Funding Gap, 2005: Low-Income and Minority Students Shortchanged by Most States" (www.Edtrust.org).

Friedman, Thomas L. 2005. *The World Is Flat: A Brief History of the Twenty-first Century.* New York: Farrar, Straus and Giroux.

Gordon, Edmund W., Beatrice L. Bridglall, and Aundra Saa Meroe. *Supplementary Education: The Hidden Curriculum of High Academic Achievement.* Lanham, Md.: Rowman and Littlefield.

Greenwald, Rob, Larry V. Hedges, and Richard D. Laine. 1996. "The Effect of School Resources on Student Achievement." *Review of Educational Research* 66, no. 3: 361–96.

Hanushek, Eric. 2006. *Courting Failure: How School Finance Lawsuits Exploit Judges' Good Intentions and Harm Our Children.* Stanford, Calif.: Education Next Books.

Hunter, Molly. 2002. "Maryland Enacts Modern, Standards-Based Education Finance System: Reforms Based on Adequacy Cost Studies" (www.schoolfunding.info/resource_center/MDbrief.php3).

24. Rebell (2002); www.schoolfunding.info.

Institute on Taxation and Economic Policy. 2005. "Achieving Adequacy: Tax Options for New York in the Wake of the CFE Case." Washington, D.C.

National Center on Education and the Economy. 2007. *Tough Choices or Tough Times: The Report of the New Commission on the Skills of the American Workforce.* San Francisco: Jossey-Bass.

New York State Board of Regents. 1993. *All Children Can Learn: A Plan for Reform of State Aid to Schools.* Albany: State University of New York.

Rebell, Michael. 2002. "Education Adequacy, Democracy, and the Courts." In *Achieving High Educational Standards for All,* edited by Christopher Edley, Timothy Ready, and Catherine Snow, pp. 218–67. Washington, D.C.: National Academies Press.

———. 2007a. "Professional Rigor, Public Engagement, and Judicial Review: A Proposal for Enhancing the Validity of Education Adequacy Studies." *Teachers College Record* 109, no. 6: 1303–73.

———. 2007b. "Poverty, Meaningful Educational Opportunity, and the Necessary Role of the Courts." *North Carolina Law Review* 85, no. 5: 1467–1544.

Rothstein, R. 2004. *Class and Schools: Using Social, Economic, and Educational Reform to Close the Black–White Achievement Gap.* Teachers College Press.

Schuck, Peter H. and Richard J. Zeckhauser. 2006. *Targeting in Social Programs: Avoiding Bad Bets, Removing Bad Apples.* Brookings Institution Press.

Soler, Mark, and Carole Shauffer. "Fighting Fragmentation: Coordination of Services for Children and Families." *Nebraska Law Review* 69, no. 2 (special issue): 278–97.

U.K. Department for Education and Skills. 2004. *Every Child Matters: Change for Children in Schools.* Report DfES-1089-2004. London.

Contributors

Sigal Alon
Tel Aviv University

Thomas Bailey
Teachers College, Columbia University

Clive R. Belfield
Queens College, City University of New York

Ronald F. Ferguson
Kennedy School of Government, Harvard University

Irwin Garfinkel
School of Social Work, Columbia University

Brendan Kelly
School of Social Work, Columbia University

Henry M. Levin
Teachers College, Columbia University

Enrico Moretti
University of California–Berkeley

Peter Muennig
Mailman School of Public Health, Columbia University

Michael A. Rebell
Teachers College, Columbia University

Richard Rothstein
Teachers College, Columbia University

Cecilia Elena Rouse
Princeton University

Marta Tienda
Princeton University

Jane Waldfogel
School of Social Work, Columbia University

Tamara Wilder
Teachers College, Columbia University

Index